CONNECTING

Like

Jesus

*Practices for Healing,
Teaching, and Preaching*

TONY CAMPOLO
MARY ALBERT DARLING

JB JOSSEY-BASS
A Wiley Imprint
www.josseybass.com

Published by Jossey-Bass
A Wiley Imprint
989 Market Street, San Francisco, CA 94103-1741—www.josseybass.com

Jossey-Bass books and products are available through most bookstores. To contact Jossey-Bass directly call our Customer Care Department within the U.S. at 800-956-7739, outside the U.S. at 317-572-3986, or fax 317-572-4002.

Jossey-Bass also publishes its books in a variety of electronic formats. Some content that appears in print may not be available in electronic books.

Unless otherwise noted, Scripture quotations are from *New Revised Standard Version Bible*, copyright © 1989 National Council of the Churches of Christ in the United States of America. Used by permission. All rights reserved.

Library of Congress Cataloging-in-Publication Data
Campolo, Anthony.
    Connecting like Jesus : practices for healing, teaching, and preaching / Tony Campolo, Mary Albert Darling.—1st ed.
        p. cm.
    Includes bibliographical references and index.
    ISBN 978-0-470-43102-3 (cloth)
    1. Communication–Religious aspects–Christianity. I. Darling, Mary Albert. II. Title.
    BV4597.53.C64C37 2010
    253—dc22

2009054230

Printed in the United States of America
FIRST EDITION
HB Printing   10 9 8 7 6 5 4 3 2 1

Contents

Acknowledgments

We are deeply grateful to the following people who helped move this book from many drafts to its final form. Our sincere appreciation goes to:

Mary's sister, Judy Albert Hunt; sister-in-law, Barbara Darling; and lifelong friend, Pat Urban Ballard, for selflessly giving their time and energy to this project. They willingly read chapters, often on a moment's notice, and provided greatly valued feedback.

Student reader, Abby Wood, for her helpful editing of early drafts, and especially for her sensitivity to potential readers.

Jenny Timm, Mary's research assistant, for continuing to fine-tune the manuscript, way beyond the agreed-on time frame, and also for her encouraging spirit.

Robbie Bolton, education librarian at Spring Arbor University, for his expert researching skills, as well as his willingness to work up to the "final hour" (twice!) on making sure references were accurate.

James Warren, Tony's executive assistant, for keeping Tony's life in order so that he could have time to write.

Robert Gauthier, managing director of Tony's missionary organization, EAPE, for helping in Tony's research.

Sarah Blaisdell, for her typing and initial editing of Tony's chapters.

Betty Videto, for transcribing Shane Claiborne's and Brian McLaren's interviews, and for typing portions of Tony's material.

All those at Jossey-Bass who made this a publishable book: our superb editor, Sheryl Fullerton, and her gifted, much appreciated staff: senior editorial assistant, Alison Knowles; copyeditor Michele Jones; and production manager, Joanne Clapp Fullagar.

Mary's dear "Friday lunch" friends: Bev, Carla, Deb, and Jan, for faithfully demonstrating what it means to care for others. And her colleagues at Spring Arbor University, especially Robert, Paul, Carol Ann, and Dr. Betty, for their ongoing support and encouragement of her writing.

We also want to thank a mutual friend, Damon Seacott, for demonstrating on a daily basis what it means to connect like Jesus in how he loves and serves others.

Special thanks to Shane Claiborne, Brian McLaren, and Mindy Caliguire, for their initial interviews for the book and for being willing to respond quickly to follow-up e-mails throughout the project.

We would have liked to thank *all* the people in both of our lives who have demonstrated that it really is possible to connect like Jesus through healing, teaching, and preaching. We are grateful to God that there are too many of you to name.

Finally, our deepest gratitude goes to our families:

To Mary's husband, Terry, for his constant encouragement and support, including his willingness to read chapters on demand; and to her two teenage boys, David and Michael, for their willingness to eat pizza several nights in a row.

To Tony's wife, Peggy, for graciously lending him out to others, and for lovingly supporting his many projects.

Let the words of my mouth
and the meditation of my heart
be acceptable to you,
O Lord, my rock and my redeemer.
—Psalm 19:14

As God's chosen ones, holy and beloved, clothe yourselves
with compassion, kindness, humility, meekness, and patience.
Bear with one another and,
if anyone has a complaint against another,
forgive each other; just as the Lord has forgiven you,
so you also must forgive.
Above all, clothe yourselves with love,
which binds everything together in perfect harmony...
And whatever you do, in word or deed,
do everything in the name of the Lord Jesus,
giving thanks to God the Father through him.
—Colossians 3:12–14, 17

An Introduction to Spiritually Charged Communication

It has been said that we live in a world in which we have created machines that act like people and people who act like machines. Most likely you have experienced both of these sources of alienation. You know how dehumanizing it is to make a phone call and realize that you are interacting with a machine, especially if the machine doesn't allow you to access the option you need. When you hear the recorded voice at the other end of the line say, "Please hold. Your call is very important to us," you may even feel like screaming, "I WANT TO CONNECT WITH A REAL PERSON!"

Worse yet, haven't you experienced times in conversations when those to whom you are speaking are absent even though they are physically present? They are somewhere else, or, even more disturbing, they are deadened souls. Trying to communicate with such people can even diminish your own soul.

This book is about relating to others in ways that satisfy the deepest needs in our souls. What we propose is more than learning what even the best communication scholars can teach us. Connecting like Jesus is a form of interacting that combines a variety of communication and spiritual practices, to engage in what we call *spiritually charged communication*. We believe that combining both kinds of practices is necessary for two reasons: those of us who claim to follow Jesus don't always connect with others in God-honoring ways, and those who have good communication skills often lack a spiritual empowerment that would result in their being able to relate to others at deeper levels. The chemistry created when we combine both practices brings about a powerful reaction that has a transforming effect on our relationships.

In the pages that follow, we will explore ways of connecting dynamically with individuals, as well as with groups large and small. In all that we have to say, we will hold up Jesus, the one with ultimate connecting power, as our model. We believe that what we can learn from Jesus will make a world of difference in how we relate to others, whether over a meal, in a more formalized helping relationship, in small groups or classrooms, or in a public-speaking context.

We hope to demonstrate how every follower of Jesus can connect in ways that change our relationships, our lives, and the world. In Part One, we lay the groundwork for what we mean by the phrase "connecting like Jesus." Part Two focuses primarily on soul healing in terms of our individual relationships with one another. In Part Three, Tony shares what he has learned and experienced as both a teacher and preacher, although you'll find that several of his suggestions also apply to our everyday relationships.

As you read, we hope you will seriously consider engaging in the spiritual and communication practices we propose. The format of the book is also conducive for small group or classroom discussions. If you decide to use the material in either of these contexts, we hope our specific suggestions at the back of the book are helpful.

Although Jesus will be our primary example for connecting with others, along the way we include segments of personal interviews from Christian speakers and writers Shane Claiborne, Brian McLaren, and Mindy Caliguire to show how certain preachers, teachers, and soul healers in our present time have endeavored to carry out these ministries one-on-one and in larger groups. We would have also liked to interview John Wesley—theologian, evangelist, social activist, and founder of the Methodist Church—as we both greatly admire his work as preacher, teacher, and healer of souls. But since he died in 1791, we could not. So instead we have taken excerpts from some of his sermons and included them in a few chapters. You will also notice some quotes from the seventeenth-century French bishop François Fénelon, whose deep spiritual insights have influenced countless followers of Jesus to move beyond themselves into deeper connections with God and others.

We invite you to come along as we explore what it means to connect to others in life-transforming ways. If you accept this invitation, we can learn together how Jesus created, and continues to create, followers who can turn the world upside down with how they love one another.

PART ONE

CONNECTING
LIKE JESUS

1

Spiritually Charged Communication

Relational Practices for Connecting Like Jesus

Two are better than one....For if they fall, one will lift up the other; but woe to one who is alone and falls and does not have another to help.
—Ecclesiastes 4:9–10

This is my commandment, that you love one another as I have loved you.
—Jesus, John 15:12

MOST OF US, from our earliest years, are taught that God existed before anything else was created. Did that mean that before creation God was a big lonely Being, all alone and surrounded by darkness? No—not if you believe in the Trinity: God, Jesus Christ, and the Holy Spirit. If the Triune God is true, God never existed in isolation; instead, God has *always* been in relationship. Genesis 1:26 in fact says, "Let *us* make man in *our* image, in *our* likeness" (emphasis ours). This divine *relationship* existed before anything else was created. And because relationship implies communication, the Triune God has always been a communicating God. As people created in the image of God, we too were made to communicate. Being alone and isolated from others goes against God's intention for all humankind.

> *God never existed in isolation; instead, God has always been in relationship.*

Alcatraz, the infamous island prison in the San Francisco Bay, was known not only for its isolated location but also for an area of cells designated for solitary confinement called "the Hole." When Mary and her family toured Alcatraz during a road trip out west, their youngest son Michael, then ten, stood in one of these cells. Mary explained how the Hole was designed to inflict what is considered one of the most extreme forms of punishment: minimal to no human contact. Michael's unexpected response, "I don't think it would be that bad," was, Mary assumed, not an argument against the awful conditions of solitary confinement, but instead a testimony to having just spent forty-five hours in a van with his parents and older brother.

Although there are times when most, if not all, of us need to be alone, extended lack of communication with others is what has driven people in solitary confinement to insanity and even suicide. God never intended for us to exist without others. That does not mean, however, that we were made to be in just *any* type of relationship with *any* kind of communication. We were created to follow the perfect example of unity found in the Trinity. As author and speaker Brian McLaren said in our interview for this book, "The ultimate reality is communication or communion between Father, Son, and Spirit. They exist in an eternal connection, eternal community, eternal communion."[1] From the beginning, God wanted creation to live that way too: in harmonious, peaceful relationships. That is what the Kingdom of God is all about.[2] Yet throughout all of history, human relationships have been much more messy and chaotic than they have been harmonious and peaceful.

Even God's chosen people, the citizens of Israel, couldn't get it right. They fell away from the good life God had planned for them and found themselves in captivity, longing to see God's peaceful plan actualized in history. They knew what it could be like because their prophets had given them very concrete images of this Kingdom. The prophet Isaiah foretold that it would be a society in which children would not die in infancy, and elderly people would be able to live out their lives in health and well-being. It would be, according to Isaiah's prophecies, a socioeconomic order in which everyone would have a good job and workers would receive fair payment for their labor. When God's Kingdom would be established here on earth, Isaiah declared, every family would build and inhabit a house of its own, and the suffering of the earth would end (Isaiah 65:17–25).

That is the Kingdom of God. A place where people are healthy, happy, and safe and everyone lives in soul-satisfying relationships. That's the life God intended for us all. God calls the church to be a model for the rest of the world of what the harmonious Kingdom will be like when Christ returns—with the hopes that others will want to be a part of that peaceable Kingdom too. As Jesus prayed in John 17:22–23, "The glory that you have given me I have given them, so that they may be one, as we are one, I in them and you in me, that they may become completely one, so that the world may know that you have sent me and have loved them even as you have loved me."

Jesus' mission was aimed at gathering followers who would be willing to join him in a radical movement that would make the Hebrew prophets' images of a peaceful Kingdom a reality for anyone who believed. In our interview, Brian McLaren said that joining Jesus means "God is setting the agenda, and we are to join in with God's agenda. It means we are to fit in with harmony rather than disharmony. The purpose of our communication with God and others is to harmonize and bring ourselves in agreement with God's Kingdom reality." Brian is echoing what the Apostle Paul wrote to the church at Rome—that they were to love one another and live in peace (Romans 12:10, 16, 18). That was their purpose in life, and it is to be ours too, as the body of Christ. Our churches are to be models of the Kingdom of God. People who observe us are supposed to say, "See how they love one another! See how they live in harmony with one another—I want to be a part of this body of believers!"

Why isn't the church perceived this way in the world today?

The answer lies in the painfully obvious fact that a peaceable Kingdom is not yet a reality for those of us who claim to be the body of Christ. As much as we might crave and even strive for the harmonious relationships God intended for us, we still find ourselves in shallow, nit-picky, and even destructive relationships. As speaker and social activist Shane Claiborne said in our interview, "People can be in love with a vision and really wreck each other trying to build that vision."[3] Far too often, others are disillusioned with how Christians relate to one another and to the world. As David Kinnaman discusses in his popular book, *Unchristian,* "Outsiders . . . think Christians no longer represent what Jesus had in mind, that Christianity in our society is not what it was meant to be."[4] Kinnaman found that strikingly high numbers of non-Christians categorize believers of Christianity as judgmental, hypocritical, and antihomosexual. From churchgoers who gossip about each other (with their concern sometimes masquerading as prayer requests) to religious leaders who intentionally misrepresent their religious opponents' views on national TV to those who protest with hate speech, Christians often relate to others in ways very much at odds with the transforming love of God.[5]

In the newsletter from an organization called the Transforming Center, founder and president Ruth Haley Barton mentioned an experience with a church elder who related to a staff member in a way that was "mean and even slanderous." She goes on to write that "When confronted with such blatantly bad behavior, the best the elder could do was to acknowledge that her communication was 'less than artful.'"[6]

Far too often, others are disillusioned with how Christians relate to one another and to the world.

Less than artful?

It's not likely negative perceptions of Christians will change if we can't see how wrong our own harmful communication patterns are. Loving others amid difficult circumstances can be extremely hard, but it's still what God commands us to do. The Bible has much to say on this topic. In his letters to the early church, the Apostle Paul wrote that everything they did was to be done out of love for one another. To limit any confusion or excuses, he got very specific with several lists of "dos and "don'ts." He told them that as followers of Christ, they were not to be jealous of anyone for any reason, and they weren't to brag about themselves either. They were not to get angry too easily or even to keep track of anything anyone did to them that they thought was wrong or unfair. They were not to complain or argue about *anything*! Instead, he told them to be kind and patient with one another; to forgive one another as God in Christ forgives them. In short, they were to be devoted to one another and humbly consider others better than themselves (1 Corinthians 16:14, 13:4–5; Ephesians 4:32; Philippians 2:3, 14). And these were not the only directives to the early church for how they were to demonstrate love for one another. There are dozens of "one another" verses in the Bible that tell followers of Christ how to relate to each other. We may wish there were exceptions written into these verses—"forgive one other *unless*" or "do not complain *unless*"—but there aren't any.

The "one another" verses in scripture can make for great sermons, Bible studies, and readings at weddings, but once the sermon, study, or wedding is over, they seem next to impossible to live out on a daily basis. Instead, we often live with disconnects between saying that we want to imitate Christ and actually following Christlike ways of communicating with one another. We sing the popular Hillsong worship chorus, "Tell the world," but what are we really telling the world with our actions toward one another? We claim to be transformed by Jesus, but cannot seem to transform the ways we relate to those closest to us, much less to the world. As Mohandas Gandhi once said, "I like your Christ. I do not like your Christians. Your Christians are so unlike your Christ."[7]

We claim to be transformed by Jesus, but cannot seem to transform the ways we relate to those closest to us, much less to the world.

It's not that there aren't any Christians who communicate in radically loving ways like Jesus. Christ followers can and do get it right. But the number of people who call themselves Christian is much larger than the number of those who intentionally and regularly practice Christlike communication in their everyday lives.

Our hope in writing this book is to change those numbers. We affirm that the meaningful, fulfilling, unifying relationships God intended before the beginning of time are truly possible. We believe that the "one another" verses in the Bible really can be lived out in how we daily communicate. The key is in learning to relate to others as Jesus did when he walked the earth. When Jesus communicated, he did so in ways that consistently *connected* him to his audience.

What Does It Mean to Connect?

As we pointed out in the Introduction, it can be one thing to communicate but quite another to connect. We can use a variety of solid communication techniques and still feel a lack of connectedness with others. Not connecting to others can be a very lonely and estranged feeling. It's possible to feel this disconnect and alienation no matter the setting or how well we know someone.

Connecting is a different level of communication than talking in an interesting manner or using solid communication techniques in our interactions. Connecting suggests a depth of mutual understanding and sharing. Saying we connect with someone means we sense a special bond, or even feel a sense of unity, with that person. We may even experience what Hasidic philosopher Martin Buber called an "I-Thou" relationship, whereby a person encounters another not as an object (I-it) but as a sacred being made in the image of God. Seeing others this way bridges our separateness. The unity that results is at the center of what it means to connect in Christlike ways. There is an intense hunger in our world for this kind of connectedness that can make the "one another" verses a reality.

Connecting Like Jesus

Throughout time and history, no one has connected to others like Jesus did. Jesus related in "I-Thou" ways not only to his peers but to those whom his culture considered beneath *and* beyond his own social class. A hodgepodge of people followed him, from outcasts to government officials to fishermen, everyone wanting, for as many reasons as there were followers, to connect with him. Roman soldiers who had been sent to arrest him returned empty-handed because they had stopped to listen to him. Jesus so powerfully connected with them, touching the very depths of their souls, that they forgot why they had been sent. They could only explain to their supervisors, "Never has anyone spoken like this!" (John 7:46). Men who had spent a lifetime as fishermen, upon hearing Jesus say, "Follow me!" dropped their nets and became his disciples. The charisma that was evident in what he said magnetized crowds so that they not only listened to him for hours but then would follow him wherever he went, hoping to hear more (Mark 6:30–33). When Jesus spoke, he changed lives. The impact was so noticeable that even his enemies could tell when his followers had been with him (Acts 4:13).

> *When Jesus spoke, he changed lives.*

What was it about the way Jesus connected with others that made him attract so many people? Even the best communication strategies are not enough to produce the powerful connections that Jesus had with others—connections that held the attention of both the simplest child and the most elite religious scholar; connections that resulted in person after person dropping everything to follow Jesus; connections so powerfully transforming that because of Jesus, all of history was changed.

The answer to the question "What made Jesus connect in such powerful ways?" might appear to be the obvious: "Because he's God!" Although it seems safe to assume that Jesus had an unfair advantage—after all, he was and is the Son of God—that is not the only reason he knew how to dynamically connect with people. He did not *automatically* know all things because he was the son of God. At four years old he did not walk around in WWJD fashion and ask "What should I do?" and then just *know.* As the Apostle Paul told the church at Philippi, even though Jesus was "in very nature God," he came to earth as a baby and "made himself nothing" (Philippians 2:6–7, NIV). Jesus was born a nobody—in a stable. He had to grow and learn just like we do. In Luke 2:52 (NIV) we are told that "Jesus grew in wisdom and stature, and in favor with God and men." At the age of twelve he was found "sitting among the teachers, listening to them and asking them questions" (Luke 2:46). He learned from his teachers; from studying and reflecting on scripture; from his times alone with God; and most important, he learned from being obedient to God and trusting God with his entire life, death, and resurrection. As the Gospel of Luke tells us, Jesus' obedience to God, along with his times alone with God, filled him with God's Spirit so that he could be prepared to do Kingdom work in the world (Luke 4:1, 14; 6:12–19).

As a result, Jesus developed what Aristotle called ethos or what we generally think of as credibility, meaning that who he was—his entire character and being—was interwoven with his message and his ability to influence others. Jesus' styles of relating flowed out of being totally committed to living for the glory of God. Through seamlessly connecting his relationship with God and his knowledge of scripture to his daily life, Jesus dynamically connected with others. He knew that times of prayer and reflecting on scripture were essential to knowing God more intimately and being spiritually prepared and empowered to connect with others in ways that would best advance God's Kingdom. And he counted on his followers to follow in his footsteps.

Developing Credibility Like Jesus

Just before Jesus ascended into heaven, he commissioned his disciples to go into all the world and spread the good news of the Kingdom of God. They must have wondered how in the world they could ever communicate his message—especially with the same credibility he had. But then he told them how. Jesus finished his commission with these words: "And surely I am with you always, to the very end of the age" (Matthew 28:20b). He told his disciples not to be troubled or afraid because he would shortly give them a spiritual power from "on high" that would enable them to do what he had done, and do even greater things (John 14:12). Jesus never expected his followers, then or now, to go out on their own. He knew we could not do it, at least not with any lasting effectiveness. Jesus knew that for us to have the same relational credibility he had on earth, we needed the same Spirit that was in him, at work in us too.

The Holy Spirit is the key. We can experience God's transforming love that connects us to others if we are empowered by the Holy Spirit through spiritual practices that include praying and "waiting on" the Spirit, just as the early disciples did. In our interview, Mindy Caliguire, president of Soul Care, said that the most important thing we can do for our relationships is "cultivate the capacity for prayer so that we can be connecting with God and others at the same time. Can you hear God's words of love and blessing and presence while you are speaking with someone? Can you silently express gratitude and even worship as you listen to a friend?"[8] Mindy believes that "we can function on both levels at once when we learn different ways of praying that help connect us to God and others."

Throughout this book, we will suggest several of these different ways of praying, as well as other spiritual practices that can help us communicate the radical love of God through the power of the Holy Spirit, not just in a moment of planned or spontaneous inspiration, but always, in all our relationships. That's how others identify that we are followers of Christ—by our love (John 13:35, Matthew 7:20). As John Wesley preached, "They who 'walk after the Spirit,' are also led by him into all holiness of conversation. Their 'speech' is always in grace, seasoned with salt; with the love and fear of God. 'No corrupt communication comes out of their mouth, but only that which is good'; that which is 'to the use of edifying'; which is 'meet to minister grace to the hearers.'"[9]

Does this mean that to effectively connect with others, the only thing we need is the power of the Holy Spirit? That even if we are not up to par as communicators, we do not need any knowledge or training in actual communication skills because the Holy Spirit will take care of that too? In fact Jesus told his disciples, "For what you are to say will be given to you at that time; for it is not you who speak, but the Spirit of your Father speaking through you" (Matthew 10:19–20). It is important to note, however, that Jesus said this to those who had been with him daily and who had already been learning from him how to love and relate to others.

Two Sides, One Coin

We need the same kind of learning that Jesus' disciples had when they were with him—the kind that prepares us to be open to the Spirit communicating through us at any moment. In 1 Peter 3:15 (NIV), we are told to "Always be prepared to give an answer to everyone who asks you to give the reason for the hope that you have." Preparation implies training. When he wrote to the Corinthians, the Apostle Paul used the analogy of training for a race to illustrate the importance of being intentional with our spiritual growth: "Everyone who competes in the games goes into strict training" (1 Corinthians 9:25, NIV). Just as physical exercise is important for our bodies, spiritual exercises are important for our souls. These exercises, or spiritual practices, are anything we do regularly and intentionally with the goal of loving God and others more. In a sermon titled "On Pleasing All Men," John Wesley said we are to "labour and pray . . . to be of a calm, dispassionate temper; gentle towards all men," and that we are to "let the gentleness of your disposition appear in the whole tenor of your conversation."[10] Notice Wesley's use of the word "labour." We are to work at developing what Richard J. Foster, who writes extensively on our life with God, calls "holy habits"—again, all for the purpose of growing our love for God and others.

Like two sides of the same coin, both spiritual practices and communication practices are necessary for transforming relationships. As we mentioned in the Introduction, without good communication skills, even well-meaning followers of Jesus can fall short when it comes to cultivating effective relationships. But knowledge and skills training alone cannot transform relationships either—no matter how well backed by good communicators, good Christians, or good research—if the training is not infused with the power of the Holy Spirit. That's why being spiritually prepared to relate to others is crucial too. As the Apostle Paul wrote, we can "speak with the tongues of mortals and of angels" and still lack the spiritual dynamic of love that connects others to the transforming message and mission of Jesus (1 Corinthians 13:1). It is the power of the Holy Spirit in our lives that sustains our ability to love and live out the radical "one another" relational demands found throughout scripture.

> *Like two sides of the same coin, both spiritual practices and communication practices are necessary for transforming relationships.*

Our goal in this book is to show how relationships can be radically transformed through integrating communication practices with spiritual practices. We call this integration *spiritually charged communication,* which we define as *the ongoing, intentional practice of connecting with others in ways that are infused with the love of God and the power of the Holy Spirit—with the goal of helping God's Kingdom come on earth as it is in heaven.* Engaging in spiritually charged communication requires that we learn from the one who did it best.

Connecting Through Jesus' Threefold Ministry

In the first week of some of Mary's communication classes, she asks students to find a passage from one of the Gospels—Matthew, Mark, Luke, or John—and tell the class what they observed about Jesus communicating in that particular passage. Students consistently notice that Jesus did not have one set way of connecting with others. Although Jesus' purpose to proclaim the Kingdom of God remained the same, Jesus took on different roles as he interacted with others. How he connected depended on his audience and the particular situation. We must do likewise. That means we need to be aware of the different ways Jesus connected to others. Consequently, we have structured the book in accordance with Jesus' threefold ministry: that of preaching, teaching, and healing. His preaching was such that his listeners testified that "never has anyone spoken like this!" (John 7:46). His teachings were so profound that they transcended Jesus' own time and are still relevant and revolutionary today. The brightest philosophers and scientists marvel at what Jesus had to say. And when it came to healing, Jesus did something more than just cure people's physical ailments. He healed people's souls. Taking on these different roles may sound like a tall, even impossible, order, but Jesus himself said that his followers are called to do even "greater things" than he did (John 14:12).

If at this point you are starting to think that this book may not be for you because you don't see yourself as a healer, teacher, or preacher, we ask you to keep reading. What we write is not meant only for those who have been identified with special gifts of healing, teaching, or preaching. Rather, our hope is that what we have to say is applicable to *all* who desire to follow Jesus. Although you may not see yourself as a healer in terms of having a gift for physical healing, our focus—on the *healing of souls*—is a call for everyone who wants to imitate Christ. It is meant for anyone who wants to go deeper in their relationships—those who crave friendships beyond surface talk; mothers and fathers who want in-depth connectedness with their children, and children who want the same; husbands and wives who want to relate in more profound ways than the romantic exchanges that first attracted them to each other; those who want to "bear one another's burdens" (Galatians 6:2) and give comfort to troubled or brokenhearted friends; and for those who need comforting themselves.

Our focus on *teaching* is in the context of the Great Commission, which requires disciples of Jesus to make other disciples through teaching them to observe all that Jesus has commanded (Matthew 28:16–20). That kind of teaching can be done through more formal classroom instruction and public speaking situations as well as more informally, in one-on-one teaching. Either way, the Great Commission calls all of Jesus' disciples, past and present, to be teachers.

And finally, our focus on *preaching* is addressed in the context of proclaiming Jesus' message and mission whenever appropriate—whether formally or informally in one-on-one conversations, groups, Bible studies, conferences, retreats, seminars, or as part of a church service.

Each chapter will address specific communication and spiritual practices that when combined produce spiritually charged communication. Please know that we are not suggesting that these particular practices are the only ones worth mentioning. There are numerous communication and spiritual practices that can help us connect like Jesus. We highlight those that have been especially meaningful in our lives and in the lives of people we know.

We start here with two practices that lay the foundation for the rest of the practices throughout the book.

Foundational Practices for Connecting Like Jesus

To connect like Jesus we need to be connected *to* Jesus. Jesus wants to be in intimate relationship with each one of us. If you have never been aware of God's great love for you and how much God wants to be in relationship with *you,* or if you have lost sight of that truth in your life—no matter the reason—then spending time with Jesus can help you discover God's immense love for you.

> *To connect like Jesus we need to be connected to Jesus.*

Prayer of the Soul

If you don't know where to start in deeply connecting with Jesus, you can picture yourself in the shelter of God's wings, or resting in Jesus' arms. Or you could picture Jesus stretching out his arms to you, saying

"Please give your burdens to me—I will take them all, no matter how large or small." Envision yourself giving everything to Jesus; see him gladly take your burdens and envelope you in his arms. As you rest in Jesus, accept his immense love for you deep in your soul. Ask the Holy Spirit to give you reassurance of God's love for you, perhaps repeating these words from a worship song for your prayer: "Spirit of the Living God, fall afresh on me."[11]

Learning About Jesus' Life

Along with connecting to Jesus in prayer, so as to be empowered by the same Spirit that empowered Jesus, we also need to become more familiar with Jesus' life. The best way to do that is to read the Gospels: Matthew, Mark, Luke, and John. You could start with Matthew and

- o Read one or two chapters a day until you go through all four Gospels.
- o Listen to a recording of the Gospels on CD when you are driving, waiting in your car, or working in your kitchen.
- o Put MP3 recordings on your iPod so that you can listen when you go for a walk, work around your house or apartment, or wait for an appointment.

Whenever you read or listen to the Gospels, we encourage you to ask the Holy Spirit to speak to you through the various ways in which Jesus connected to others.

Trinity Prayer

If you want to delve further into relationship with the Trinity, we suggest a prayer that may strike you as a little odd at first, but we ask that you consider trying it. Imagine yourself in conversation with the Trinity—God, Jesus Christ, and the Holy Spirit. To do this, you can form an image in your mind of each of them. You could use whatever image you have when you think of the Holy Spirit or Jesus or God, as long as those images are loving ones instead of troublesome to you. If any are troublesome, such as a picture of God as Father when you have had problems with a father figure in your life, then you may want to hold off on this prayer until you experience each member of the Trinity genuinely loving you. If that is the case, we recommend going back and spending time in the first prayer we just suggested, as well as talking to a trusted spiritual mentor, pastor, or friend.

When you are ready to pray this second relationship prayer, imagine yourself sitting at a table with the Trinity, having a meal. If you are having trouble envisioning that scene, you could take an idea Mary's pastor, Mark Van Valin, introduced in church one day. He wanted the congregation to better understand the nature of the Christian life through focusing visually on *Holy Trinity,* the painting by Andrei Rublev (1415). In this painting, God, Jesus, and the Holy Spirit are sitting at a table with a golden chalice. Pastor Mark encouraged the congregation to meditate on Jesus coming into our life and "eating with us" and asked us to think about how these images might help us understand our Christian life and our relationship with Jesus. He then told us to reflect on the words of Jesus from Revelation 3:20: "Here I am! I stand at the door and knock. If anyone hears my voice and opens the door, I will come in and eat with him, and he with me."

After reflecting on this verse and the scene at the table, have an actual conversation with the Trinity. You might ask questions that come to you, or tell them something that is on your mind; don't be hesitant to wait in silence and see if they have any comments or questions for you. Perhaps they will say things to one another and you will listen. Let the scene unfold and see what happens. After anywhere from a few to several minutes, you can tell them how good it was to eat with them.

Praying this prayer can give you a new or renewed appreciation for the relational aspect of the Trinity and how that relationship can feed your soul. It can also create a desire in you for better relationships with others.

Learning the "One Another" Verses

To build a more personal foundation for connecting like Jesus, we recommend becoming familiar with the "one another" verses in the Bible. You'll find them throughout the New Testament. We've also provided a list of several of them at the back of the book.[12] Because they are short, you could pick a few each week to commit to memory and reflect on throughout the week. The spiritual and communication practices throughout the book are intended to help you live out these verses in concrete ways in your relationships. To help you remember to think of the verses you have chosen for the week, you could post them where you can easily see them. If you have Facebook, you might consider putting them on your profile. (Then others can help you be accountable in trying to live them out!)

In our interview, Brian McLaren echoed the importance of having one of our initial spiritual practices focus on scripture: "There are a lot of ways to define spiritual practices, but one way is to say that it is to practice obeying scripture, like 'Be kind to one another.' Then the question is, 'How do I practice kind words?' Every social interaction is communicative, so every social action becomes a spiritual practice. I'm either practicing bad behavior or practicing Christlike behavior."

Practicing Christlike behavior means learning how to obey scripture (such as the "one another" verses) in concrete ways, through solid communication practices empowered by the Spirit of God. The deliberate combination of the two is critical if we want to connect like Jesus. As Mindy Caliguire said in our interview, "The gravitational pull of daily life typically draws my attentiveness away from God, so that's why I need to be intentional with these various practices."

It is our hope that in the following chapters, you will discover how integrating several spiritual and communication practices results in a dynamic combination that can transform all our relationships and, in turn, transform the world.

2

Soul Healing

Connecting Like Jesus Through Care of the Soul

Be kind, for everyone you meet is fighting a great battle.
—Philo of Alexandria

He restores my soul.
—Psalm 23:3

IN ONE OF HIS PARABLES, Jesus tells the story of a son who left home, spent all of his inheritance, and found himself homeless. Destitute and devastated, with no options left, he wondered if he should try to go back to his father's house. Believing he didn't deserve to live any longer as his father's son, he decided he would ask his father if he could live as one of the hired hands instead. Here's what happened next:

> When he was still a long way off his father saw him. His heart pounding, he ran out, embraced him, and kissed him. The son started his speech: "Father, I've sinned against God, I've sinned before you; I don't deserve to be called your son ever again." But the father wasn't listening. He was calling to the servants, "Quick. Bring a clean set of clothes and dress him. Put the family ring on his finger and sandals on his feet. Then get a grain-fed heifer and roast it. We're going to feast! We're going to have a wonderful time! My son is here—given up for dead and now alive! Given up for lost and now found!" [Luke 15:20–24, The Message]

We are not told how the son responded at that moment. We can only imagine the healing that took place deep in his soul after realizing his father still loved him and wanted him back *home,* in spite of what he had done. This parable is a powerful story of God's redemptive love. It is also a powerful reminder of how Jesus' love and acceptance of us can restore our souls.

Jesus and the Healing of Souls

One day when Jesus sat down to teach a crowd of people, the teachers of the law and the Pharisees brought a woman to Jesus who had been caught sleeping with a man who was not her husband. They reminded him that the law of Moses commanded that such a woman be stoned to death. They asked, "Now what do you say?" This question was not about the woman; they didn't care about her. Its purpose was to trap Jesus. If they could get Jesus to admit that his message of love and forgiveness was in conflict with the law, they would then have a reason to accuse him. But Jesus did care about the woman—he cared deeply, even though he knew what she had been caught doing. Instead of answering the question, Jesus knelt down and wrote on the ground. Then he stood up and said, "Let anyone among you who is without sin be the first to throw a stone at her" (John 8:7). Again he wrote on the ground. No one knows what Jesus wrote. Whatever it was, it had quite an impact on the teachers and Pharisees because they all walked away. In fact, everyone walked away, leaving only the woman and Jesus, the only one without sin who could have actually thrown a stone. Jesus then asked her, " 'Woman, where are they? Has no one condemned you?' She said, 'No one, sir.' And Jesus said, 'Neither do I condemn you. Go your way and from now on do not sin again' " (John 8:10–11).

Imagine being that woman. There you are, condemned by the religious leaders for doing something that was by law to result in your death. You are terrified. But then this man you don't even know not only shows you compassion but saves your life. With his noncondemnation of the woman, Jesus set the stage for healing deep in her soul.[1]

Another day, Jesus was passing through Jericho where a hated, wealthy tax collector named Zacchaeus lived. Zacchaeus wanted to see Jesus; because he was short and the crowd was blocking his view, he climbed a tree. When Jesus reached the tree, he looked up and said, "Zacchaeus, hurry and come down; for I must stay at your house today" (Luke 19:5). The crowd was not at all happy that Jesus had invited himself to the home of someone they considered a sinner. But Zacchaeus was happy. Because Jesus not only acknowledged but also affirmed him by wanting to stay at his house, Zacchaeus in turn wanted to change his whole life.

He told Jesus, " 'Look, half of my possessions, Lord, I will give to the poor; and if I have defrauded anyone of anything, I will pay back four times as much.' Then Jesus said to him, 'Today salvation has come to this house, because he too is a son of Abraham. For the Son of Man came to seek out and to save the lost' " (Luke 19:8–10).

Imagine being Zacchaeus, a man people hated and whose occupation put him in the "sinner" category. Then Jesus shows up. With his non-condemnation in the midst of Zacchaeus's judgment from the crowd, Jesus healed his soul, freeing Zacchaeus to leave his self-serving life to serve others instead.

Jesus as Healer

Both of these situations involve Jesus healing, although they may not be what typically comes to mind when we picture Jesus as healer. When we read in Matthew that "Jesus went through all the towns and villages . . . healing every disease and sickness" (Matthew 9:35, NIV), we most likely think of physical healing because there are numerous accounts in the Gospels: in Matthew 8 alone we find Jesus healing a man with leprosy, a man who was paralyzed (he even did this one from afar), and a woman with a fever.

Much has been written on Jesus and his ministry of physical healing. Our focus, however, is on the kind of healing Jesus did with the woman caught in adultery and with Zacchaeus: the healing of souls. As Matthew wrote, Jesus healed *every* disease and *every* sickness—body and soul. And although physical and soul healing can go hand in hand, Tony had an intense experience several years ago that we believe illustrates the difference between the two.[2] Here is the story in his words:

> *Our focus is on the kind of healing Jesus did with the woman caught in adultery and with Zacchaeus: the healing of souls.*

Once when I was a visiting preacher at a church in Oregon, halfway through my sermon I noticed there was a small bottle of oil on a shelf inside the back of the pulpit. I knew immediately that it was put there by the pastor of the church who had a weekly healing service. On what I believe was the impulse of the Spirit, at the end of my sermon, I invited any who wanted me to pray over them and to anoint their heads with oil, as the Bible prescribes in James 5:14–16, to stay after the worship service was over and come forward for prayer. I explained to the congregation that any who did stay for healing should not be in a hurry because before I would pray for healing for anyone, I wanted to spend enough time listening to the burdens on their hearts so that I might have some basis on which to connect with them spiritually and emotionally. I made it clear that I was not like those healers we see on television who can lay hands on people, knock them over and then raise them up healed of their physical ailments or handicaps. Furthermore, I explained, I had never done this sort of thing before, and they shouldn't expect too much from my healing ministry.

Surprisingly, almost thirty people came forward for healing, in spite of my warnings. Most of them had nothing physically wrong with them, but reported psychological and moral maladies from which they wanted deliverance. There were several, however, who were suffering from physical illnesses and problems. I did what I promised to do, entering into intensive but short conversations with each of them; anointing the head of each with oil, in accord with the instructions written in James 5:14; and then, with my hands on their heads, praying for healing.

About three weeks later, I received a call from a woman who told me that on the Sunday that I prayed over people who came for healing, her husband had come forward for prayer. She said he *had* cancer.

I immediately picked up on the word "had"—past tense. I asked her what had happened, and she said, "He died."

Needless to say, I was distraught at that answer and told the woman how sorry I was that my prayer for healing had not been effective.

"Oh! Don't apologize," she said. "I called to thank you for your prayer. You see, when my husband went into church that day, he knew he had cancer and didn't have long to live. He was angry with God because he was dying, and the angrier he got at God, the meaner he was to everybody around him. Nobody wanted to be in the same room with him—and least of all me. But you anointed his head with oil and you prayed over him. After that he was changed. He went out of that church a different man.

"The last two-and-a-half weeks we had together were the best days of our marriage. If I had to choose between the past two-and-a-half weeks and the previous thirty-one years of our marriage, it would be an easy choice. I'd choose the last two-and-a-half weeks. We laughed together, prayed together, and even sang together. We talked almost nonstop about meaningful things and about the things that were really important to us."

Then she said, "After you prayed over him, he wasn't cured—but *he was healed.*"

Of course the woman was referring to the healing of the heart and soul of her husband. Cures are only temporary deliverance from death, but the healing in our souls has everlasting significance.

Jesus healed souls not only for the afterlife but for this life too. He cared about others' souls in ways that powerfully healed their deepest hurts. This is what we mean when we use the term *soul healing.* It is the process of caring for our own as well as others' souls in ways that help free us to live the full, abundant life Jesus wants for us all (John 10:10).

> *Jesus healed souls not only for the afterlife but for this life too.*

Jesus' Purpose in Soul Healing

Everything Jesus did was focused on bringing freedom to *others* through healing in their souls. He didn't think about how an encounter was going to serve him; instead he thought about how it would help others hear and experience the good news of God's Kingdom. If we want to be like Jesus, we too are to pay attention to others. The purpose of our spiritual journey is, in the words of M. Robert Mulholland Jr., "for the sake of others."[3] In Romans 15:2, the Apostle Paul writes that "Each of us must please our neighbour for the good purpose of building up the neighbour." What does it mean to please and build up our neighbor? John Wesley, in his "On Pleasing All Men," said the Apostle Paul intentionally limited what it means to please our neighbor because

> were it pursued without any limitation, it might produce the most mischievous consequences. We are directed to please them *for their good;* not barely for the sake of pleasing them, or pleasing ourselves; much less of pleasing them to their hurt; which is so frequently done by those who do not love their neighbour as themselves. Nor is it only their temporal good, which we are to aim at in pleasing our neighbour; but what is of infinitely greater consequence, we are to do it *for their edification;* . . . make them wiser and better, holier and happier, both in time and in eternity.[4]

Caring for our neighbors as Wesley described requires that we move beyond ourselves into a self-sacrificing love for others. But that is not necessarily an easy task. Until we face the variety of demons in our own souls and surrender them to God, it can be very difficult, if not impossible, to focus on others.

Jesus as Healer of the Demons in Our Souls

An area of soul healing often mentioned in the Gospels is Jesus' healing people from demons (Matthew 4:23–25, 8:14–17, 8:28–34, 9:32–34, 12:22–32; Mark 16:9; Luke 7:21, 13:10–17). Interpretations of this kind of healing vary greatly, ranging from a literal casting out of evil spirits to "demons" being a metaphor for severe emotional and psychological issues. Some who believe Jesus and his Apostles literally cast out evil spirits also believe that this kind of healing was applicable only to that specific period in history; others believe that this literal casting out is for us as followers today too.

Our intent is not to get into a theological battle over the issue of demonic influence. But regardless of one's definition of or beliefs about what demonic influence actually means, the Gospels are clear that Jesus "cast out demons," resulting in people's being healed from deep soul disturbances. In Luke 8, for example, we are told the account of Jesus casting out several demons from a man who, after the healing, was found "sitting at the feet of Jesus, clothed and in his right mind" (v. 35).

The way demonic influence takes place in a modern scientific world is different from the way it took place in the first century. In the first century, people saw demons more in terms of personality. They had names. Our modern mind-set and worldview lead us to dismiss the idea that certain creatures with personalities and names invade and possess us. The way in which demonic influence expresses itself today is less about being possessed by actual evil beings and more about struggling with certain sinful conditions. Even by the Middle Ages, these modern forms of demonic influence were already beginning to emerge. The Christian community began to refer to them as the seven deadly sins of pride, envy, gluttony, lust, anger, greed, and sloth. Our Pentecostal friends would agree, for they speak in terms of these specific demons, as in "the demon of greed" or "the demon of pride." We believe that these *conditions of the soul* are a modern form of what the Bible refers to as demon possession. When we allow any of them to take hold in our souls, we can be hindered or even prevented from living for God's Kingdom.

Is It Well with Your Soul?

Perhaps you can answer that question immediately. Perhaps you need to reflect on it awhile. Either way, it's an important question to ask ourselves, for we all have hurt or "dis-eases" in our souls. These soul diseases can hinder our ability to connect with Jesus and others. If it's not one or more of the seven deadly sins, then it might be guilt, shame, or self-loathing. Or it may be something else that causes us deep pain. Any one of these can deeply harm our souls. As Wesley scholar Stephen Blakemore wrote, "So vast is the rupture in our human personhood that the power of sin can only be broken in one's life by a total 'healing' of our souls."[5] That's why being open to receiving, as well as giving, soul care is so crucial. As Mindy Caliguire said in our interview, "When I care for my soul, that increases my openness to God, and I more readily experience the flow of God's spirit in and through me."

Admitting to others the brokenness in our own souls opens the door for our own soul healing—and theirs too. As Shane Claiborne said in our interview, "It's through our own brokenness and pain that we are able to speak into the lives of others. A woman who is connected to our community told me, 'Even though Jesus rose from the dead, he still had his scars.'" Jesus was not bound by his scars—instead he used them to help free others, like Doubting Thomas (John 20:19–29), who was freed when Jesus let him touch his scars. Again, freedom is what the Kingdom of God is about. As Paul wrote to the Galatians, "It is for freedom that Christ has set us free. Stand firm, then, and do not let yourselves be burdened again by a yoke of slavery. . . . You, my brothers, were called to be free. But do not use your freedom to indulge the sinful nature; rather, serve one another in love" (Galatians 5:1–2, 13, NIV).

We can all experience freedom from whatever enslaves us if we accept the saving grace of God. Then we need to live in that grace. Having people to talk to who have experienced freedom through grace—and continue to do so—can help us live in that freedom, as can practices like the ones we suggest throughout the book. After Mindy emphasized the importance of caring for our souls, she went on to say that she believes we do that by "intentionally placing ourselves—our souls—in a place of connection with God. This happens through a wide variety of practices, but they all have in common the desire for me to connect authentically with God—because only God can infuse life, grace, energy, peace . . . everything that my soul thirsts for."

Yes, only God can give us what our soul thirsts for. But we don't always live as if that were true. That's why we need people and practices to help point us to God and away from the biggest hurdle to our soul healing, a hurdle that is always close by: our own selves.

Freedom Through Dying to Self

One day when Mary was at one of those "one-stop shopping" stores with her two boys, her son David, then about four years old, was insistent on getting a toy. He kept asking if she would buy this or that toy, which started to really annoy her. Finally she said to him firmly, "David, I am not buying anything for you today, so you can just give it up." She did not expect the response she got. Instead of arguing, David immediately looked relieved; he relaxed and then seemed very content the rest of the time in the store.

Being released from focusing on our perceived desires can be the most freeing feeling in the world. It seems paradoxical, doesn't it? But giving up our own desires really does lead to freedom. It is what Jesus calls us to do when he says we are to lose our lives for his sake (Luke 9:24). This "dying to self" means giving up our agenda for God's agenda; it means recognizing our place in God's plan and submitting to that place. That is what John the Baptist did when Jesus started his public ministry. When John was with two of his own disciples one day and Jesus walked by, John pointed to Jesus and said, 'Look, the Lamb of God!' (John 1:36, NIV). As soon as John's disciples heard this, they started following Jesus. John did not run after them and try to get them back. Instead he said, "[Jesus] must increase, but I must decrease" (John 3:30). We also are to point people to Jesus instead of to ourselves. But since we can't point to Jesus literally, as John did, our calling is to become more and more like Jesus so that when people are with us, they are drawn to him.

As freeing as it is to die to self, we do not give ourselves up easily. French theologian and poet François Fénelon wrote, "Many think that 'dying to themselves' is what causes them so much pain. But it is actually part of them that still lives that causes the problem. Your imagination exaggerates how bad death will be. Let all that is not born of God within you die."[6] As we reflect on what might be in us that is not from God, we may find that we fear losing control over our lives, including certain wants and desires for people and possessions or recognition and respect. If that is the case, the best advice from lovers of Jesus who have gone before us is this: trust Jesus. Trust that there is life-transforming freedom in losing ourselves for the sake of God and others. If you don't know where to begin, let us recommend two different ways you can pray to develop trust in Jesus. The first is one that Mindy Caliguire described in our interview: "I quiet myself and yield to the Holy Spirit in silence to come to a place of peace and centeredness to reestablish a connection with God and get clear, once again, why I'm doing whatever I'm doing.

I focus on my utter dependence on God for making any difference in people's lives. Using scripture like 'hiding myself in him' from Psalm 143:9 helps me here. It's the idea of becoming invisible so that God is more visible through my life."

As freeing as it is to die to self, we do not give ourselves up easily.

The second prayer is one Shane Claiborne recommended, called "Radiating Christ." It was written by Cardinal Newman and used in slightly altered form as a daily community prayer by the late Mother Teresa and the Sisters of the Missionaries of Charity.

Dear Jesus,
help me to spread Thy fragrance everywhere I go.
Flood my soul with Thy spirit and life.
Penetrate and possess my whole being so utterly
that all my life may only be a radiance of Thine.
Shine through me,
and be so in me that every soul I come in contact with
may feel Thy presence in my soul.
Let them look up and see no longer me
but only Jesus!
Stay with me,
and then I shall begin to shine
as Thou shinest,
so to shine as to be a light to others;
the light, O Jesus, will be all from Thee;
none of it will be mine;
it will be Thou shining on others through me.
Let me thus praise Thee in the way Thou dost love best
by shining on those around me.
Let me preach Thee without preaching,
not by words but by my example,
by the catching force of the sympathetic influence
of what I do,
the evident fulness of the love my heart bears to Thee.
Amen.

Regularly praying one or both of these prayers can help us lose our selves for the sake of God's Kingdom, and therein discover our true selves in Christ. This discovery frees us to really care for the souls of others.

Our Role in Soul Healing

As imitators of Christ, the greatest servant of all, each one of us is called to the healing of souls. That does not mean that we try to figure out exactly what someone needs and then "fix" him or her—that's the Holy Spirit's job. Our calling to care for others' souls is not about our projecting onto someone else what we think that person needs. Even if we are convinced we are right, we could still be wrong. We cannot know the depths of what makes people act and react the way they do. Even what someone shares with us could be but a glimpse of something much larger than we could ever imagine. That's why we are to put our trust in God, not ourselves, to speak into a person's soul. Our role is to be a vessel, available for the Holy Spirit to work through.

The Holy Spirit is the real healer of souls. If we ever think we are the ones doing the healing, then we are on very dangerous ground. It is *always* the Spirit who heals. We are helpers, midwives if you will, for the rebirthing of souls. We are not to be like a global positioning system (GPS) that tells others which direction to go. Instead, we are to help guide others to listen and respond to what we could call the True GPS—the global positioning Spirit—who knows the way. Learning to be more in tune with the Spirit so that we are worthy guides is the aim of this book.

> *The Holy Spirit is the real healer of souls. If we ever think we are the ones doing the healing, then we are on very dangerous ground.*

Although in this book our focus on soul healing is primarily in the context of conversations with others, we do not take lightly the importance of wordless actions in caring for one another's souls. What we do for others when their souls are aching or weary is just as important as what we say. Making meals and mowing lawns—or helping someone find a job, acquire the skills for a job, or leave a harmful situation—are all ways we can help those whose souls are hurting. Mary's lifelong friend Pat has been going through an extended period of serious health struggles with her husband, Carl. Here is what she told Mary about being on the receiving end of soul care that goes beyond words:

> For as long as I can remember, I have been part of the meals ministry and felt that I helped people through tough times by doing something so simple as bringing them a meal. However, I have now experienced that in a receiving way, and it confirms the healing that happens by the simple act. Someone bringing a meal refreshes me, calms my day full of doctor appointments and treatments, touches me in a way far beyond the physical nourishment. It is spiritual, emotional, and mental nourishment as well. It is an act of love that I feel as I anticipate the love they are putting into the planning and making of the meal, driving it over to my house, while I'm eating, and when I feel the energy come back to my weary body after the meal. It is absolutely one of the blessings that has kept me going. I will always love doing this for others with a renewed sense of passing on God's love and strength in this way.

Mary has another friend, Carla, who is very action oriented when it comes to caring for others' souls. If Carla thinks someone may need help, she doesn't say, "Let me know if I can do anything." Instead she asks questions like "What food can I bring?" or "Who can I call for you?" Specific offers like these are what a stressed or hurting person needs, especially if the person has trouble accepting help, because these questions require answers. Again, being able to *receive* soul care is essential for our own soul healing. We do not want to refuse soul care, as Peter initially did when Jesus was about to wash his feet (John 13:1). May our sense of self-sufficiency or pride never prevent us from allowing others to show love through acts of service.

Preparation Versus Spontaneity in Soul Healing

The Apostle Peter tells us in 1 Peter 3:15 (NIV) to "Always be prepared to give an answer to everyone who asks you to give the reason for the hope that you have." If we look at this verse in the context of soul healing, then preparation for our encounters with others is essential. The spiritual and communication practices we propose throughout the book can not only alert but also prepare us for soul-healing encounters. Sometimes, however, these practices may come across as too planned or even controlling, leaving little or no room for spontaneity. It is not our intention to script all conversations or kill spontaneity. If our purpose is to connect with others like Jesus, with intentionality fueled by the Holy

Spirit, we can communicate with "planned spontaneity," meaning that we can be prepared to give and receive God's love in all our encounters, whether those encounters are expected or not.

But how?

We believe the answer lies in the verses just prior to 1 Peter 3:15, where Peter writes that we are to keep our tongues from evil and our lips from deceitful speech as we "seek peace and pursue it" (1 Peter 3:10–11). If we develop a *habit* of spiritually charged communication that results in Christlike qualities such as honest speech and the pursuing of peace, then being prepared takes on new meaning. It's not that we will have scripted conversations to fire up at a moment's notice, adapted specifically to a specific encounter. We will, instead, be people whose spirits are more in tune with Jesus' spirit, resulting in increased love and compassion for others. People may come to us for soul care because they sense that love in our souls, not because we have said anything in particular. Or we may seek someone out, sensing that his or her soul is hurting. But that doesn't mean we view *every* encounter as a time for intense, planned healing. Soul healing does not have to imply invariable seriousness or extreme intentionality when we are with others. Jesus was always about advancing the Kingdom of God, but that did not mean that all of his encounters were somber or structured. He spent lots of time walking and talking, and eating with others, and we know of at least one wedding he attended. It is safe to assume that Jesus had spur-of-the-moment fun amid his more serious conversations, and that even serious conversations often arose out of informal gatherings.

In Ecclesiastes 3:1–8, we are told that there is a time for everything, which means there is a time to be intense and a time to be lighthearted, a time to carefully plan and a time to be spontaneous. We do not always have to be anticipating who we might meet and what we might say. That would drive us crazy (not to mention those with whom we come in contact).

As we hope will be implied throughout the book, the healing of souls is a process that includes spontaneity and structure as well as solemnity and levity. Any of these times can be conduits for soul healing. It is important, however, to be alert to what time it is when connecting with another's soul. If we are always joking, our relationships will not connect at a deep soul level. If we are always serious, our relationships will be off balance too. If we always plan how we intend to specifically communicate, we leave no room for the serendipitous healing moments that can surface from spontaneity.

If we remember that there is a time for everything, a healthy balance can emerge as we interact with others for the purpose of soul healing. There should be plenty of room for spontaneity within any intentionality we suggest in this book. It is our hope that as we are guided more and more by the Holy Spirit, spontaneity in our words and actions will flow out of us from that Spirit. We also hope we will be open to the Spirit "expanding our territory" in terms of whose souls we encounter. May we never look past someone God yearns for us to see. Jesus not only saw but focused in on those whom society considered undesirable, like Zacchaeus and the woman caught in adultery. He knew they had deep needs in their souls and spoke to them with revolutionary words of healing. May we all endeavor to take time to see and to know the kinds of people Jesus hung out with, whether that person is our neighbor close by, a person in another part of our town, or someone on the other side of the world.

May we never look past someone God yearns for us to see.

There truly is a time for everything. The practices addressed in the next several chapters are designed to help us become better at telling what time it is so that we can connect like Jesus in ways that honor and glorify God.

PART TWO

PRACTICES FOR SOUL HEALING

MARY ALBERT DARLING

3

It *Is* About You

Knowing Yourself as the Starting Point for Soul Healing

Oh it's so hard to see, when my eyes are on me.
—from "Make My Life a Prayer," sung by Keith Green

May I know myself, may I know Thee.
—Augustine

ALTHOUGH "IT'S NOT ABOUT YOU" is a popular line, it is not entirely true. It *is* about you, especially if you want to help care for others' souls. The Golden Rule, given to us by Jesus, states, "In everything do to others as you would have them do to you; for this is the law and the prophets" (Matthew 7:12). Jesus goes on to say in Matthew 19:19 that the second greatest commandment, just after "Love the Lord your God" is to "love your neighbor as yourself." The assumption in both of these verses is that we want to be loved and treated in healthy, life-affirming ways, and that's how we are to treat others too. These verses also imply that we know what is best for ourselves and that we are consciously aware of how *we* want others to care for *our* own souls.

> *It* is *about you, especially if you want to help care for others' souls.*

But that may not be true for everyone. Some people may not know or love themselves and therefore do not know the best ways to treat themselves, much less others.

That is why focusing on how we want to be treated is important. But it still may seem too self-centered. This kind of self-awareness is not selfish, however, *unless* we figure out how we want to be treated—and then stay there. As we have seen, if we want to be like Jesus, then our eyes must inevitably move from ourselves to others.

Exceptions to the Golden Rule?

Even though we may believe the Golden Rule in theory, there may be certain people who we do not think deserve to be treated in loving and edifying ways. But Jesus did not put any exceptions or qualifications on the Golden Rule. He did not say, "Do to others as you want them to do to you unless it is someone who is mean to you, irritates you, or even does something harmful or hateful." I often wish he did. But long before Nike came along, Jesus told his followers to *just do it*. That is why it is called the Golden Rule, not the Golden Suggestion. If it were a suggestion, when someone does something unloving to us, we would not have to be loving in return. Mean people are not easy to like, much less love. Yet if we want to follow the Golden Rule, we must be loving and kind. That is the path to soul healing, and it's not always an easy one. It is interesting to note that right before stating the Golden Rule in Luke 6:31, Jesus tells us to "Love your enemies, do good to those who hate you, bless those who curse you, pray for those who mistreat you" (Luke 6:27–28). In Romans 12:17–21, Paul expands on what it means to love others: "Don't hit back; discover beauty in everyone. If you've got it in you, get along with everybody. Don't insist on getting even; that's not for you to do. 'I'll do the judging,' says God. 'I'll take care of it.' Our Scriptures tell us that if you see your enemy hungry, go buy that person lunch, or if he's thirsty, get him a drink. Your generosity will surprise him with goodness. Don't let evil get the best of you; get the best of evil by doing good" (The Message).

> *But Jesus did not put any exceptions or qualifications on the Golden Rule.*

I find it easy to romanticize these verses. Loving my enemy seems noble as a concept and at a distance. I can pray for my enemies as faceless entities. But when they become real people, sometimes the last thing I want to do is love them.

I have a friend, Jacob Atem, who is one of the "lost boys" of Sudan. Both of his parents were killed in Sudan's 1987 civil war. As their village was burning, six-year-old Jacob and his older cousin fled to the jungle, and then along with thousands of other boys whose parents had been murdered, soon began the thousand-mile walk to Ethiopia and then Kenya. Only half of them made it. Jacob was carried much of the way on his cousin's back, and the two of them barely escaped death several times.

Jacob told me that he has forgiven the people who killed his parents and caused horrific pain and death to thousands. I asked him if he could say that he not only has forgiven but also loves these people. He immediately replied, "Oh yeah! If I forgive them, there's no reason I shouldn't love them." Jacob said that the only reason he does not hate them is because of his relationship with Jesus. On his own, he never could. "Based on my life story, how can anybody honestly convince me that I am to love them? There is no way, except with the Holy Spirit in me. I call this the Holy Spirit communication. It's the Holy Spirit in me. I see the people who killed my parents through the Holy Spirit. I am so thankful that God is in me." Jacob went on to say that "Other Christians helped change my view, but the Holy Spirit changed my view most. I am in love with God and God is helping me through other people."[1]

Jacob's attitude may be hard to grasp and even harder to put into action. But as theologian Wendy M. Wright wrote in *The Rising*, "We may not like the other but we are called to love. We may certainly not validate or condone his or her actions. But we are called into a radical sense of our interconnectedness as creatures and children of the same God. To perceive this deeplevel of interdependence, especially with those . . . who would seek to harm or destroy our worlds, seems a nearly impossible task. Yet the Gospels prod us on. . . . At the furthest reaches of our capacities to love, we are urged, 'Love even your enemies.'"[2]

Jacob was able to forgive, and now he is helping heal others' souls because the Holy Spirit profoundly healed his soul. Jacob's kind of transformation is only possible if you are willing to become fertile ground for the work of the Spirit. That can't happen without an understanding of another possible enemy: you. If you don't love yourself, you can get in your own way and not be able to love others in the ways God intended. You can learn to love yourself by accepting God's love for you—available at *any* moment. Then you can start the transformational process of becoming aware of how you truly and lovingly want to be treated so that you can treat others that way too. The following communication and spiritual practices can help you gain this awareness so that you can live out the Golden Rule and become focused on others— for the purpose of helping heal their souls.

The Practice of Noticing

Noticing how and why you think, feel, believe, talk, act, and react the way you do opens the door to discovering your true self—an image bearer of God—so that you can treat others in soul-healing ways. Without this awareness, we can too easily get stuck in faulty, unhealthy relationships and never know why, much less know how to fix or even get out of them. When I asked Mindy Caliguire in our interview what she saw as the role of self-awareness in connecting with others, this is what she said:

> Because I see sharing my faith as sharing what is real—like my experience of faith, of trusting God, and of being confident in the Kingdom—rather than sharing a core set of doctrinal statements, self-awareness is critical. I need to ask myself how exactly am I trusting God right now? In what way am I choosing faith? What is the basis of my confidence? Where am I struggling to have faith or to believe in God's presence, goodness, purpose in a given situation?

Being able to honestly answer questions like these requires a great deal of awareness. Socrates, the great Greek philosopher, understood the importance of self-awareness when he said, "the unexamined life is not worth living." But David, the Psalmist, understood that *self*-awareness alone was not enough. In Psalm 139 he wrote, "Search me, O God, and know my heart; test me and know my thoughts. See if there is any wicked way in me, and lead me in the way everlasting" (Psalm 139:23–24). David knew that God must guide his self-awareness if he was to discover his true self. Jesus promised that God's Spirit would be available to guide us, too (John 14:16–17). The Holy Spirit can reveal any unhealthy patterns in ourselves, as long as we don't block the Spirit's work in our lives.

One night, when the temperature had gone down to seven degrees, our furnace stopped working. When the technician came, he could not find anything wrong with the furnace, although it was not blowing out any heat. When he went outside, he found that the entrances to our exhaust pipes were covered with ice, blocking the pipes from getting any air. We can be like those pipes, shut off from the work of the Spirit due to our hardened hearts or to aspects of ourselves we have never noticed (but others may have). Asking the Holy Spirit to help us look honestly at ourselves, just as David did in Psalm 139, opens us to the redemptive work of the Spirit in our lives. Healing from the Spirit then enables us to help heal others.

Jesus often invited others to become more self-aware. As Brian McLaren noted in our interview, "Jesus tried to help people see themselves. He would tell a parable, and the Pharisees would know that he was speaking of them [Luke 18:9–14]. . . . In the parable of the prodigal son, after he left home, squandered his money, and ate with pigs, the prodigal son 'came to himself' [Luke 15:16–17], which is another illustration Jesus used to help people see themselves in a different light." Not all who Jesus invited accepted his invitation to increased awareness.

Jesus often invited others to become more self-aware.

Brian's first example with the Pharisees illustrates the problem of a hardened heart. His second example is more hopeful—the prodigal son became more self-aware. But before we decide to leave home and go through the trials and mistakes that lead us to eat with pigs, let's first try looking at reasons the prodigal son may not have been self-aware enough in the first place.

Difficulties in Becoming More Aware

Becoming aware of how we relate to others can be difficult for a variety of reasons. Some of us may not think much at all about how we come across to others—in the field of communication, such people are called "low self-monitors"—whereas others of us, "high self-monitors," may think about it a lot. A good exercise to determine where you might fall on this high-to-low continuum is to visualize yourself as a bystander as you go through your most recent twelve waking hours. How might your words, the tone of your voice, your eye contact, and other body language have been interpreted by others? How much did you show that you are interested in seeing them? How often were you supportive? Angry? In a bad mood?

If you are surprised by what you recall, you are probably more toward the low-self-monitor end of the continuum. If you are not surprised by observations of your behavior, you are most likely on the higher end of the continuum. Our ability to self-monitor is an aspect of what is called *impression management,* which is our attempts to influence how others see us, including that all-important first impression. In an old "Far Side" cartoon by Gary Larson, Tarzan is anticipating meeting Jane. In his mind he is going over the various ways he might greet her, including "How do you do. My name is Tarzan, and I believe you are known as Jane?"

and "Allow me to introduce myself . . . I am Tarzan, Lord of the Jungle
. . . And you?" When he actually sees her, he blurts out, "Me Tarzan!
You Jane!"

We use impression management in a variety of ways, from trying to
impress a love interest to getting a job. The idea of impression management may seem disingenuous, but if our goal is to connect with others
in the best ways possible, then it is important to be purposeful about
how we come across. Intentionally creating false impressions is, of
course, wrong. But we can *uninten-*
tionally create false impression too.
Although high self-monitors can see
themselves as very self-aware, that
does not guarantee that they are
accurate in their awareness. How
we see ourselves coming across does
not necessarily match how others
see us.

> *How we see ourselves*
> *coming across does not*
> *necessarily match how*
> *others see us.*

If you have ever watched the popular show *The Office*, you might
have noticed that the main character, Michael Scott, appears to be trying
to be very intentional in how he communicates. He thinks he is a great
manager who relates well with his staff, but many of his employees see
him as incompetent. They often roll their eyes when he talks, or they
take offense or are confused by his words; but he seems to be clueless
about his communication style.

You may know someone like this—someone who believes he knows
how he is coming across, but does not. If you don't know anyone like
this, you may want to consider what Steve Carell, who plays Michael
Scott, said in an interview on *Larry King Live*, June 17, 2008: "If you
don't know a Michael Scott, you are a Michael Scott." If you start to
think you may lack some self-awareness—perhaps even like a Michael
Scott—the practices in the rest of this chapter can help you know what
to do with this newfound awareness.

For followers of Jesus, any impression management and increase
in self-awareness are to be for the purpose of connecting to others in
ways that help usher in God's Kingdom. But even if that is our goal,
it doesn't mean that self-awareness comes easily. There are things
we may not want to see in ourselves. Self-protection is a strong force
that often produces self-deception. The result can be harmful, discon-
nected relationships with others, as well as with God. That is why it is
vitally important for us to strive to be as honest with ourselves as
possible.

The first obstacle to self-awareness is that it can be just as difficult to recognize our strengths as to admit our weaknesses. For some of us, we may think that not admitting our strengths shows humility, but in fact this could be false humility. For others, an honest assessment of strengths can be especially challenging if their self-esteem is unrealistically inflated, meaning that they feel good about themselves in ways they perhaps ought not to. My husband related a tongue-in cheek term he heard, "pronoia" (the opposite of paranoia), to describe those who think others like them when they really don't! In their book, *Psychology Through the Eyes of Faith*, renowned Christian social psychologist David G. Myers and psychology professor Malcolm A. Jeeves give several examples of inflated self-esteem.

Myers and Jeeves write that "In virtually any area that is both subjective and socially desirable, most people see themselves as better than average. . . . Most businesspeople see themselves as more ethical than the average business person. Most community residents see themselves as less prejudiced than their neighbors. . . . When the College Board asked high school seniors to compare themselves with others their own ages . . . [i]n ability to get along with others, *zero* percent of the 829,000 students who responded rated themselves below average, while 60 percent saw themselves in the top 10 percent and 25 percent put themselves in the top 1 percent. If Elizabeth Barrett Browning were still writing she would perhaps rhapsodize, 'How do I love me? Let me count the ways.'"[3]

There are numerous inventories, including several inventories of spiritual gifts, that can help us become more aware of both our limitations and our strengths. We can also ask others their opinions of our strengths; what they *don't* say can clue us in to our limitations. As Shane Claiborne said in our interview, "Knowing the things we are good at and the things we are not is crucial. Self-awareness makes us ready to collaborate and build on someone else's gifts."

Whereas some of us may need to bring our self-esteem down a notch in certain areas, others don't come close to having exaggerated self-esteem, or any self-esteem at all, for that matter. These people cannot seem to find anything in themselves that resembles a strength. There are at least three possible reasons for this. First, it can be especially hard to see the good in yourself if others have downplayed, ignored, or criticized your positive characteristics. If you grew up in a home where a parent or sibling treated you in one or more of these destructive ways, you know what I am talking about. You may even have come to believe that you did something to deserve that treatment. But *nobody* deserves to be treated in these dehumanizing ways. The good news is that God can help you identify your strengths—if you trust in God's Spirit instead of your own. One of the best ways to identify your strengths is through a spiritual practice called the *prayer of examen,* highlighted at the end of this chapter.

The second reason you may find it difficult to see the good in yourself is that there is something you have done, or that has been done to you, that consumes you with so much shame and guilt that you don't believe there is any good in you. If that is the case, God really can free you. God loves you in spite of what you have done or what has been done to you. Believing this truth will free you to accept and receive God's gift of grace. As the Apostle Paul wrote to the church at Ephesus, "For by grace you have been saved through faith—and this not your own doing; it is the gift of God—not the result of works, so that no one may boast" (Ephesians 2:8–9).

The third reason you may have trouble seeing the good in yourself is that you possess a certain characteristic that you despise about yourself but can't change. Your embarrassment and negative self-talk might make it almost impossible to see any positive traits. I know someone who used to base almost his entire identity on a physical deformity. It embarrassed him greatly, but I never even noticed the deformity until he pointed it out to me. Yet it loomed so large for him that he was barely aware of his many strengths, even though others often praised him for them. What he did not realize is that although he could not change the deformity, he could change the way he felt about it. This is true not only with physical deformities but also with many other perceived areas of weakness in our lives. God's grace can bring about a change in attitude in ways we too often do not believe possible. The Holy Spirit can help us refocus and even help us see that our weaknesses can be strengths when God is in them.

The Apostle Paul had an affliction that he prayed to God to rid him of, but God did not. Instead God said, "My grace is sufficient for you, for power is made perfect in weakness." Paul responded, "So I will boast all the more gladly of my weaknesses, so that the power of Christ may dwell in me. Therefore I am content with weaknesses, insults, hardships, persecutions, and calamities for the sake of Christ; for whenever I am weak, then I am strong" (2 Corinthians 12:9–10). Accepting our weaknesses, however, does not give us permission to refuse to become more aware of our shortcomings. It does not give us license to give up on working toward fixing those shortcomings. But it does give us permission to receive God's grace for those areas that we cannot change. As the Serenity Prayer says so well, we need God's wisdom to know the difference between what can be changed and what cannot.[4]

Although intentionally becoming more aware of our weaknesses is not easy or pleasant, again, it is essential if we want to find what is hindering us from relating to others in soul-healing ways. As John Wesley preached, "Be deeply sensible of your own weaknesses, follies, and imperfections; as well as of the sin remaining in your heart."[5] That might not be what we want to hear, as it's easier to be aware of others' weaknesses instead. But we are to begin within ourselves. As Jesus said in Matthew 7:3–5, "Why do you see the speck in your neighbor's eye, but do not notice the log in your own eye? Or how can you say to your neighbor, 'Let me take the speck out of your eye,' while the log is in your own eye? You hypocrite, first take the log out of your own eye, and then you will see clearly to take the speck out of your neighbor's eye." In other words, we need to notice and change our own faults before we even think of pointing out others' weaknesses. Noticing our own faults should help make us much more understanding of the faults of others. And even then, if we think we are doing someone a favor by pointing out his or her weaknesses, it may be hard to know if our motives are pure. In reality, we may want to make ourselves look good or the other person look bad (or both).

What bothers us about someone can actually be an indicator of what bothers us about ourselves. A sign of impatience in another person can trigger distaste for our own impatience, without our conscious awareness. Or we may be put off by something that is really more a difference in preference than a fault (such as the way a person chews his or her food). French theologian and poet François Fénelon believed that if someone's faults are bothersome to us, it may well be that we are "too fussy and hard to please,"[6] and *we* are the ones who need to change, not the other. Besides, others are more drawn to connect with us when we are a personal example of change rather than a pronouncer of how someone else should change.

Others are more drawn to connect with us when we are a personal example of change rather than a pronouncer of how someone else should change.

Six Crucial Questions for Increased Self-Awareness

The following questions can be useful tools in helping you discover your own level of self-awareness. It may be hard to answer some of the questions honestly, for a variety of reasons. Perhaps certain significant people in your life were not very self-aware, and you picked up their patterns. Or you could be unconsciously protecting yourself from potential hurt. Or there may simply be blind spots in the way you relate to others. Asking the Holy Spirit to reveal hard truths about yourself can free you from harmful patterns so that you can connect with others in more God-honoring ways. I also recommend discussing these awareness questions with a spiritual mentor, spiritual director, or mature friend. One caution, though: do not ask someone for feedback about your level of awareness unless you really want to know. It would not be fair or loving if a person was trying to be honest with you and you got angry at him or her for doing what you asked.

1. **How good do you think you are at seeing situations from someone else's perspective?** I knew of a mother and daughter, I will call them Elaine and Sara, who were having problems living together. Elaine would often complain to me about Sara, and Sara would often express her frustration to me about how much Elaine expected of her. Because I could, at times, observe them living together and agreed with Sara that Elaine's expectations were unreasonable, Sara and I felt it best that I talk to Elaine. I asked Elaine if there was *anything* about the way she related to Sara that she thought might bother Sara. Elaine paused, looked at me sincerely, and said, "No, I don't think so. If there was, I would know it, because it would bother me." It was not the response I was expecting. I had assumed that Elaine would reflect and then have at least some realization of how her expectations might be coming across to Sara.

Elaine was not good at *perspective-taking,* which is the ability to see a situation through the other person's eyes without justifying one's own actions. If she had taken time to look beyond herself and consciously put herself in her daughter's shoes, Elaine might have been able to see and admit at least some of the role she played in their conflict. There are lots of Elaines in the world. It may be easy for us to spot them, but not so easy to admit that we may be an Elaine. The real test of how good we are at looking at situations from other people's points of view is seeing if we can give specific examples, *involving conflicts that weren't resolved our way.* If you have trouble coming up with examples, you may need to rethink how good you are at seeing things from others' points of view, especially in conflict situations. In the chapter on listening (Chapter Five), we propose an empathy exercise that can help with perspective-taking.

2. **Are you willing to say you are or could be wrong?** One of the problems in Elaine and Sara's relationship was that Elaine rarely, if ever, admitted she was wrong. It is difficult to have a clear perspective on someone else if you do not admit your own mistakes. There are four possible reasons for this failure: you sincerely believe you are usually right; you are too proud to admit your mistakes; you are too scared; or you are God. Let's assume it is one of the first three. One of the best examples I have seen of someone who sincerely thought she was usually right came from the 1980s film *Broadcast News*. The main character, Jane Craig, worked in the TV primetime news business and was very idealistic about how the news should be portrayed. At a business cocktail party one evening, she was earnestly telling the station's executive director her ideas. He stopped her at one point and dryly asked what it's like to be the only one in the room who knows the right thing to do. She immediately replied in a very weary tone that it was "awful." She did not realize that he was being sarcastic. She also did not realize how freeing it is to not always have to be right.

> *It is difficult to have a clear perspective on someone else if you do not admit your own mistakes.*

The other two reasons for possibly not admitting your mistakes involve pride and fear. We may not want people to think we are weak ("Never let them see you sweat"), or we may be afraid that if we admit mistakes we will have to do something about them. Both of these attitudes prevent us from experiencing the freedom that comes through these simple but potentially relationship-changing words: "I could be wrong," "I was wrong," or even "Was I wrong?"

3. **Do you *more often than not* see the negative things that happen in your life as the fault of someone or something other than you?** In other words, if your family life, social life, job, school situation, or physical or emotional health is not what you want it to be, do you see the reasons as mostly beyond your control? "More often than not" and "mostly" are essential terms with these questions, considering that external forces can certainly cause you harm or dissatisfaction. But if you

usually blame others for negative circumstances in your life, chances are that you are a *reactor* to life situations, which means you take little to no responsibility for what is happening. If you find yourself often saying things like "My manager expects too much," "The teacher didn't make the assignment clear," or "He's so difficult to get along with," chances are that you are a reactor. When students tell me that they have had several bad roommates, I start to wonder who the bad roommate might actually be.

4. **Do you often cut yourself slack in situations, but do not cut others slack who are in similar situations?** This is often called a *self-serving bias* and is evident when we attribute bad motives to someone for an action, but attribute good motives to ourselves for the very same action. Have you ever thought that the person who cut you off in traffic was a jerk, but then when you mistakenly cut someone else off, you hope he or she understood that you did not do it intentionally—that you really are a nice person? That is the self-serving bias. Unfortunately, I could give lots of personal examples of succumbing to this bias, but I will keep it to one. When I took the milk out of the fridge one afternoon, I was upset that the last person to use the milk did not finish it, as there was such a tiny amount left and the container was taking up much-needed space. I figured that whoever did it was being lazy and did not want to take the time to rinse it out for recycling. Then I remembered that I was the one who had left that amount after measuring for a recipe. I was no longer irritated with the person.

These final two questions may be the most difficult to answer:

5. **Do you have the tendency to think of other people instead of yourself when responding to any of the previous questions?**

6. **Do you believe you are the exception who doesn't show the behavior pointed to in any of the previous questions?**

Answering yes to one or both of these last two questions is probably the best indicator that you have awareness issues to deal with. If you are willing even to admit that *maybe* you do, you are on the right track. If you thought of other people when going through the first four questions, I encourage you to go back through those questions again, this time focusing on yourself. If you believe you had legitimate reasons for being an exception to one or more of those questions, you may want to see if a spiritual mentor or friend agrees with you. Connecting like Jesus requires an honest awareness of ourselves so that we can be free to be more aware of others.

Moving Toward Change

Even when we identify areas where we have lacked awareness, that does not mean we will automatically do something about it. Changing self-perceptions does not automatically lead to behavior change. Transformation is a lifelong process, not a one-time awareness exercise, in which we commit to building on our strengths and changing ineffective and harmful ways we have of relating—including harmful ways we relate to ourselves. As we've seen, those ways not only hurt us but also destructively spill over into how we treat others.

Changing how we see and relate to ourselves and others is worth it, though not easy. If you try doing it on your own, you will probably find that you are the hardest person in the world to change. In fact, trying to change on your own won't work—just as trying to be more self-aware without the Spirit's guidance won't work—if your goal is to connect like Jesus. We could never on our own produce the kind of change Jesus requires of his followers, the kind that totally transformed my friend Jacob to be able to say that he loves those who killed his parents. Radical changes like that can only come through the love of God and the power of the Holy Spirit.

The good news is that these radical changes are entirely possible.

You can, as the Apostle Paul says in Romans 12:1–2, offer yourself as a living sacrifice, "holy and acceptable to God"; you can "be transformed by the renewing of your mind." You can actually live in more dynamic communion with God, yourself, others, and the world, as you speak and act out of the transforming love of God. In fact, as you continue to be transformed by God's love, you will most likely find that certain harmful patterns you had in relating to others become foreign to you. As John Wesley preached in a sermon titled "On Love," "And if you love your neighbor as yourself, you will not be able to prefer yourself before him. Nay, you will not be able to despise any one, any more than to hate him."[7]

Through the Holy Spirit's power in your life, you can become someone who, in the words of the Apostle Paul, does "nothing out of selfish ambition or vain conceit" but in humility "consider[s] others better than yourself." You can become someone who consistently looks "not to your own interests, but to the interests of others" (Philippians 2:3–4). As Henri Nouwen said, "True joy, happiness and inner peace come from the giving of ourselves to others. A happy life is a life for others."[8] You can have that kind of fulfilling life, as you learn to engage in spiritually charged communication. You sustain attitudes of love through a heart change fueled by the Holy Spirit. The fruit of that heart change will be the ways in which you connect with others for the healing of their souls.

Holy Spirit–Guided Awareness Through the Prayer of Examen

Although the Holy Spirit can use any means to help us become more self-aware, a particular prayer called the prayer of examen has been known throughout the centuries to be one of the best ways to discover our true selves so that we can live more for the sake of others. It is a way for the Holy Spirit to heal our own souls so that we can help heal others. St. Ignatius of Loyola, the person who advocated this prayer back in the sixteenth century, believed that if we could pray only one prayer in a day, it should be the prayer of examen due to its transformational power in people's lives. The prayer of examen is a Holy Spirit–guided self-awareness prayer based on several verses in the Psalms (Psalm 139:23–24, Psalm 26:2, Psalm 4:4). The following method for this prayer comes from the teachings of St. Ignatius.

Because the prayer of examen involves an intentional reflection on your day, St. Ignatius advised praying it at the end of the day. It can also be prayed in the morning, with the reflection being on the previous day. The first part of the prayer involves thanking God for all the blessings of the day, from being thankful for the taste of food to expressing gratitude for specific relationships in your life. Beginning and continuing the prayer in a spirit of thankfulness is crucial, as cultivating a spirit of gratefulness will help you positively approach whatever the Holy Spirit brings to your mind during the prayer. As a matter of fact, expressing gratefulness is a valuable spiritual practice in and of itself; when cultivated, it changes how we relate to others. Brian McLaren said in our interview that "The practice of gratitude and praise and thanksgiving in our prayer life can send us into the world less on a fault-finding mission and more on a virtue-finding mission—less full of complaint and more full of grace and encouragement."

After you express gratitude to God, the prayer of examen then has two major parts, which need to take only about ten minutes total. The first part involves asking the Holy Spirit to bring to mind those times when you lived out of love and freedom in Christ that particular day. Think about those things you said and did that were in line with what the Apostle Paul wrote in Philippians 4:8: "Finally, beloved, whatever is true, whatever is honorable, whatever is just, whatever is pure, whatever is pleasing, whatever is commendable, if there is any excellence and if there is anything worthy of praise, think about these things." Like playing a movie in your head, visualize what you said and did that led to harmony instead of disharmony as you went through your day.

The first major part of the prayer is also what sets you up for the second part, in which you reflect on those times when you did not live out of love and freedom in Christ. But remember: only after you have strengthened your faith by reflecting on the positive side of how you lived the day should you take upon yourself the task of facing up to any negative things you did. Otherwise, you can drive yourself into a negativity that is not of God.

When you are ready for this second part of the prayer, ask the Holy Spirit to bring to mind any of your weaknesses or failures in the ways you related to yourself or others that day. For the prayer of examen to truly transform you, it is important to commit to praying this second part of the prayer with a genuine desire to have your weaknesses made known. Then you are to confess any revealed weaknesses with a "contrite heart" (Psalm 51:17), not as a way to get down on yourself or to become unduly upset. The difference is in intention. Fénelon explained this crucial distinction when he wrote that our faults "will not be cured by being upset about them. The only thing you can do is bear the humiliation your sins bring to you. It is not humble to resist being humbled. Be sorry for your faults, repent of them, make no excuses for them, but don't become bitter or discouraged over your imperfections." He goes on to say, "It is not when you notice your faults that you are most wicked. You never really see your sins until they are beginning to be cured. Neither flatter yourself, nor be impatient with yourself. Despondency is not humility. Actually, despondency is the despair of your wounded pride. Your faults may be useful to you if they cure you of the vain confidence you have in yourself. God only lets you feel your weakness so that you may seek your strength in Him."[9]

When we confess our failures with a sincere heart, Christ's cleansing, healing power moves in. We can even confess as David prayed in Psalm 51:10, "Create in me a clean heart, O God, and put a new and right spirit within me." Confession and cleansing will, in Tony's words, "go a long way toward making you into a clearer lens through which the power of God can be focused

> *When we confess our failures with a sincere heart, Christ's cleansing, healing power moves in.*

through you onto others. The cleansing from sin through the prayer of examen is crucial for the kind of spiritual connecting that God wills for those who would be like Jesus in their ministry of healing souls."

After this time of cleansing, close your time of examen by thanking God for all the Holy Spirit brought to mind, and by asking the Spirit to help you take any new awareness of both your strengths and weaknesses into the next day.

A note on being receptive. For the prayer of examen to be fruitful in our lives, being open during our prayer time to receive *whatever* the Holy Spirit reveals is crucial. If we are not open, we can pray this prayer every day of our lives and not be transformed. In C. S. Lewis's book *The Screwtape Letters,* Uncle Screwtape (the Devil) said to Wormwood (his apprentice devil), "You must bring [your patient] to a condition in which he can practice self-examination for an hour without discovering any of those facts about himself which are perfectly clear to anyone who has ever lived in the same house with him or worked in the same office."[10]

Another way to know we are being receptive, outside of our regular prayer time, is if we find that the prayer of examen has become a deterrent of sorts, stopping us at times from speaking or acting in ways that are not out of love and freedom in Christ. More than one person has told me that knowing they are going to pray this prayer later has stopped them from responding in less than loving ways. That's awareness! If we stay receptive to the work of the Holy Spirit in our lives, then we will discover what God wants us to discover. We will also find fruits growing in our lives.

Fruits of Holy Spirit–Guided Self-Awareness

Jesus said we would be known by our fruits (Matthew 7:16). When we engage in the practices of noticing and the prayer of examen, we can expect tangible changes in how we relate to others. In our interview, Brian McLaren had this to say about how we track those changes in our lives, related specifically to confessing our weaknesses:

> We want to quantify everything so much, but it's a qualitative issue rather than a quantitative issue. You can pray a lot, but in a phony way that probably will make you a phonier person when you talk to other people. You could probably pray a whole lot less in a very authentic way, and that act of authenticity, nakedness, and honest and humble contrition with God would send you into all of your

other relationships with a different kind of transparency and vulnerability. That's where spiritual practices like the confession of sin
become extremely important. If we could learn to take the practice
of confessing our sins more seriously, we would become so much
more gracious with other people.

Along with growing more gracious toward others, we may start to see
the following fruits in our lives as a result of noticing and of praying the
prayer of examen.

An Increase in Other-Centeredness

We are most likely moving from self- to other-awareness if we find we
are becoming more able to focus on others, to be present with them, and
to be content to yield to the Holy Spirit's agenda instead of our own.
There is much freedom in these fruits. Having less desire to change others
opens us up to be vessels of the Holy Spirit for however the Spirit wants
to work. We may even find that we have more patience, tolerance, and
mercy toward those who annoy or even anger us with certain behaviors.
As the reality of how much God loves us in spite of our own weaknesses
soaks into our souls, we are freed to love others in spite of weaknesses
we may perceive in them. As McLaren went on to say, "When we have
been telling God what a mess we are and how much mercy we need,
how can we not be merciful to others, especially if we pray the Lord's
Prayer: 'forgive us our sins as we forgive others'?"

Unfortunately, others may not see your mercy as a fruit; instead they
might accuse you of being too passive and not working as hard toward
changing a person as they think you should. Don't let that kind of accu-
sation get to you—you have a good role model for "appropriate passiv-
ity." Jesus did not force people to change. He was patient, sometimes
even silent; he presented people with truth about the Kingdom of God
and then left it up to them as to whether or not they wanted to be a part
of that Kingdom. For instance, Jesus knew what the rich young ruler
needed, but at the end of their interaction, Jesus let him walk away (Luke
18:18–30). There may be times that we, too, after much prayer and
careful discernment, are to let someone walk away.

A More Selfless Way of Relating

Although uncovering more areas where you were not aware may feel
more like a failed tree than a fruitful one, one of the best ways to know
you are becoming more aware of who you are in God is that you con-

tinue to discover ways you could more selflessly relate to others. As Fénelon wrote, "Whatever revelations you receive or whatever emotional experiences you have are worthless unless they lead you to the very real and constant practice of dying to your self-nature."[11] Discovering more areas in ourselves that need pruning is not only common but a necessity for those who are being transformed. Jesus himself said, "I am the true vine, and my Father is the gardener. He cuts off every branch in me that bears no fruit, while every branch that does bear fruit he prunes so that it will be even more fruitful" (John 15:1–2, NIV). The more areas you discover that need to be pruned, the more God can take those areas, redeem them, and continue to purify you to have the kind of relationships that are glorifying to God—as long as you stay connected to Jesus. Jesus made this point clear when he said, "Remain in me, and I will remain in you. No branch can bear fruit by itself; it must remain in the vine. Neither can you bear fruit unless you remain in me" (John 15:4, NIV). That is why the practices discussed in this chapter and throughout the book are not one-time practices. They are practices that countless lovers of Jesus have regularly engaged in to know God and themselves in ways that produce the kind of spiritually charged communication that helps them connect like Jesus.

It can be easy to understand why as followers of Christ we need to rid ourselves of whatever hinders us from helping God's Kingdom come on earth. But there is something that needs special attention—something many of us succumb to that more than anything else can prevent us from connecting with others in soul-healing ways. It is something so inhibiting that although Jesus tells us not to hold on to it, we often feel powerless to follow his instruction, even after we are aware of its hold on our lives and confess that hold to God. That something is *fear,* which is the topic of the next chapter. Until we recognize and learn to deal with some of the fears in our own souls, we cannot experience the kind of freedom that results in our ability to deeply connect with others.

4

From Fear to Freedom

Overcoming What Keeps
Us from Others

---

*The only thing we have to fear is fear itself—nameless,
unreasoning, unjustified, terror which paralyzes needed
efforts to convert retreat into advance.*
—FDR, first inaugural address, March 4, 1933

*For God has not given us a spirit of fear, but of power and of
love and of a sound mind.*
—2 Timothy 1:7 (NKJV)

IN A "PEANUTS" CARTOON STRIP, Linus is getting advice from Lucy, who
is sitting in her "psychiatric" booth. In this particular scene, Lucy focuses
on what she believes is keeping Linus in his depressed state: fear. She
names several unusual phobias, finally arriving at Pantophobia.
Linus asks, "What's Pantophobia?"
Lucy replies, "The fear of everything."
"THAT'S IT!!!" Linus shouts.[1]
Even if you feel like Linus at times, chances are you don't have
Pantophobia. Still, most of us are afraid at one time or another. What
are you afraid of? Perhaps you fear losing a certain relationship or
job. Maybe you fear failing at something or getting sick and even
dying. Or you may fear that what you believe about God isn't true. If
you have any of these fears or phobias, at least you can rest assured that
you aren't alone. Lucy named only six fears when attempting to diagnose
Linus, but there are over *five hundred* phobias indentified in reference
or medical books.

Fears That Can Keep Us from Others

Any fear, large or small, rational or irrational, can hinder and even prevent us from connecting with others in ways that advance God's Kingdom. Some people won't join a small group for fear of having to "share" or being asked to pray out loud in the group. Some fear one-on-one interactions and will avoid situations where they may be in a room with only one other person. Others fear society in general and may stay away from social situations even if there are no specific expectations of having to interact with anyone. There are many reasons for these kinds of fears and phobias: some of us are born with an extra dose of anxiety (that we can, unfortunately, access too quickly), some have situations in their lives that result in certain fears, and some have a combination of these factors.

Most likely you are familiar with at least one phobia: the fear of public speaking (Glossophobia). According to some surveys, the fear of speaking in public is so prevalent that it rates as the number-one fear in America, meaning that it's even more common than the fear of dying (Thanatophobia). Comedian Jerry Seinfeld observed that if you're that afraid of speaking in public, at a funeral you'd rather be in the coffin than delivering the eulogy.

> *The problem with any fear is that it can make us so self-focused that we can't get beyond ourselves to love and serve others in soul-healing ways.*

It is important to note that the majority of the population would not be *clinically* diagnosed with any of the phobias I've mentioned. But that does not mean we don't struggle with some degree of fear in certain areas. The problem with any fear is that it can make us so self-focused that we can't get beyond ourselves to love and serve others in soul-healing ways.

Although it might seem odd for me to say, as someone who speaks in public and teaches communication at Spring Arbor University, I was *almost* deathly afraid of speaking in public from my earliest years. Although I admired certain public speakers and wanted to speak with the confidence I saw in them, I didn't think that would ever be a reality for me. I didn't know at the time that being willing to speak and being good at it didn't mean there wasn't nervousness involved. I also didn't know that what I was going through as a young person was in the range of normal. It would be many years before I would read in speech textbooks that the physiological reactions I experienced—pounding heart, sweaty palms, and shaky voice—were considered normal. Those who are not afraid to speak in public are, in fact, the unusual ones.

Although the best piece of advice for overcoming any fear of talking in social settings is to talk, that didn't work for me. Each time I was told I had to speak in front of a class or small group, I would experience the same overwhelming nervousness. My fear did not go away; rather, it got worse, at a time when many things get worse in one's life—junior high. At the close of one meeting of my small youth group, our youth leader told us to go around the circle and each say a prayer. My nervous anxiety immediately kicked in. I managed to form two sentences in my mind about a current event, and kept silently going over them. Then the person just before me "stole" my lines. I had nothing. When it was my turn, I said something that didn't come out right, and a couple of people snickered. I was frozen in embarrassment and never wanted to pray out loud again.

No one could have convinced me that day that I would eventually emerge from my fearful shell and be able to comfortably pray in a small group, much less teach communication classes, including public speaking. And no one could have convinced me that I would love speaking in public. I believe God has a sense of humor, but more important, I now *know* that God has the power to change us in ways we can't dare to believe or even imagine. God is *always* bigger than our fears.

We don't need to look far in the Bible to see examples of God's will at work in spite of people's fears. When God called Moses to go to Pharaoh to bring the Israelites out of Egypt, Moses said to God, " 'O my Lord, I have never been eloquent, neither in the past nor even now that you have spoken to your servant; but I am slow of speech and slow of tongue' " (Exodus 4:10). God then replied, " 'Who gives speech to mortals? Who makes them mute or deaf, seeing or blind? Is it not I, the Lord? Now go, and I will be with your mouth and teach you what you are to speak' " (vv. 11–12). Even after God's reassurance, Moses still didn't want to do it. He asked God to send someone else, which resulted in God's appointing Moses' brother Aaron to speak for him. (Don't count on a similar solution if you are asked to give a speech at work or for a class.)

Moses wasn't the only one who did not want to speak when God asked him to. Perhaps you know Jonah as the one who spent three days in the belly of a whale, but have forgotten what got him there in the first place. God had called Jonah to go to an unfamiliar country and tell them of their wickedness and need for repentance. In Jonah 1:3, we are told that the first thing Jonah attempted to do was to "flee" from the Lord. In the end, Jonah was eaten by a fish, and eventually went to Nineveh, just as he was commanded to do.

Facing Our Fears

Like Jonah, we are often put in situations where the only thing we can do is face our fears. Popular evangelist Joyce Meyer often encourages her listeners to "Do it afraid!" In many situations, it is about stepping out of our own comfort zones and doing what we have been called to do. In 2 Corinthians 12:9 (NIV), the Lord tells Paul, "My grace is sufficient for you, for my strength is made perfect in weakness." We are not to run from our fears but to face them, continually asking God for grace to rise above them in every situation. Easier said than done, right? Especially for those of us with more intense fears. But we really can learn to deal with our fears and even rise above them. The best place to start is with Jesus.

I am not alone in believing that Jesus experienced fear. I believe that in the garden of Gethsemane, when he asked God to "take this cup from me" (Luke 22:42, NIV), Jesus was greatly troubled by the pain and suffering he was about to endure. After all, he was human as well as divine. But when the cup wasn't taken from him, he didn't run from it. Instead he faced his fear—even to the point of death—and trusted God for the outcome.

We, too, need to face our fears, which includes becoming aware of the many possible reasons we may have those fears. We may fear certain interactions due to previous experiences of being rejected or criticized or of having anger directed toward us by others. Like Peter, who three times denied knowing Jesus, we too may fear being associated with Jesus in front of certain people. But that is all the more reason to learn to deal with our fears. It's not that we shouldn't be wise in how to respond to others, but if we fear being rejected, criticized, or yelled at to the point of not being authentic in our interactions, we cannot have the kind of relationships that honor God and others. John Wesley once preached, "If you would please all men for their good, at all events speak to all men the very truth from your heart. When you speak, open the window of your breast: let the words be the very picture of your heart."[2]

Wesley is talking about having authentic, honest relationships with one another so that we can help each other grow into the kind of relationships God intended from the beginning of time. But even if you are graciously speaking a difficult truth "in love," as the Apostle Paul tells us to do in Ephesians 4:15, that doesn't mean that what you say is met with a gracious response. You can be met with rejection, criticism, denial, or anger even when you have allowed the very same person to speak difficult truths to you. Or it may be that the other person graciously accepted your difficult words, but you did not return the favor when the situation was reversed. That person could even be one of your closest friends. It is often with those closest to us that we have the most difficulty with gracious dialogue. As Professor Dumbledore of the Harry Potter series said, "It takes a great deal of courage to stand up to your enemies, but a great deal more to stand up your friends."[3] We need to learn to engage more graciously and honestly in dialogue with friend and foe, especially in confrontation and disagreement, if we want to help others and ourselves grow in Christ.

Speaking the truth in love can be next to impossible if we don't trust one another. Tragically, our own faith communities might be where some of us feel the least "safe." Brian McLaren spoke to this issue in our interview when he said, "If we're in a faith community that isn't characterized by grace, then we learn 'You'd better not show a sign of weakness or you'll be shamed.' So many communities create a social field of anxiety and fear of being out-grouped and shamed and excluded. This is a very, very deep problem. For a lot of us, our faith communities are the scariest places we've ever inhabited. It shouldn't be that way, but it's definitely true." The reason for this may be that many faith communities are actually communities bound more by fear than by faith. Grounding our beliefs in fear—whether it's fear of being wrong, fear of judgment, fear of going to hell, or all of these—instead of love will have disastrous results. Fear of being wrong can cause us to judge others; fear of losing a person or possession can cause us to be jealous or full of greed; fear of losing control over our lives can cause us to control others. None of these results are loving. Love cannot coexist with unhealthy fear. We are told in 1 John 4:18 that "There is no fear in love, but perfect love casts out fear." Perfect love requires us to treat one another with the fruits of the Spirit, such as patience, kindness, faithfulness, and self-control—just as God treats us. As Shane Claiborne said in our interview, "Healthy communities are where people of grace have created an environment where you know you're safe."

Many faith communities are actually communities bound more by fear than by faith.

A note on healthy fear. Not all fear is bad. So before we delve into ways to rid ourselves of unhealthy fears, it's important to note that there are times when fear is beneficial.

Have you ever known someone who takes too many risks? People can endanger their own lives and the lives of others when they "have no fear." Healthy fear can keep us from getting too close to the edge of the Grand Canyon, from giving in to a dangerous dare, and from spending more money than we have. Fear can also motivate. A fear of growing apart from a dear friend who moved away can cause us to keep in regular contact with that person, and a health scare can kick-start us into taking better care of our bodies. A complete lack of fear can result in complacency and inertia. Lack of fear of consequences can cause us to perform badly in a variety of circumstances. I'm thankful for a little nervousness when I'm asked to speak in public. Those nerves can be a good motivator for being prepared, and they can be channeled to produce positive energy when it's time to connect with my audience. There's an old saying that it's normal to have butterflies; you just need to get them to fly in formation. Opera singer Luciano Pavarotti once said, "Am I afraid of high notes? Of course I am afraid. What sane man is not?" Learning to value our healthy fears and to rid ourselves of those that are unhealthy will help free us to better connect with God and others.

Communication and Spiritual Practices to Turn Unhealthy Fear into Love

When any fear causes us to live in bondage instead of freedom, it is an unhealthy fear. We cannot concentrate on loving God and others when we are too focused on our fears. I know this from personal experience, as I have dealt with many more fears and anxieties than just a fear of speaking. From abnormal fears when my first child was born, to tendencies toward being a hypochondriac, to a period of intense anxiety after my dad died suddenly on the golf course, fears in my life have often caused my focus on God's Kingdom to take a distant backseat. Even though I have tried more than a few techniques in the fields of both communication and psychology known to help people deal with their unhealthy fears, it was not until I combined those methods with spiritual practices that I saw my fears consistently lessen. In particular, I found that combining four of these techniques

> *We cannot concentrate on loving God and others when we are too focused on our fears.*

with four corresponding spiritual practices creates a powerful dynamic that releases us from binding fears, thereby freeing us to connect with others in ways that glorify God.

I believe these practices can help you experience an intimacy with God that empowers you to live in a freedom in Christ you may not have thought possible. Fear loses its grip when we focus on God, who gives us the Spirit of love, power, and a sound mind (2 Timothy 1:7, NIV). It is this Spirit that empowers us to focus more on others and live for the Kingdom of God. It is my hope that no matter what your fear, the following combined practices can help make this verse the rule, not the exception, in your life.

Relaxation and Centering Prayer

One of the best methods for dealing with fear involves a process of being gradually exposed to your fear while remaining relaxed. *Gradually* and *relaxed* are key terms for this method, which is called "systematic desensitization." Vital to this process is learning how to relax your body, because researchers have discovered that you cannot be anxious if your body is completely relaxed. Ways to relax include tensing and relaxing your muscles, and practicing slow, steady breathing. Next you are exposed to a lesser version of your fear. For example, if you are afraid to talk with someone who quickly becomes angry, your first step might be to imagine a picture of that person, as you simultaneously stay relaxed. Then if you can remain calm, the exposure is gradually increased; for example, you might imagine the person calling you to talk. Whenever you become fearful, you go back to the previous step until you can once again be relaxed enough to go on. Eventually you get to the point where you can have a real conversation with the person while remaining calm.

Although systematic desensitization alone has been known to work well in helping people face their fears, it did not work well for me until I learned a form of praying that includes aspects of this technique. It was when I learned to be calm in the power of the Holy Spirit, through engaging in centering prayer, that I began experiencing freedom from many of my fears.

Centering prayer is a way to quiet our souls and be still before God. Throughout history, church fathers and mothers have prayed in wordless silence. I believed this is one of the ways Jesus prayed. We are told in Psalm 46:10 to "Be still" before God, and Psalm 62:5 tells us, "For God alone my soul waits in silence, for my hope is from him." Jesus knew these scriptures. He often went away alone to be in prayer with God

(Matthew 14:22–23, 26:36; Luke 6:12). We can assume that part of his prayer time included waiting in silence before God because that is, in part, how scripture taught him to pray.

In centering prayer, we yield to God in silence, opening the door for the Holy Spirit to work. Here is how I was taught to do centering prayer:

1. Find a quiet place where you will not be disturbed. This usually takes intentional planning, such as knowing when you will be alone or putting a sign on the door telling people you are not to be disturbed.

2. Sit comfortably and calm yourself through tensing and relaxing your muscles and engaging in slow, steady breathing for a few minutes, while you empty your mind of distractions by focusing your thoughts on being in God's loving presence.

3. Pray an opening prayer, like this one: "Dear God, I pray for your help and divine protection as I rid my mind of any distractions so that I can yield to your Holy Spirit in silence. In Jesus' precious and powerful name I pray."

4. Sit in silence for ten to twenty minutes. When distractions come (and they will), release them to God; do not get down on yourself for being distracted—it's normal. Have a certain word in place, like "Jesus" or "peace," that you can repeat when you are distracted.

5. End your time with the Lord's Prayer.

Centering prayer is what I call a "trust" prayer, because we may not experience any immediate freedom from fear. What *is* often experienced immediately is a calmness in our souls that will continue to grow in us the more we practice this prayer. Eventually, we will find that we can access this calm in the midst of a fearful situation by intentionally relaxing and focusing on God. This stillness in our soul is from the Holy Spirit and will continue to produce in us the kind of "holy relaxation" needed to face our fears.

Cognitive Restructuring and Reflecting on Scripture

Stuart Smalley was a fictitious self-help character created by Al Franken, from *Saturday Night Live*. Smalley advised looking at yourself in the mirror and reciting daily affirmations, his most famous being: "I'm good enough, I'm smart enough, and doggone it, *people like me*." Although this was meant as a spoof of those who take positive thinking too far, there really *is* something to this kind of affirmation. It's called *cognitive restructuring* and involves changing the way we think by replacing negative self-talk with positive statements—including the way we frame our fears.

You may already be sensing how this form of turning negative thoughts into positive thoughts meshes with being a Christ follower. In Philippians 4:8 (NIV), we are told to think about "Whatever is true, whatever is noble, whatever is right, whatever is pure, whatever is lovely, whatever is admirable" as well as anything that is "excellent or praiseworthy." We can learn to think in terms of these uplifting attributes, in relation not only to life in general but also to ourselves. Reciting daily affirmations that are grounded in scripture can help us restructure how we think about, and deal with, fear.

An especially powerful way to have scripture reframe our fears is through a spiritual practice called *lectio divina,* which is Latin for "holy reading" or "divine reading." Lectio starts with choosing a verse from scripture—in this case one related to fear—and reading it slowly, at least twice, to help draw you into the passage. You then take a few minutes to reflect on, or "sit with," the verse, asking the Holy Spirit to bring to mind whatever thought or image God might want to reveal to you. If a thought or image comes to mind, you take that with you throughout your day. Because lectio involves reading the text more than once, you may be surprised to find that if you engage in lectio on the same verse for a few days, you have inadvertently memorized the verse. If you have not, I encourage you to continue focusing on the same passage until it is memorized, because then you will be able to bring the verse to mind during a fearful time.

The following verses are only a sampling of those you can choose for this kind of scripture reflection:

> "Even though I walk through the darkest valley, I fear no evil; for you are with me, your rod and your staff—they comfort me" (Psalm 23:4).

> "Cast your burden on the Lord, and he will sustain you; he will never permit the righteous to be moved" (Psalm 55:22).

> "Trust in him at all times, O people; pour out your heart before him; God is a refuge for us" (Psalm 62:8).

> "Trust in the Lord with all your heart, and do not rely on your own insight. In all your ways acknowledge him, and he will make straight your paths" (Proverbs 3:5–6).

"Surely God is my salvation; I will trust, and not be afraid, for the Lord God is my strength and my might; he has become my salvation" (Isaiah 12:2).

"Therefore I tell you, do not worry about your life, what you will eat or what you will drink, or about your body, what you will wear. Is not life more than food, and the body more than clothing? Look at the birds of the air; they neither sow nor reap nor gather in barns, and yet your heavenly Father feeds them. Are you not of more value than they? And can any of you by worrying add a single hour to your span of life?" (Matthew 6:25–27).

"So do not worry about tomorrow, for tomorrow will bring worries of its own. Today's trouble is enough for today" (Matthew 6:34).

"Do not let your hearts be troubled. Believe in God, believe also in me" (John 14:1).

If you do memorize some verses like these, then when you find yourself approaching or in a fearful situation, you can go over one or several of them in your mind. Adding in relaxation breathing, while slowly repeating the verse over and over, can be especially powerful in calming you and helping you reframe your fears.

Visualization and Ignatian Contemplation

Visualization or positive imagery is a method highly recommended for improving functioning in a variety of settings that cause us to fear. Numerous studies have found that when we visualize ourselves performing successfully prior to an event, we will perform better in the actual event. In anticipating public speaking situations, for example, visualizing yourself confidently approaching the situation and then confidently speaking has been known to greatly reduce fear during the actual speaking event.

There is a spiritual practice, one that St. Ignatius of Loyola highly valued and taught, that incorporates visualization. It is a form of meditating on a scene in scripture. Although Ignatius called it contemplation, it is often more commonly known as imaginative prayer. This type of prayer involves putting yourself in a particular story of scripture and visualizing yourself as one of the main characters or as a bystander in the scene. Before you begin, you ask the Holy Spirit to help guide you to discover what God wants you to discover as the scene plays out in detail in your imagination. In the context of dealing with unhealthy fears, you would choose a passage of scripture that involves a fearful situation, to help prepare you to deal more effectively with fearful situations in your own life. Although I encourage you to find passages of scripture that you especially relate to, here are a few suggestions for characters in whose place you might imagine yourself:

- Peter, who denies knowing Jesus for fear of being punished (Mark 14:66–72)
- The woman who becomes fearful after Jesus discovers that she is the one who touched his garment (Luke 8:40–48)
- The woman caught in adultery, terrified that she is about to be stoned (John 8:1–11)
- The disciples on the boat when the storm develops (Luke 8:22–25)

When visualizing yourself as a main character or bystander in each of these passages, make sure you include Jesus as part of the scene. Imagine Jesus standing with you—what might you say to him and he to you? Then picture yourself making the decision to trust Jesus with your fears.

You can also choose to picture Jesus with you in any fearful situation you may be facing. Go through the entire situation with Jesus by your side, picturing yourself handling every detail with a calm that you know is from the Holy Spirit at work replacing your fear with love.

Picture Jesus with you in any fearful situation you may be facing.

Implosive Therapy and Service

Although the jury is out as to how well implosive therapy works with phobias, there is still something to be said for its success in other areas. Implosive therapy is a way to deal with fear that is just about the opposite of systematic desensitization. It is throwing yourself right into the middle of your fear, such as by jumping out of an airplane if you fear flying or holding a big snake if you suffer from Ophidiophobia. When it comes to connecting with others, it could be taking someone you don't like out to dinner to hear their story or volunteering for a service project in an environment you fear.

When I was in a two-year spiritual direction program, we had what was called an "immersion" weekend where we were required to participate in a particular ministry with the goal of interacting with others on more than surface levels. We could choose to visit a prison and talk with prisoners, go to a homeless shelter and start a conversation with residents in the lounge, or go to a hospital emergency room and ask people who were waiting if we could pray with them. Some of us who read the list didn't want to do any of these activities because the thought of initiating what my friend called "cold calls" was a scary prospect. Yet each one of us came away from the day so thankful that we were forced to face our fears—fears that ended up being insignificant compared to the blessings that came from stepping out of our comfort zones and connecting with people with whom we would otherwise not have come in contact.

Fruits of Facing Our Fears

When you take active steps to face your fears through combining communication and spiritual practices, the following fruits will most likely become a reality in your life:

1. *You are less fearful overall.* Although Jesus tells us not to worry (Matthew 6:25–27), that's not always easy. But after committing to these practices over time, you are highly likely to find that you do, indeed, worry less!

2. *You handle fearful situations better.* It's not that all your fears will necessarily go away with these practices, but they will not have the grip on you they once had. When a fearful situation emerges, you may be surprised to find that you handle it in ways you never thought possible. Remember the Apostle Peter being afraid to admit he knew Jesus when challenged by a teenage girl the night before Jesus was crucified? This same Peter, whose words and actions became empowered by the Holy Spirit, went on to become a dominant spokesperson for the Kingdom of God, and even died a martyr's death. That depth of spiritual empowerment really is possible, not just for those in the early church but for us today.

The spiritually charged communication that comes from engaging in the kinds of practices suggested throughout this chapter can cause your fears to "grow strangely dim," as they are overpowered by God's Spirit, resulting in your being able to connect with others in ways that powerfully advance God's Kingdom. When your fears are no longer your main focus, you will have the freedom to focus on helping care for others' souls, which is the subject of the remaining chapters in this part of the book.

5

Sacred Listening

Hearing with the Ears of God

Hear and your soul shall live.
—Isaiah 55:3 (KJV)

The soul speaks its truth only under quiet, inviting, and
trustworthy conditions.
—Parker Palmer, *Let Your Life Speak*

I WILL NEVER FORGET meeting Olivia Newton-John years ago at a charity event—not because she was so beautiful (which she was), but because of how she treated our two little boys. When my husband and sons and I were introduced to her, she immediately knelt down in front of the boys so that she was at eye level with them. She then looked at both of them, asked them how they were, and listened intently to their responses. I did not expect her to treat our children in such attentive and affirming ways, especially when there were so many adults standing around waiting to meet her.

Listening attentively is one of the most powerful ways to connect with another human being. When we listen to the deepest needs and concerns of another's soul, we affirm his or her very personhood. And isn't that what we all want, to be validated as persons of worth? As fiction writer Taylor Caldwell once wrote, "our most desperate need is for someone to listen to us as a human soul."[1] Listening to someone as a human soul requires that we look beyond superficial appearances and assumptions to the realization that this person has been created in the image of God. That awareness has a powerful effect on how we listen. Our listening becomes a sacred act in which we see another person through the lens of God's love—beyond the surface to his or her

soul. In our interview, when I
asked Mindy Caliguire how she
would describe sacred listening,
she said, "When we listen, we
invite someone to share their
story—and that's holy ground.
We honor others' stories by listening to them and looking for
the fingerprints of God in their
story."

*When we listen to the
deepest needs and concerns
of another's soul, we
affirm his or her very
personhood.*

My friend Bev, who has been trained as a spiritual director, is especially gifted at sacred listening. When I talk to her, she listens intently,
remembers what I say, sifts through my words, and seems to know what
to focus on for me to process. I can almost see her silently checking with
the Holy Spirit to discern when to listen and when to respond. Oftentimes
when we have been together, I feel incredibly calm, as if my soul has just
been to the spa. Bev knows how to listen sacredly in ways that help heal
souls.

If we want to learn to listen in these sacred ways, a good place to start
is with the best sacred listener of all—Jesus. As the Son of God, he had
a great deal he could say. Yet Jesus often listened to others before doing
much, if any, talking himself.

On the first day of the week after Jesus had been crucified, two of
Jesus' followers were walking to the village of Emmaus. They were
talking about everything that had happened in the last few days, when
Jesus himself "came up and walked along with them" (Luke 24:15, NIV).
Luke then says that "they were kept from recognizing him" (v. 16) and
that Jesus asked them, "What are you discussing together as you walk
along?" They proceeded to sadly tell Jesus what had been happening in
the last few days involving him, still not recognizing who he was.

It's interesting to note that before Jesus communicated in any other
way with the two men on the road to Emmaus, he listened. There are a
lot of verses in the Bible that stress the importance of listening—to others
and to God. Here is a small sampling:

> "And now, my child, listen to me, and do not depart from the
> words of my mouth" (Proverbs 5:7).

> "To draw near to listen is better than the sacrifice offered by
> fools. . . . Never be rash with your mouth, nor let your heart be
> quick to utter a word before God, for God is in heaven, and you
> upon earth; therefore let your words be few" (Ecclesiastes 5:1–2).

"[Jesus said,] "Let anyone with ears listen" (Matthew 11:15).

"You must understand this, my beloved: let everyone be quick to listen, slow to speak, slow to anger" (James 1:19).

Even though the Bible has much to say on listening, it's really no wonder that most of us do not pay more attention to how we listen. It is not how we've been taught. In our educational system, emphasis is given to reading and writing, but not to listening—although we do more listening than both reading and writing combined. There is also the issue of our own self-focus. Sacred listening, in particular, requires us to get beyond ourselves to focus on the other person—not an easy task, even for those of us familiar with good listening skills.

Tony tells the story of a time when he was teaching at the University of Pennsylvania. He had just finished a lecture on the theories of sociologist Emil Durkheim. After the lecture, Tony was followed to his office by a student who sat down and asked a rather trivial question about the lecture. Because Tony was tired and busy catching up on some details, he only half listened. He said he didn't listen as Jesus would have, or else he would have realized that the student had not come to talk about Durkheim. Tony answered the question in an offhand manner and then said, "Is that all?" The student left Tony's office. He went back to the high-rise building where he lived, went to the roof, and jumped to his death. Tony realized too late that the student's visit was not to talk about sociology, but sociology was all Tony heard.

Paying attention to what lies beneath the surface of people's words, reaching to their souls, is an essential element in sacred listening. A friend of mine, Pastor Brandi Kendall, put it this way: "True listening has little to do with the ears and a whole lot to do with our hearts, our own spirit, and a connection with the Holy Spirit within. It is an intentional process of being open and aware, of having ourselves prepared for hearing and discernment long before the first words are ever spoken."[2] Each of us can enhance our abilities to listen in these ways so that we do not miss an opportunity to help heal someone's soul.

Two of the best ways to listen sacredly are what I call *active soul listening* and what is known as empathic listening. Both are forms of active listening, which is attentive, purposeful listening—as distinguished from a more casual, less focused listening. Although we can actively listen for a variety of purposes, including listening to music for pleasure or listening to a lecture to learn something, the purpose of active soul listening and empathic listening is to connect with others on deeper levels. In the sense that both of these are purpose driven, they are "managed" by the listener more than in other types of listening—meaning that the listener is deliberately engaging in ways that can help draw out soul issues in another person. The listener is not, however, supposed to figure out what the other person needs to say. That is the role of the Holy Spirit. Besides, even if we think we know what a person needs from us as a listener, it is better not to assume, because we could be wrong. As Shane Claiborne said in our interview, "It's important we come as listeners, learners, and friends instead of assuming we know everyone else's problems and pain. That's what is most restorative and healing."

Tony recently told me that a friend asked if he could meet with him to talk. Because of difficult circumstances the person had been going through, Tony was sure the person needed him to be a sympathetic counselor. Tony knew they didn't have much time together, and because they didn't see each other often, he was ready to talk about these difficult circumstances right off the bat. It's a good thing he listened first instead, because Tony quickly realized that his friend had come through those circumstances well and wanted Tony's advice on a certain career change he was considering.

Because people want others to listen to them for a variety of reasons, if *how* someone wants us to listen isn't clear, we can ask a form of this question: "What would you like from me—an understanding ear, advice, or both?" Some will know what they want. For those who don't, we can quiet our spirits and ask the Holy Spirit for guidance in our listening and in any responses we offer. This is especially important when it comes to giving advice, because as we'll see later in the chapter, there are good reasons to be careful about giving advice.

Knowing how to listen isn't easy. The practices of active soul listening and empathic listening can help us to hear from the Spirit and respond to others in soul-healing ways.

Active Soul Listening

Active soul listening involves paying careful attention not only to what a person is saying but also to possible meanings that may lie beyond the actual spoken words. It is the kind of listening that Tony said he desperately wishes he would have done with the student who followed him to his office. It is how Jesus listened to the men on their way to Emmaus. Jesus' purpose was to have the two men discover who he was and how the realization of his death and resurrection would speak to their souls, thereby changing their entire lives. Listening with that purpose meant that Jesus not only heard their words but understood that beyond those words was an unspoken hunger to live for the Kingdom of God. It was said of Jesus that "he knew what was in a man" (John 2:25, NIV); nevertheless, Jesus listened, not for what he needed to hear, but for what others needed to say and to have him hear. Although we cannot assume that we know what is inside someone, we can still learn to listen to others' souls with the active intent and purpose that Jesus did. The following key skills can help us in our endeavor to actively listen to others' souls.

> *Jesus listened, not for what he needed to hear, but for what others needed to say and to have him hear.*

Listening for Both Literal and Implied Meanings

What people say and what they mean are not always the same. A friend left me a phone message one evening, but instead of her usual "Give me a call sometime," she said, "Will you call me?" Both sentences could easily mean the same thing, and the tone of her voice sounded the same as usual. Still, the nuance in wording caught my attention. I wondered if something might be wrong. Although I would normally have waited until the next day to call her back, I called her immediately and found that my hunch was right. Paying attention to even minor changes in usual wording can help us discover unspoken meanings. The Holy Spirit can also alert us to when something is wrong by making us more sensitive to hearing those minor differences. I don't know if that is what happened with me, but I would like to believe that it was the Spirit prompting me to notice.

Listening to What Is Not Being Said

A close cousin to listening to the implied meaning is listening to what is *not* being said. When Jesus talked with a Samaritan woman at a well, he listened beyond her words to what was unspoken in her spirit. When the woman realized that Jesus knew she had had five husbands and that the man she was now with was not her husband, she tried to get Jesus off track by replying, "Sir, I see that you are a prophet. Our ancestors worshipped on this mountain, but you say that the place where people must worship is in Jerusalem" (John 4:19–20). But Jesus wasn't derailed; he took what she said and seamlessly connected it to the good news he knew she needed to hear to transform her life. We too can listen for possible unspoken needs in the souls of others by asking the Spirit to make us aware of possible tangents they might be taking, and help us bring them back to soul issues, as Jesus did.

Clarifying by Reflecting Content Back to the Person

Reflecting content means that we repeat or paraphrase what the person said, in order to confirm that we understood. Such phrases as "You want me to pray specifically for . . . is that right?" or "Did you say you have a week to decide?" will help ensure that what we thought we heard is really what the other person said. Of course not all content needs to be clarified (imagine how annoying that would be). In sacred listening, we reflect content to help make sure that we understand the person's core focal points. We wouldn't want to sidetrack someone by honing in on an inconsequential point like "So you said you had an extra-large mocha caramel latte when you met with her, is that right?"

Clarifying by Reflecting Feelings Back to the Person

To reflect feelings implies that we are able to recognize possible emotions in others (like joy, excitement, anger, or jealousy). The problem here is that how people feel may not be accurately portrayed in their words or through their nonverbal expressions (whether or not they are conscious of that). Even a smile can be deceiving. One time a friend of mine came into my office and, with a smile on his face, said in an angry tone, "I am *so* mad." Such phrases as "It sounds like you were frustrated by what happened—is that how you felt?" or "What I hear you saying is that you were angry" can help us not only confirm the feelings behind someone's words but also discern any contradictions in expressions.

As you can see, active soul listening is a focused, purposeful way to help us sacredly listen. Empathic listening, the second type of sacred listening, is an even more focused listening. It is one of the best ways to help us not only hear but understand what is in another person's soul.

Empathic Listening

Have you ever listened to someone and sensed that you were feeling what that person was feeling? That is empathic listening. It is a form of active listening with the goal of understanding a perspective different from, and possibly opposed to, your own. Empathic listening entails listening without judging, and coming to understand why someone thinks and feels the way she or he does. The great American sociologist Charles Cooley called this kind of listening *sympathetic introspection,* which, he said, requires the listener to take on the role of the "significant other" and imagine what it is like to be hearing what is said from another person's point of view. The old saying that we cannot identify with others until we have walked a mile in their shoes fits well with empathic listening.

In one of my communication classes, I assign students an "empathy interview," in which they try to understand why someone might hold a point of view or have a way of life that is vastly different from theirs. I tell students they can be up front (in a nice way) and tell the person why they are asking him or her in particular for an interview. The students then give an in-class report focusing on their own reactions during and after the interview. Topics they have chosen include roles of women, racial issues, abortion, homosexuality, living together before marriage, capital punishment, and other "hot" topics. Although empathic listening can include sharing our own thoughts and feelings,[3] for this assignment students are to listen without injecting their own opinions, so that their own perspectives do not get in the way of trying to understand the other person.

To help students listen empathically, I encourage them to ask questions that are nonjudgmental in both tone and wording and that lead to more than a one- or two-word response, because questions like these invite more open sharing. Here are some examples:

> How do you think your views developed on this issue?
>
> Who or what has been influential in how you feel or think about this topic?
>
> How have significant people in your life treated you as a result of your views?
>
> How has your life changed as a result?
>
> What do you understand the Bible to say (or not say) in reference to this topic?

I tell students that if a question they ask is answered briefly, they can be ready with a follow-up question. If the response to "When do you first remember feeling that way?" is "I think it was two years ago," a fitting follow-up question might be "Can you describe the circumstances around that time?"

Again, asking nonjudgmental questions will encourage a person to share thoughts and feelings. Disapproving or discrediting questions such as "How could you *possibly* think that was right?" or "Do you *seriously* think that's what that Bible verse means?" rarely, if ever, result in either open sharing from the person or increased empathy from the interviewer.

It might not surprise you that this assignment makes some students very uncomfortable and even fearful. They are afraid that listening empathically will imply that they agree with something they are against, although most find that their problem is not implied agreement, but a struggle to listen without judgment. I remind students that they can admit they do not necessarily agree, but must make it clear to the person that they are trying to listen nonjudgmentally. Other students fear that they will listen so empathically that they will actually change their core beliefs on a particular issue. I tell those students that holding a belief that cannot stand up to scrutiny is a belief they may want to consider reinforcing or reconsidering.

My students are not the only ones who have these fears. Many of us struggle with listening to those with whom we disagree. Like my students, we may fear that listening implies agreement, or that we'll be tempted to change our minds about something we are against—especially if it's a position on a crucial moral issue that we believe would be a sin to change. This may be especially true if we think that being Christian primarily means standing up for our beliefs and convincing others of those beliefs. As important as standing up for beliefs can be, what defines us as Christians, according to Jesus, is whether or not we live out the two greatest commandments, love for God and love for others (Matthew 22:37–39). Loving involves listening. According to Dietrich Bonhoeffer, "The first service that one owes to others in the fellowship consists in listening to them. Just as love to God begins with listening to His Word, so the beginning of love for the brethren is learning to listen to them."[4]

Suspending judgment and listening empathically is the first step in what Bonhoeffer calls the "first service" of understanding one another. Shane Claiborne talked about the importance of this kind of listening in our interview: "I want to be marked as being part of a group of people who have respect for dialogue. I believe that begins with listening and learning from other people with whom we disagree. It's important to connect that way. I've tried to do that with people, like with one of the fresh voices within the church who I disagree with—we've gone to dinner together and talked and prayed together, but still, that doesn't cheapen what either of us believes to be true."

In his book *Love Is an Orientation,* author and speaker Andrew Marin writes about empathic listening in relation to certain Christian and gay, lesbian, bisexual, transgendered (GLBT) communities. Through his own experiences as a straight man living with his wife in a gay community in Chicago, he discovered how difficult it is for members of some Christian and gay communities to really listen to one another without each trying to prove he or she is right. He observes, "Each group talks past the other rather than to the other group."[5] Marin's challenge for both communities is to "elevate" the conversation, which means moving away from argument, and trying to better understand the other side's thoughts and feelings. It doesn't mean never taking a stand on an issue. What it does mean is to live out the Biblical command to do *everything* without arguing (Philippians 2:14, NIV). Marin's book is, in essence, an empathy assignment for communities who seriously differ on issues.

Brian McLaren, in our interview, gave this example of what elevating a conversation looks like.

> There is that beautiful verse in Ephesians: "Let no evil talk come out of your mouths, but only what is useful for building up, as there is need, so that your words may give grace to those who hear" [Ephesians 4:29]. That is a very helpful concept when I'm in a social setting because it means I should ask myself, "What can I contribute that would add grace?" To me, that's a spiritual practice. Although there have been too many times when I got it wrong, here's an example when I finally got it right: I was in a setting where several people were insulting another group of people. I knew there were some other people in the room who were being really wounded by insulting language, and I was one of the speakers invited to this group. So I spoke up and said, "I really feel terrible right now because you're attacking people for holding a whole set of views, some of which I hold, and I feel really out of place right now." I didn't criticize them. I didn't say, "That's bad what you're doing. You're wrong to do that." I just made a vulnerable statement. I self-reported. As soon as I spoke up, person after person said, "I feel the same way." And what that allowed us to do is to respond to a situation with vulnerability as opposed to anger. It's self-reporting as opposed to either clamming up and feeling excluded or fighting back. It was a redemptive moment.

When these empathic conversations happen, Shane, Andrew, and Brian all find what many of my students find too—not necessarily a change in belief on either side (though that can sometimes happen), but changes in how both parties respond to one another. Instead of dominating or manipulating, both parties try to understand each other's perspective. Students repeatedly testify coming away from their empathy interviews with a more informed understanding and even appreciation for why someone might feel and think differently than they do. Experiencing that understanding and appreciation is a crucial step in opening doors to more meaningful and elevated empathic conversations.

I recommend empathy interviews anytime we want to connect better when we disagree with others. They don't have to be formal interviews; we can have an informal empathy interview with anyone at any time, as long as we are careful to ask our questions and to respond in loving ways. We can also seek to understand an opposing viewpoint by researching why theologians and other scholars think it is a valid position. Even when we are good at knowing the reasons we think our position is valid, which sadly is not always the case, we often can only identify weak or "straw" arguments for the other side. Being able to discuss solid pros and cons on either side can help us have more loving and reasonable conversations with others.

Too Much Tolerance in Empathic Listening?

Does all this talk of suspending judgment and being tolerant as a listener mean never expressing disagreement or never voicing your own opinions or standards for life? If I said yes, I would be contradicting the very premise of this book: that connecting with others in Christlike ways means proclaiming and advancing God's vision for the world. God's vision involves believing and acting in certain ways—such as living out what Jesus taught and preached in the Sermon on the Mount (see Matthew 5–7)—and teaching others to do the same, as Jesus commanded in the Great Commission (Matthew 28:19–20). But advancing a way of life does not have to mean expressing intolerance or arguing with someone.

The best approach to proclaiming a way of life is being consistent in how we ourselves live that life and teaching others how to do the same. The best teachers are also good listeners. When people disagree with one another, what is most loving is to remain engaged in conversation and listen to one another. Expressions of intolerance are guaranteed to start an argument or stop a conversation.

We may see declaring intolerance as a virtue, but if the goal is to encourage people to love God and others in truly transforming, Kingdom-building ways, then intolerance is not the best path for winning people

How many people have ever really had their minds changed by an intolerant attitude?

over. Think about it: How many people have ever *really* had their minds changed by an intolerant attitude? As Tony told me when we were talking about this issue, "No one is ever converted to Jesus by losing an argument."

But what if the other person is going against what we believe are clear Biblical principles? How we respond depends in part on the specific issue and whether or not the person claims to be a Christian. If that person does not, then we listen to the reasons for those opinions or ideas before we tell her or him what we believe. If that person is a Christian, again, we listen. Because there are different interpretations of Biblical principles, listening to how each of us has arrived at our own beliefs connects us and opens the door to further conversations in ways that intolerance and judgmental attitudes never will.

Tony said that his colleagues at the University of Pennsylvania were always very surprised that he could get away with making strong evangelical statements in class without his secular and Jewish students objecting. He explained that he always prefaced his statement by saying, "This is what evangelicals believe." Students were interested in what evangelicals believed. What they didn't want was to be told that this is the absolute truth, even though they knew that Tony believed that it was.

Tony's approach doesn't work only for him, but for much less seasoned communicators too. A few years ago, I was asked to speak at an interfaith conference in Washington DC on prayer practices that I believe help us become more sensitive to justice issues. I told Tony I didn't think I could do it: I couldn't talk about how these prayer practices have impacted my life without talking about Jesus, but I thought that would offend those of other religions who would be at the conference. Tony told me, "No problem. You just need to add one sentence to what you say. Tell your audience, 'I want to tell you how certain prayer practices in my faith tradition have helped me,' and then you can talk about Jesus as much as you like." The feedback I received from participants showed me that Tony was right. No one seemed offended by what I said when I expressed my faith in those terms.

Again, it's not that we aren't to take positions on issues, but we are to remember that showing love is what first and foremost defines us as Christians.

The Prophetic Exception

But what about prophets? Prophets, especially in the Hebrew Bible, never seemed to hold back from expressing intolerance. It's true that many of them did express intolerance, and even judgment—sometimes very strongly—but that does not mean we can assume they did it with loveless condemnation in their voices. Both Jewish theologian Abraham Joshua Heschel and Christian Old Testament scholar Walter Brueggemann agree that a true prophet weeps (as Jesus does in John 11:35). A true prophet is also full of love and compassion, as demonstrated in these words of Jesus: "Jerusalem, Jerusalem, the city that kills the prophets and stones those who are sent to it! How often have I desired to gather your children together as a hen gathers her brood under her wings, and you were not willing" (Luke 13:34). If the hard sayings that prophets proclaim do not leave the listeners with the sense that the words are being said with great pain and love, then what is heard will be treated as arrogant condemning. If we feel led to express prophetic words, especially words of intolerance, we would do well to remember that not everyone is called to be a prophet. Even though my son Michael decided when he was four years old that he wanted to be a prophet when he grew up (after hearing the story of young Samuel in the Bible), most of us would agree that his decision still needs to be "tested" if he feels that way as an adult (1 John 4:1). Likewise, even though we may believe we have prophetic words to proclaim, that belief would need to be verified. It would be wise to have others who are committed to following Jesus help us "test the spirits." One of those tests may well be whether or not what we are drawn to proclaim makes us weep.

There are few better ways to connect with others than through actively and empathically listening to them and having them do the same for us. Listening helps us discover common ground on which we can connect and allows us to share our own beliefs, for true connecting implies a mutual understanding and sharing. But as you can see, sacred listening takes a lot of work. Engaging in either kind, even for a short amount of time, can be draining, which is why being physically prepared to listen is so important.

Physical Preparation for Sacred Listening

The author of a textbook I used in graduate school claimed that when we listen, our senses should be as heightened and engaged as they are when we are giving a speech. When I first read that statement years ago, at the height of my fear of public speaking, I was intrigued but skeptical. Because my senses were usually in overdrive when I spoke, speaking was mentally, emotionally, and physically exhausting. After thinking about it awhile, I realized that this was perhaps the author's point: we are to be so hyperengaged when listening that it drains our energy.

I see his point for active and empathic listening, but it doesn't seem practical or necessary to be so intensely focused in *every* listening context. It can be too draining to listen to every single thing we hear. We all have what could be called a "physical threshold" in listening—the degree to which we listen before burning out. That's why both listeners and talkers need to be discerning as to when active soul listening and empathic listening are appropriate. Otherwise we can drain ourselves listening with high levels of intensity inappropriate for the situation. There are times we will know that sacred listening is called for because the person has told us that he or she needs to talk about something serious. Other times, a conversation may start with a different purpose and evolve into a time of soul sharing—for example, an exchange at a party that starts with chitchat and moves into deep spiritual matters. But if we are with a person who *keeps* chattering away and we are exhausted, we may want to leave the intensity of active listening for another day. My poor husband has had to make this decision with me at times. When I used to come home from work, the first thing I wanted to give Terry was a play-by-play of my day. I didn't really think about whether or not what I shared was of any value. For me it was a kind of purging, my way to unwind. But I don't think that was really fair to Terry—to be on the other end of my stream of consciousness about what errands I ran and what I had for lunch. As talkers we need to be careful as to what we share and when we share, so that we do not unnecessarily burden a listener with idle chatter.

Because we won't always know in advance when a sacred listening situation might present itself, it's important to develop a habit of being physically healthy so that we are prepared to expend the energy this kind of focused listening can take. Exercising, eating a healthy diet, and getting enough sleep are all important here. Not having enough sleep may be the most important in terms of being able to engage in listening, as we can't listen well when we are barely awake. Studies show that it is a good idea to commit to getting at least eight hours of sleep every night.[6] If that isn't feasible, then scheduling a time of rest sometime before a planned or possible interaction can help us be prepared for any listening encounter. If we do find ourselves in a sacred listening situation and at least one person involved seems too tired to focus (if he or she has fallen asleep, that's a good hint), we may need to decide that it's better to postpone our time together.

What Keeps Us from Sacred Listening

In addition to not being rested, there are other common barriers to sacred listening. The fact that they are so common can make them dangerously tolerable. Becoming aware of these barriers in ourselves can help us break free from them so that we can listen to others in ways that connect with their souls.

Inappropriate Responses to the Situation

One of the biggest barriers to listening is failing to pay attention to *how* we are listening. When involved in sacred listening to others, it is important to ask ourselves the following questions:

- How might my responses be coming across? For example, if the other person is angry or saddened by something, am I contributing counterproductive negativity to the encounter through my own negative responses?
- Am I joking too much and not allowing the other to be serious?
- Am I being too serious and not allowing for any levity?
- Am I distracted, not giving the other person my full attention?

You may have noticed that I haven't mentioned two of the most inappropriate responses: talking too much and interrupting. They are such big barriers to listening that each gets its own section.

Talking Too Much

Years ago, an elementary school friend who used to walk home every day with another friend of mine, Annie, complained to Annie's mom, "Mrs. Smith, every time I try to talk, Annie puts her hand over my mouth." Although adults typically use more socially accepted means than Annie's literally in-your-face strategy, the results are the same: others don't get a chance to speak.

Some people talk too much. The fact is, if we are talking, we cannot listen. If you aren't sure whether or not you talk too much and you want to know, think about your ratio of talking to listening compared to that of other people. Then ask four important questions:

1. Do I put a lot of responsibility on myself for making sure the conversation flows?
2. When there are more than a few seconds of silence, do I feel uncomfortable and try to think of something to say?
3. Do I find myself giving advice often?
4. Do I think that what I have to say is more important than what the other person is saying?

Answering yes to the first two or three questions may indicate a fear that the other person won't think your time together was worthwhile if no one is talking. The prayer of examen, highlighted in Chapter Three, can help you discover why you might feel this way. In addition, taking a slow, deep breath and intentionally making yourself not say anything for five seconds or so can help you learn to be more comfortable with silence. In addition, the spiritual practices discussed later in this chapter can help you become more comfortable with silence.

Answering yes to the third and/or fourth questions could indicate a heightened sense of self-importance. If this is the case, intentionally reducing the number of comments you make or the amount of advice you give can help you move beyond the tendency to believe that your words are more important than what the other person has to say. As François Fénelon wrote, "A humility that is still talkative does not run very deep. When you talk too much your self-love relieves its sense of shame a little."[7]

For those of us who are natural talkers, it is hard to realize that sometimes a person would prefer that we be with him or her but that we not talk. As a friend of mine, Susan Hric, said, "It is easy to underestimate the power of presence and overestimate the power of words."[8]

Knowing when it's time to talk and when it's time to listen is crucial in caring for others' souls. Thinking about the purpose for an encounter is a crucial starting point for this art. If someone wants guidance or counsel, as in spiritual direction, listening is our main task. If we are having an informal conversation, we are more likely to take turns talking and listening. If a person has a specific problem to discuss, it is important to ask whether he or she wants advice. If the answer is no, we need to honor that response and not give it. Sometimes people want us to listen and that's it. But even if the answer is yes, it's a good idea to be careful giving advice. If, for example, someone is sharing about a broken relationship and we dive in with our opinion that it's better that the couple is no longer together, how awkward if they do get back together. It is usually better to listen first than to offer advice right away. In silent reflection, others often discover important insights on their own that they wouldn't have discovered otherwise. We don't want to block that process with premature advice. There is also unexpected freedom for the listener who holds off on giving advice: release from feeling that it is always our responsibility to tell someone else what he or she should do.

Knowing when it's time to talk and when it's time to listen is crucial in caring for others' souls.

Interrupting

In any conversation, so much of what people say can trigger things *we* want to say, making it too tempting not to interrupt. We may want to argue or agree with something they said, or even show how similar we are by launching into what we believe is a relevant point or story. But interrupting implies not listening well, because to interrupt means we have been thinking about something we wanted to say instead of really listening. It also means we aren't letting the other person finish voicing his or her own thoughts. We are told in Proverbs 18:13, "If one gives answer before hearing, it is folly and shame."

Although there is a time to argue and a time to share our own stories, most often that time is not while someone else is talking. Even if our interruption seems appropriate, it can too easily derail another person's train of thought. If we think we can get the person back on track after our interruption, we may be wrong, as he or she might not have been going where we thought they were.

There are times when interrupting, instead of being a listening liability, may actually be a necessity. There is an unspoken rhythm and flow to conversations that can be broken when someone dominates a conversation and talks over others, instead of taking his or her turn at listening. This can happen not only in a business meeting or a classroom but also in a more sacred listening situation when a person may get so animated, adamant, or agitated that another person needs to gently interrupt, even midsentence if necessary. Interrupting with something like "Let's stop there for a minute—let me summarize what I think you are saying," can help the person settle down and listen better to others. If it's a group setting and the talker is offended by being interrupted, a private conversation in which the person is asked to consider how he or she comes across could lead to greater self-awareness and better connecting with others.

External and Internal Noise

In the field of communication, *noise* is a technical term that refers to anything, internal or external, that interferes with communication. We can be so used to both internal and external types of noise that we are not aware of how they negatively affect our souls and our ability to listen, not only to others but to God.

Any distraction our senses pick up that hinders our ability to listen is an external noise. We live in a time of massive external noise: cell phones, iPods, computers, and video games (to name just a few). All of them can easily capture, steal, or command our attention while we're listening to others.

Noise may not even be something you hear—it can also be visual, as I found when we were visiting a church during vacation. I noticed something strange about the pastor's mouth, but could not quite put my finger on what it was. Finally I leaned over and asked my husband, who whispered back to me, "He has too many teeth in his mouth." That was it! But then I could no longer listen to what the pastor was saying because I was too obsessed with his teeth. I finally had to distract myself from this "noise" by taking notes so that I would not look at him anymore.

If the goal is to connect through listening, it's crucial to have strategies to counter external noise. A combination of intentionally focusing on the other person, turning off electronics, and, when possible, removing ourselves from any other distractions (such as by leaving a noisy restaurant) takes care of most external barriers to listening.

Even when there is no external noise, our own internal thoughts and feelings can hinder the ability to listen. Our minds can wander off on tangents for a variety of reasons, including lack of interest in, or disagreement with, the conversation; we may also be distracted by stereotypes (good or bad) we may hold with regard to the other person's status, age, race, religion, gender, lifestyle, and physical characteristics. Our self-centeredness, defensiveness, and self-esteem, whether high or low, can produce loud internal noise that prevents us from listening well. Being preoccupied with something else going on, such as not feeling well physically or thinking about some disturbing or exciting news, can also make it difficult to listen attentively. But it *is* possible to overcome internal

noise through self-awareness
and discipline. Like those who
are able to "live in the moment,"
we can learn to "listen in the
moment" no matter what is
going on in our lives. Being
present, a spiritual practice discussed toward the end of the
chapter, can help us learn to do
just that.

We can learn to "listen in the moment" no matter what is going on in our lives.

Gender Differences

Both personal experience and research show us that males and females
often have different ways of listening. One study found that when females
are listening, they interject such phrases as "I understand," "Wow!" "Go
on," "Yes," and "I know" to show their attentiveness. Men, in contrast,
stay silent to indicate they are paying attention. See the problem? Women
may perceive a man's silence as lack of interest; men may perceive a
woman's verbal interjections as wanting to take over the conversation.[9]
Being aware of, and tolerant toward, these differences in listening can
greatly reduce gender barriers. And if we fit the average gender profile,
we could try being a little quieter if we are a female listener, and interject
a few encouraging verbal responses if we are male.

Semantics

Tony often tells a story of saying to an audience, "While you were sleeping last night, thirty thousand kids died of starvation or diseases related
to malnutrition, and most of you don't give a shit. What's worse is that
you're more upset with the fact that I said 'shit' than the fact that thirty
thousand kids died last night." Tony is always right about that last statement. The first time I heard his illustration was when I was coordinating
the chapel program at Spring Arbor University. After chapel, several
students came up to me and said "Can you believe he swore in chapel?"
Not one said, "Can you believe that thirty thousand kids die each day
of starvation?"

When we allow certain words to stop us from listening to what a
person is saying, we succumb to a semantic barrier. The barrier could
be what we consider an "unseemly" expression, such as in Tony's
example; what are called value-laden terms, such as "family values" or

"evangelical"; use of poor grammar; or what we consider sexist or racist language or other loaded language that conveys judgment or somehow violates what is considered appropriate. When we find a word or phrase troubling or offensive, it is important to resist the tendency to discredit the entire message. Unlike Tony, who was using an obscenity intentionally, the speaker may not be aware of how it is coming across. Even if a problematic word or phrase is being used intentionally, that is not a cue to stop listening. One bad word does not have to spoil a whole message. Listening beyond an emotionally charged word does not mean we agree with its usage, just that we are willing to suspend judgment and give the benefit of the doubt to the rest of what that person has to say. Besides, if we stop listening, we may miss out on a profound and even life-changing message. As speakers, we need to become aware of and sensitive to emotionally laden terms, but it's equally important for us as listeners not to allow semantics to stop us from listening. Semantics can be an even more serious problem now that so much communication is done with the written word through electronic media. But there is also an upside to electronic forms of communication.

A note on electronic "listening." Although the examples I've been giving have been in the context of face-to-face listening, the concepts apply equally to "listening" to people's words through the various forms of what is called computer-mediated communication. There are both benefits and drawbacks to this kind of listening. Those who are better at expressing themselves in written form may much prefer interacting through the computer. (The drawback: not everyone has good writing skills.) Another benefit is that the listener does not have to necessarily respond immediately, giving him or her more time to reflect on what the person wrote, as well as on their own response back. (The drawback: the writer might wish for a speedier response.) Finally, even though it may seem that not seeing someone face-to-face and being unable to read his or her expressions and body language can be a major hindrance to listening, that is not necessarily the case. In fact, we aren't always as good at reading nonverbal communication as we think we are. For instance, we may have learned that if someone crosses his or her arms, it means that the person is "closed off" emotionally, when in fact it could be cold in the room. Physical appearance can also be distracting to one or both parties involved. In addition, cultural and gender differences often affect our ability to effectively interpret nonverbal communication.

Listening with the Ears of God

It should be obvious by now that sacred listening is hard work. Along with good listening skills, we need our listening to be infused with the power of the Holy Spirit. As Dietrich Bonhoeffer wrote in *Life Together,* "Christians have forgotten that the ministry of listening has been committed to them by Him who is Himself the great listener and whose work they should share. We should listen with the ears of God that we may speak the Word of God."[10] The following spiritual practices can help us listen to God and God's Word so that we are empowered to listen to the souls of others.

Centering prayer, discussed in Chapter Four, is a powerful spiritual practice for "settling our souls" so that we are better prepared to sacredly listen to others. In addition, listening to Jesus in our daily lives, praying specifically for our listening encounters, and cultivating intentional times of solitude in the midst of busy days are all ways for us to be more focused in our listening to God and others.

Listening to Jesus

One of the best ways to sacredly listen is to learn to listen daily to Jesus, the ultimate listener. Pastor and author John Ortberg teaches a spiritual practice he calls "Spending an Ordinary Day with Jesus."[11] The idea is to imagine Jesus with you for an entire day. You could start by visualizing Jesus sitting in a chair by your bed when you first awaken. Then as you move through your day, picture Jesus going where you go and doing what you do. As you envision yourself with Jesus, along with talking to him, make sure you listen to him as well. Notice what, if anything, he says or asks you as the two of you go through the day.

Another way to listen to Jesus involves the spiritual practice of imaginative prayer discussed in Chapter Four. You can picture yourself in a Gospel story from Matthew, Mark, Luke, or John when Jesus is talking to an individual, a group, or a crowd. Imagine you are one of the main characters or a bystander. Put yourself in the scene, noticing the various sights and sounds. One way I do this exercise is to imagine that I am in the crowd listening to Jesus give the Sermon on the Mount (Matthew 5–7). I start with the Beatitudes in Matthew 5 one day, then go to the following section. I have found that listening to Jesus' words this way makes them come alive in ways that reading them without the visualization never has. However, it's important to be aware that this spiritual practice may challenge how you currently live. As Oswald Chambers wrote in *My Utmost for His Highest,* "Jesus Christ says a great deal that we listen to, but do not hear; when we do hear, his words are amazingly hard."[12] Hard as they may be, if we want to be a part of helping realize God's vision for the world, we will listen with the intent of obeying even the hardest teachings of Jesus.

Praying Before Listening to Others

I have found it extremely beneficial, whenever possible, to take a few minutes before meeting with someone to quiet myself and reflect on the upcoming appointment. That reflection time includes asking the Holy Spirit to help me recall what is important to remember from the last encounter, as well as praying for the person and our time together. Because listening is such an important part of spiritual direction, a fruit of that time of reflection is the ability to enter into the encounter in a spirit of sacred listening. Even though we cannot do this for every listening encounter, when we know that we will be seeing someone and that our role is to be a sacred listener, a brief time of reflection will help us listen more intently.

Cultivating Silent Moments

Cultivating silence in our lives, perhaps more than any other spiritual practice, can make us more attuned listeners. Having times in our lives when we intentionally try to block out external and internal noise helps us learn to listen in ways we cannot when our lives are too full of distractions.

> *Cultivating silence in our lives, perhaps more than any other spiritual practice, can make us more attuned listeners.*

I experienced my first silent retreat several years ago as a required part of a two-year program in spiritual direction. I never would have gone on a silent retreat on my own, as I used to be very uncomfortable with any extended period of silence. Although I struggled with the silence in the first retreat, during the second retreat, silence quickly became not only calming but incredibly freeing. I found freedom both in not talking and in not feeling that I had to avoid silence. After the retreat, I realized it was easier to listen more attentively to others without my mind wandering off. I also discovered that I *wanted* periods of silence in my daily life when I was alone, whereas before I would always try to fill the silence by playing music or turning on the radio, just to have background noise.

You can intentionally cultivate silence in your own life by scheduling times alone, whether it's ten minutes in a day or an intentional half-day, full-day, or several-day silent retreat. You can also practice silence by not turning on your MP3 player, phone, computer, TV, or radio during certain times of the day. I think you will find, as I did, that these intentional practices help you listen to others in more focused, sacred ways.

Silent Walking

Just as power walking is good for our bodies, meditative walking—slow, silent walking while paying attention to our environment—is good for our souls. It helps us learn to listen more attentively to ourselves and others through listening more attentively to our environment, which is an ability many of us have lost. Just before the tsunami of 2004 hit the Sri Lanka and India coastlines, there were eyewitness reports of animals sensing something was about to happen. Elephants headed for higher ground, and flamingos fled their low-lying breeding areas. The theory is that animals have an acute hearing that allows them to sense the earth's vibrations.[13] If humans once had this acute kind of hearing, we have lost it. There are far too many distractions in today's world that block us from hearing what is really important and perhaps even lifesaving. Meditative walking is one way to become more in tune with our natural surroundings, which then helps us become more in tune with ourselves and with one another.

Meditative walking may at first be difficult, especially for those of us who walk for exercise, because the walking I'm proposing here is intentionally and deliberately slow. While we walk, we are to breathe in a relaxed fashion while paying attention to our surroundings (which means no ear buds). We are to thank God for the sights, sounds, and smells we encounter while we practice being fully in the moment.

Fruits of Listening

After engaging in some of these or other communication and spiritual practices for listening, you may be surprised to find you are less tempted to talk while another is talking. You may even feel a sense of freedom (or relief) from self-imposed pressure to say something important. It's not uncommon to experience increased freedom in these areas as you are becoming more attuned to the guidance of the Spirit about when to speak and when to stay silent.

When you focus on listening more intently to the Spirit and to others, you may also find it easier to hold distractions at bay. In addition, you may notice more people coming to you, wanting you to listen to them. Even if this isn't the case, you don't need to worry. If God wants to "increase our territory" with regard to others, we can trust God to put it on their hearts to seek us out. We need only continue to be alert and ready to receive opportunities to sacredly listen to others.

6

Connecting Through Questions

Why Asking Is Better Than Telling

For if you love those who love you, what reward do you have?
—Jesus (Matthew 5:46)

What do you want?
—Jesus (John 1:38, NIV)

ON THE POPULAR TV SHOW *Whose Line Is It Anyway?* there was a sketch called "Questions Only," involving two participants acting out a scene in which they could only communicate through questions. It would go something like this:

"How are you?"

"What would you say if I told you I was better than normal?"

"What if I didn't know what to say?"

"Why wouldn't you know what to say?"

"Why would I?"

"You don't know?"

"What don't I know?"

And on it would go, until someone either mistakenly answered with a statement or could not think of a question in a reasonable amount of time. When playing "Questions Only" with my family while waiting in line at a restaurant, I discovered that it is a good exercise for honing skills in the important art of asking questions.

Without Questions . . .

Asking questions is essential to all of life. Questions are starting points for learning more about ourselves, others, and the world. Think of how different life might be if some of these questions were never asked:

Will you go out with me?

Will you marry me?

Are you OK?

Are you sure?

What happened?

What do you think?

Why did you do that?

Where does it hurt?

How did that make you feel?

What would Jesus do?

Who do you say that I am?

My husband, Terry, has understood the value of asking questions longer than I have. For instance, when our boys entered high school, he advocated the use of questions as a way to help David and Michael take more ownership in curfew decisions. He suggested that at the beginning of each school semester we ask them, "What do you think is a reasonable time to be home and in bed on school nights and on weekends?" I did not like that idea at all. I thought it would give them too much license to negotiate a less than ideal time and was skeptical that they would come up with reasonable suggestions and arguments. To my surprise, their responses have consistently been in agreement with what we thought was appropriate. Most important, they have done a much better job of sticking to the agreed-on times than when Terry and I set the time without asking for their input.

Questions can be used to invite people into important decision-making processes; questions also provoke us to think more intently about important issues. Questions challenge and change lives in ways that statements and directives rarely do. That is why learning to ask good questions is so important when it comes to matters of the soul.

Questions challenge and change lives in ways that statements and directives rarely do.

A Conversation of Questions

In her book *The 7 Powers of Questions*, speaker and author Dorothy Leeds writes, "It is the act of questioning that causes us to go deep inside and examine our emotional selves and questioning that causes us to take actions that turn our lives around."[1] Examining our own lives and helping others examine theirs is often best done in the context of asking questions instead of directing and *telling*. It was Socrates who is credited with advocating the patient asking of questions as the best route to self-discovery and even truth.

Although the Socratic Method is most often recommended in the context of teaching, it is also a valuable tool for the healing of souls; it goes hand-in-hand with sacred listening. Asking the right kinds of questions is much better than telling others what we think they should do to care for their own souls (even if they say they want advice and we want to give it). Good questions create an environment of openness, fostering dialogue that invites others to discover the condition of their soul. In fact, "What is the state of your soul?" is a question John Wesley encouraged people to regularly ask one another.[2]

In our interview, Mindy Caliguire talked about the importance of using questions in caring for others' souls: "The questions I tend to ask most are the ones looking backward at someone's life and experiences, since I sometimes wonder about connections between the past and current circumstances or future scenarios. Also, I love asking people how they are experiencing God in the midst of their current circumstances. Sometimes I find it best not to ask many follow-up questions and let the person decide what to tell me next. Leaving silence helps them to continue their own thought process." Mindy's point about not asking too many questions is an important one. As valuable as questions are in guiding and encouraging others to express their thoughts and feelings, we do need to be careful not to ask so many questions that we sidetrack others from adequately expressing themselves.

Jesus as a Model for Soul-Healing Questions

Jesus often used questions to connect with others. Instead of directly telling people what to believe and do, Jesus would ask questions that fostered conversations to help others arrive at truths. In John 20 we read that Mary Magdalene went to Jesus' tomb and discovered that he wasn't there. She was devastated, thinking that someone had taken his body. When Jesus appeared to her, she thought he was the gardener. Instead of telling Mary it was he, Jesus asked her, "Woman, why are you weeping?

*Jesus often used questions
to connect with others.*

For whom are you looking?" (John 20:15). He invited Mary to discover for herself, through his questions, that it truly was he; and when she did, she was overcome with joy.

Not surprisingly, when we look to Jesus for examples of the art of asking questions, we find solid communication practices that are as effective today as they were back then. Although some of the questions Jesus asked were for the purpose of confronting the religious leaders of his day, the focus of this chapter is on the characteristics of the questions he asked those who he knew had a desire to follow him—whether or not *they* knew it. In this context, his questions

- *Intentionally began the interaction with the purpose of expanding the conversation.* When Jesus first encountered the Samaritan woman at the well, he asked, "Will you give me a drink?" (John 4:7, NIV). It was a question that led to a conversation that changed the woman's life.

- *Fostered dialogue rather than defensiveness.* When Jesus first approached the two men on the road to Emmaus, he did not ask "Are you talking about me?" which could have led to a defensive (and confused) response. Instead he asked, "What are you discussing together as you walk along?"(Luke 24:17), another question that resulted in lives changed for the Kingdom.

- *Were open, meaning that they encouraged answers of greater depth than closed questions that could be answered with a one- or two-word reply.* As we saw with the previous example, Jesus' open questions often began with "What." In John 1:38 (NIV), Jesus asked two of John's disciples, who started following Jesus, "What do you want?" In Matthew 20:21, he asked the mother of Zebedee's sons the same question: "What do you want?" Her response then set the stage for Jesus to talk about what it means to be part of God's Kingdom. When a closed question is asked, such as "Are you OK?" it might be wise to follow up with another question, such as "What happened that upset you?"

- *Challenged the status quo.* Jesus asked numerous questions that challenged the usual way of responding to a person's particular circumstances or to life in general. Questions like the following encouraged Kingdom ways of believing and living:

"For what will it profit them if they gain the whole world but forfeit their life? Or what will they give in return for their life?" (Matthew 16:26)

"For if you love those who love you, what reward do you have? Do not even the tax-collectors do the same?" (Matthew 5:46)

"And can any of you by worrying add a single hour to your span of life? And why do you worry about clothing? Consider the lilies of the field, how they grow; they neither toil nor spin, yet I tell you, even Solomon in all his glory was not clothed like one of these." (Matthew 6:27–29)

"Why do you see the speck in your neighbor's eye, but do not notice the log in your own eye? Or how can you say to your neighbor, 'Let me take the speck out of your eye,' while the log is in your own eye?" (Matthew 7:3–4)

In our interview, Shane Claiborne expanded on how asking questions can help change the status quo:

> Most of our questions arise around pain, doubt, dysfunction, and despair. A part of what we have to do is enter in the brokenness and pain of others. It's easy, for example, to have answers to world poverty if you don't know poor people and we don't ask questions, like "What leads to homelessness?"—instead of assuming that all homeless people either just need to go out and get a job or they are mentally ill. I know so many homeless people who are hard working, but they can't make enough money to take proper care of their kids. Our questions are shaped by what we see out our windows, so to avoid a narrow view of why people are homeless, some questions we can ask ourselves and others are "Do we know any homeless people?" and "Have we talked to them about why they are homeless?" If we don't know any homeless people, we may not be asking the right questions about the conditions of their lives and their souls.

If we want to connect with others the way Jesus did, we'll want to develop a habit of intentionally asking the kinds of questions Jesus did.

A note on tone. We do not know how Jesus sounded when he asked a question, but we can draw on what we do know about vocal inflection, rate, and loudness to be mindful of the most appropriate way of speaking in a situation. As a general rule, asking a question with a calm voice works best. There are exceptions, however. It may be that Jesus used exasperated or sarcastic tones at times. In a previous example, when Jesus asked the question "Why do you see the speck in your neighbor's eye, but do not notice the log in your own eye?" he could sound frustrated or sad, depending on how the passage is read. And when Jesus asked, "You of little faith, why are you talking about having no bread? Do you still not perceive?" we don't know if he used a sarcastic or a sympathetic tone. Either one *could* be appropriate, but we must be careful with our own use of frustrated or sarcastic tones when asking questions (or with any type of communication). Taking a deep breath to get a handle on our emotional state and being aware of whether or not we are acting out of love for God and the other person can help us determine and use the best tone. Even a sarcastic, dry tone can work if the other person gets and enjoys sarcasm. But sarcasm does not work for everyone. A frustrated tone can also work to motivate, but caution is needed there too. If we often use a sarcastic or frustrated tone, we may be demonstrating that *connecting* to another is not our goal. Nor will it likely be the result.

Developing the Habit: From Comments to Questions

If we are not in the habit of asking questions, the solution to changing this habit is probably obvious: start asking more questions. A good warm-up exercise might be the "Questions Only" approach mentioned at the beginning of the chapter. When you are in a conversation, instead of responding to a comment with another comment or story, ask a question. Continue to avoid the temptation to add your own comments or stories. Focus on appropriate questions you can ask that are relevant to the situation. In our interview, Mindy Caliguire shared some specific questions she has learned to ask when attempting to connect at a soul level with others.

> I often ask people about their motives. . . . what made you want to study that in school? Why were you interested in joining the army? What made you want to see a spiritual director at that time? Whenever someone tells me of a choice or a decision they've made, recently or long ago, I always find it interesting to understand why they chose that particular direction. That way, it goes beneath the details of their lives and into the realm of the heart. I also try to imagine myself in those circumstances and imagine what I would feel, wonder about, be afraid of, and then ask questions to check out my assumptions. I

believe these conversations extend Jesus' grace, his concern, his presence, his love into another person's life through us.

Ever since my training in spiritual direction, I have been collecting questions to draw on when in "soul conversations" with someone. I have memorized some of them, and sometimes I glance at the list before meeting with someone. Of course they are to be used in context, meaning that we prayerfully consider, even in the midst of a conversation, whether it might be appropriate to ask one of them, given what the other person is saying (as opposed to blurting one out when we can't think of anything to say). Here they are:

- What is your image of God or Jesus in everyday life? When you pray?
- How have you been sensing or noticing God's presence and activity?
- When (or where) in your day do you feel that you experience or encounter God the most?
- Where is a difficult place for you to see God in your life?
- Is what you just talked about growing your heart for others? How?
- What might be God's invitation to you through what you just shared?
- Have you taken the situation you described to me to Jesus in prayer?
- Is it well with your soul? Or Wesley's question, "What is the state of your soul?"

Be Careful What You Ask

Not all questions are good questions. Some questions are not appropriate for the purpose of the particular conversation. Asking someone "What is the state of your soul?" could be inappropriate depending on the setting or the amount of time you have to listen to the person's response. Asking for prosaic details while listening to an emotionally charged personal account would also be inappropriate. No matter how tempting it might be to ask irrelevant questions, try to ask only questions that stay on topic, especially when people are sharing intimately.

We also need to be discerning in how personal our questions are. People share at different levels, and even if we might be quick to share intimate details about ourselves, that doesn't mean everyone else has those same boundaries. If we aren't sure, we can ask whether or not the person is comfortable talking about a certain topic: a simple "Do you mind talking about this?" can be enough. It is important to get a sense of how comfortable the other person is at different levels of sharing, and then to be sensitive as to the kinds of questions you ask.

It's also important to consider our possible motives for asking questions. You'll want to avoid asking a question if you are interested in finding out information more for curiosity's sake than for the sake of the other person.

Jesus was also alert to people's motives when *responding* to questions. In our interview, Brian McLaren spoke to how Jesus responded to certain questions: "Jesus refused to answer a badly framed question. I think we could learn something from that. Often he would answer a question with a deeper question. He would reframe the whole issue. Or if there was a question being asked to trap him, he would sort of 'booby-trap the trap' so that those who were trying to trap him would be trapped in their response to his answer."

Here is an example from Luke 20:1–8 of how Jesus reframed certain questions.

> One day, as he was teaching the people in the temple and telling the good news, the chief priests and the scribes came with the elders and said to him, "Tell us, by what authority are you doing these things? Who is it who gave you this authority?" He answered them, "I will also ask you a question, and you tell me: Did the baptism of John come from heaven, or was it of human origin?" They discussed it with one another, saying, "If we say, 'From heaven,' he will say, 'Why did you not believe him?' But if we say, 'Of human origin,' all the people will stone us; for they are convinced that John was a prophet." So they answered that they did not know where it came from. Then Jesus said to them, "Neither will I tell you by what authority I am doing these things."

Responding to Questions

As the religious leaders discovered with Jesus, we cannot control another person's response to our questions—nor should we. We may hope that if we ask certain high-quality questions, others will discover answers deep down in their souls that result in their lives being radically changed for God's Kingdom. That would be wonderful. But if that is what we count on, we will burn out fast. We are to be faithful to whatever may lead to soul healing in others, but we must always leave any responsibility—or credit—for change with God and the other person. Besides, if we always want a certain response, we will be disappointed. A person may respond antagonistically or defensively and a soul-to-soul connection may not take place, no matter how high-quality we thought our questions were. Still, we are called to be faithful to asking questions that we hope will foster soul connections.

We cannot control another person's response to our questions—nor should we.

Whatever response we get from a person, one thing is sure when connecting with others: we must listen to the response. Most likely we have all experienced asking a question and not paying attention to how the person responded. As bad as this is in a casual conversation, it is worse when someone is sharing intimate information. Whenever we use questions as a way to connect with others, we must be sure to listen. As we have seen, committing to helping heal souls involves the sacred act of listening.

What if we ask a question and the other person does not respond? It is a matter of discernment as to whether or not we push for a response. It may be that we need to ask a different question, or we may need to respect the person's right to be silent and to reflect. Not everyone responds immediately, nor should they have to. It might do all of us good to reflect more before responding. Asking if we can come back to a question later may be appropriate, but it is important not to push harder than might be best for the situation. Some people may not respond because they didn't understand the question. If we think that could be the case, we can ask whether our question was clear, and if it wasn't, rephrase it.

Some questions are asked without the intention of yielding a response. Jesus often asked rhetorical questions, which are questions not meant to be answered, at least not out loud, but intended to get people thinking about a topic. When Jesus asked his disciples, "What does it profit them if they gain the whole world, but lose or forfeit themselves?" (Luke 9:25), he did not intend for them to start discussing possible answers. Jesus was using the question to challenge their thinking.

Reflecting on Questions Jesus Asked

Intentionally reflecting on questions Jesus asked is a valuable spiritual practice for helping us understand the importance of a powerful question and enabling us to ask similar life- and world-changing questions. One method of intentional reflection involves choosing a question that Jesus asked (sample questions are listed at the end of this section) and spending time reflecting on it; you could choose one question a day, or you might stay with a certain question for one week and then go to the next. At the beginning of your reflection time, spend a minute or two resting in God's presence, asking the Holy Spirit to reveal to you whatever God desires you to know. Then either reflect on the question as it relates to your life today, or imagine yourself back in Jesus' day. Don't try too hard to think up answers to the question; instead, "sit with" the question and see what emerges. Trust the Holy Spirit to reveal what needs to be revealed. After five to fifteen minutes, you can write down any thoughts and feelings that came to you. If nothing did, don't worry about it; just show up again tomorrow for the same or a different question.

There is one question Jesus asked that I often come back to during times of reflection. In John 1:35–38 (NIV), we are told that the day after Jesus was baptized, John was at the same place again with two of his disciples. They saw Jesus passing by, and John said to his disciples, "Look, the Lamb of God!" (v. 36). In response, John's disciples started following Jesus. When Jesus turned around and saw them following him, he asked them this question: "What do you want?" They responded with another question, "Where are you staying?" They wanted to go where he was going so that they could be with him. Jesus' reply was "Come, and you will see." So they went (v. 39).

What do you want? is an important question for each of us. I recommend imagining yourself in that scene, following Jesus. Picture Jesus turning around and asking you that question. Then spend time reflecting on how you might have responded. You could also reflect on the question as if Jesus were asking it to you today. I have found it to be a profound question that either helps me stay focused on following Jesus or convicts and motivates me to want to get off my own path and get back on his.

> *What do you want? is an important question for each of us.*

For subsequent times of reflection, you could see if one of the questions from the following list "jumps off the page" more than others. That may be a good way for you to continue to choose questions. You may also want to explore other questions Jesus asked; there are many more in the Gospels than are listed here.

"Why are you afraid, you of little faith?" (Matthew 8:26)

"And can any of you by worrying add a single hour to your span of life?" (Matthew 6:26)

"Why do you see the speck in your neighbor's eye, but do not notice the log in your own eye? Or how can you say to your neighbor, 'Let me take the speck out of your eye,' while the log is in your own eye?" (Matthew 7:3–4)

"For if you love those who love you, what reward do you have? Do not even the tax-collectors do the same?" (Matthew 5:46)

"Do you love me?" (John 21:17)

"Is there anyone among you who, if your child asks for a fish, will give a snake instead of a fish? Or if the child asks for an egg, will give a scorpion?" (Luke 11:11–12)

"You of little faith. . . . Do you still not perceive?" (Matthew 16:8–9)

"But who do you say that I am?" (Matthew 16:15)

Fruits of Asking Questions

The more we learn to ask appropriate questions and the more we discover how we respond to questions Jesus asked, the more we will recognize the value of questions for soul healing. As a result, you may notice that

1. *You talk less and listen more.* Those who learn the art of asking questions find that they become less interested in hearing themselves talk and more attuned to listening to others.

2. *Others open up to you more.* When you develop the habit of asking good questions and genuinely listening to responses, people will more likely than not become more responsive to you. Nothing causes others to share with us more than when they sense our interest through the kinds of attentive questions we ask.

Asking questions is one of the more powerful ways to connect with others. We can use soul-healing questions with one another to help each of us discover who we are in Christ so that we can live more consistently for God's Kingdom. And as we will see in the next two chapters, good questions can help us deal with conflict in more redemptive ways, a praiseworthy goal for any follower of Christ.

7

Conflict

An Opportunity to Connect

A scoffer who is rebuked will only hate you; the wise, when rebuked, will love you.
—Proverbs 9:8

One of our most important contributions and witnesses to the rest of society is our ability to disagree well.
—Shane Claiborne

RADIO TALK SHOW HOST Dr. Laura Schlessinger has made a living out of giving people advice on conflict. One afternoon I heard a young woman call in with a question about her upcoming marriage. She told Dr. Laura that she wanted to have children but her fiancé did not—ever—and she asked Dr. Laura what she should do. Dr. Laura told her not to marry him. The woman responded as if Dr. Laura had not understood. She said she was not asking if she should marry him; she was asking what to do about their disagreement about having children. Again Dr. Laura responded, in no uncertain terms, that the woman should not marry her fiancé: their differing values on such a critical issue would not make for a good marriage.

This example may seem a little extreme, but the truth is, we all have differing values that can and do result in incompatible desires within relationships. Even those of us who are very similar, including twins and couples who wear matching sweatshirts, will not see eye-to-eye on everything. Conflict is an inevitable part of life. But that does not mean we have to settle for less than the kinds of loving relationships God has always wanted for each of us. God never intended for us to be estranged from one another, which is why separation due to conflict is disturbing at best and heartbreaking at worst. No matter how relationships in your life may be damaged by conflict, there is good news. You can learn to deal with conflict in ways that preserve your relationships. You can even learn to connect at deeper levels with others *through* conflict. More than any other way of relating, how we handle conflict determines how well we connect with others. Because of this, we devote two chapters to this critical topic.

> *More than any other way of relating, how we handle conflict determines how well we connect with others.*

Christians and Conflict

Those of us who claim to be followers of Christ should be especially interested in how to deal well with conflict. That's because we live in a fallen world full of disharmony that we are called to help unify (John 17:20–21). Conflict entered the world when we chose to disobey God and thereby created discord instead of harmony (Romans 12:16; 1 Peter 3:8). We were never supposed to live in conflict, so if you dislike conflict and yearn to live conflict free, *that* is what is natural. It is not natural to thrive on conflict or to want to stir it up (which some people do). Jesus stirred up controversy, not because he liked conflict, but because how he lived and taught others to live was radically different from the status quo. His actions often undermined what the religious leaders of his day taught and how they lived. In Mark 3 we find the Pharisees "looking for a reason to accuse Jesus" for this very reason. When they saw Jesus heal on the Sabbath (considered unlawful because it was an action and not rest) they "began to plot with the Herodians how they might kill Jesus" (Mark 3:6).

It didn't take long for even Jesus' own followers to have disagreements with one another and with Jesus himself over his teachings. In one instance, misunderstandings about what it meant to be a part of God's Kingdom caused ten of Jesus' disciples to get mad at James and John for asking Jesus if they could sit at his right and left in heaven (Mark 10:37, 41). In another instance, Peter "rebuked" Jesus for Jesus' own teachings on his death and resurrection (Matthew 16:22, NIV). After Jesus' death and resurrection, conflict continued to emerge among believers over the "right" ways to follow and help accomplish Jesus' mission. Paul writes to the Galatians about his conflict with Peter, whom Paul accused of being a hypocrite for eating with Gentiles only when certain Jews, who didn't think Gentiles were part of God's chosen people, weren't around (Galatians 2:11–12). Conflicts among believers have continued to grow to the point that we now have three branches of Christianity—Eastern Orthodox, Catholic, Protestant (whose very name denotes conflict)—and more than *thirty-three thousand* denominations.[1]

Those of us who claim to follow Jesus are not immune to conflict, nor should that be our goal. Instead, as representatives of Jesus Christ, we should strive to be excellent role models for handling conflict. Yet history confirms that conflicts among those who claim to follow Jesus have led people not only to part company and form different communities but even to kill one another in the name of Christ. As we pointed out in Chapter One, many people today classify Christians as mean-spirited, judgmental, and antagonistic when it comes to how they express their differences among themselves and with the world. Shane Claiborne echoed these sentiments when he said in our interview, "I never knew that people could be so mean to each other, trying to build a perfect world."

Ironically, the negative stereotypes many people have of how Christians respond to conflict are in sharp contrast to how these same people see Jesus. Instead of being described as judgmental or hypocritical, Jesus is often characterized by nonbelievers as "a friend of sinners, relentlessly pursuing the downtrodden," and "embracing truth."[2] Jesus didn't relentlessly pursue the downtrodden to push them even lower, but to love them. If that is who Jesus is and how he acts, then his followers should be described in those terms too, especially when it comes to conflict. How we treat others with whom we are in disagreement on *any* issue is a reflection of the state of our relationship with Jesus, who calls us to love, first and foremost—especially in the midst of disagreement about our beliefs. Heeding Jesus' words does not mean that our beliefs aren't important. They are. But what we *do* with those beliefs when others disagree with us is much more important. The Apostle Paul gave crucial advice on this very issue to the church at Corinth:

> *How we treat others with whom we are in disagreement on* any *issue is a reflection of the state of our relationship with Jesus.*

> Now I appeal to you, brothers and sisters, by the name of our Lord
> Jesus Christ, that all of you should be in agreement and that there
> should be no divisions among you, but that you should be united in
> the same mind and the same purpose. For it has been reported to me
> by Chloe's people that there are quarrels among you, my brothers
> and sisters. What I mean is that each of you says, "I belong to Paul,"
> or "I belong to Apollos," or "I belong to Cephas," or "I belong to
> Christ." Has Christ been divided? Was Paul crucified for you? Or
> were you baptized in the name of Paul? [1 Corinthians 1:10–13]

Notice that Paul said they were to be in agreement and united, indicating that being united is a higher value than resolving conflict—even regarding conflict over what teachings to follow. And Paul's words to the church at Corinth are not the only ones in scripture that tells us that how we deal with conflict is more important than the actual conflict.

When *How* Is More Important Than *What*

There is often more said in the New Testament about *how* we are to handle conflict than there is about *what* we are to believe about the actual point of disagreement; at times we are not even told the point of disagreement. In his Sermon on the Mount, Jesus told the crowds that if a "brother or sister" has something against them, they are to first reconcile with the person before leaving an offering at the altar (Matthew 5:23–25). Jesus didn't even give examples of possible conflict; he only said how to handle it in terms of the relationship. In Philippians 4:2–3, Paul writes, "I urge Euodia and I urge Syntyche to be of the same mind in the Lord. Yes, and I ask you also, my loyal companion, help these women, for they have struggled beside me in the work of the gospel, together with Clement and the rest of my co-workers, whose names are in the book of life."

Because we are not told what their disagreement was, we could assume that the issue between Euodia and Syntyche was not important, but we have to be careful here. What we think is not important could be of vital importance to someone else. Because we are not told of any specific issues in either of these examples, I think it's safe to assume that the most important aspect of handling the conflicts was to preserve the relationships of those involved. That means it is more important to be loving than to be right. Jesus said that the greatest commandments are to love God and others, not to make sure our beliefs are exactly right. John Wesley picked up on this in his "Preface to the Sermons" when he wrote, "For, how far is love, even with many wrong opinions, to be preferred before truth itself without love! We may die without the knowledge of many truths, and yet be carried to Abraham's bosom. But, if we die without love, what will knowledge avail? Just as much as it availeth the devil and his angel."[3] In other words, love trumps truth. As the Apostle Paul writes in 1 Corinthians 13:2, "If I have prophetic powers, and understand all mysteries and all knowledge, and if I have all faith, so as to remove mountains, but do not have love, I am nothing." It is not that right belief isn't important, but when searching for how to live "right" for Jesus, we must have at the forefront how to live in harmony with other believers. Trappist monk Thomas Merton even believed that if we reject someone until he or she agrees with us, our faith is inadequate.[4]

It is more important to be loving than to be right.

In a post Brian McLaren wrote for Sojourners' blog, God's Politics, he suggested that along with the Evangelical Council for Financial Accountability established in 1979,[5] perhaps there should also be a council established that promotes accountability for how Christians disagree with one another. His suggestion came after reading an article in which a prominent Christian leader attacked a Christian presidential candidate. It wasn't the Christian leader's disagreement with the candidate that bothered Brian; it was *how* he disagreed, including name-calling. Brian wrote, "In times like these—dangerous times, election seasons, and so on—we must not only scrutinize what people say and whether we agree with it, but also how they say it and whether we agree with their means of persuasion. . . . One wonders what it will profit evangelicals—or religious people of other traditions—to have financial accountability while they squander their rhetorical integrity as honest and trustworthy bearers of truth."[6]

As representatives of Christ, the words we speak, even in conflict, are to flow out of us from God's spirit of love. In addition, we are to be very careful who we talk to, and why, regarding any conflict in which we are involved.

The Matthew 18:15 Principle

We all have people in our lives who talk to us about certain conflicts they have with others. I don't see a problem with that if the person's motivation in talking to me first is to process how to handle the conflict in a Christlike manner before going directly to the other person; but if a person is complaining, gossiping, or hoping that I will offer to deal with the conflict, then he or she is not handling the situation the way taught. Nor am I, if I do the same, no matter how good I might be at justifying myself as an exception. In Matthew 18:15–17, Jesus' words are straightforward: "If another member of the church sins against you, go and point out the fault when the two of you are alone. If the member listens to you, you have regained that one. But if you are not listened to, take one or two others along with you, so that every word may be confirmed by the evidence of two or three witnesses. If the member refuses to listen to them, tell it to the church; and if the offender refuses to listen even to the church, let such a one be to you as a Gentile and a tax-collector."

Notice the intentional sequence. Jesus said to go first to the person. If that doesn't work, then take one or two with you; if that doesn't work, take it to the body of believers; if that doesn't work, treat the person as a nonbeliever, which doesn't mean shunning the person, but doing what you can to love the person back into the Kingdom. In our interview, Shane Claiborne spoke about these verses:

> When people don't follow Matthew 18, it's just out of line with our empowerment to be people of God. In community at a micro level, we call it straight talk. You've really got to talk directly to one another, not around each other. I think one of the things that cultivates healthy community is the idea that there's no room to talk around each other. If you hurt someone, you talk directly with them. If you've been hurt or offended by someone, then you talk directly with them. Other people protect that, too, so if someone comes up to you and says, "Man, Robin's not doing her dishes, huh?" that's the yeast of the Pharisees. You need to tell the person to go talk to Robin.

Conflict with Believers Versus Nonbelievers

Many New Testament verses on conflict, like the ones I've mentioned, refer specifically to conflict *within* the body of believers. These verses suggest that the rules for dealing with conflict may be stricter among those within the body of believers than between believers and nonbelievers.

When relating to nonbelievers, we are to draw them into dialogue that demonstrates the love of Christ, not alienate them with words of judgment (or hate). Although we may feel good about ourselves for protesting or boycotting "in the name of Jesus," most often, our protesting only solidifies our base and further alienates our enemies, as opposed to showing love for them—the very thing Jesus calls us to do. As author and Emmy-winning TV producer Bob Briner wrote in *Roaring Lambs*, "Participating in a boycott of the products of companies sponsoring trashy television programs might make us feel good and righteous, but it has very little to do with being salt in the world. . . . Christians must penetrate key areas of culture to have a preserving effect." Briner goes on to recommend that instead of boycotting, we take Jesus "everywhere and show His relevance and the relevance of His Word to every aspect of modern life."[7]

Choosing the Best Style for the Situation

We each have different ways of dealing with conflict: some of us are very intentional (whether the methods or results are actually effective or not); others do not give much thought to it. No matter how we have dealt with conflict in the past, we can learn to handle our differences with others in ways that actually promote harmony for the Kingdom of God.

One of the best-known models describing different conflict styles was developed by researchers William Wilmot and Joyce Hocker.[8] They identified five predominant styles that people use in conflict: avoidance, accommodation, competition, compromise, and collaboration. Although some of these sound better to use than others, each one can be appropriate or inappropriate depending on the situation. Unfortunately, when in a conflict, many of us tend to default to one style, whether or not it's effective for that context. The key to handling conflict effectively is to be able to choose and use the best method for a particular situation. As you read the following descriptions, think about which one(s) you use the most. Then consider trying others in the future, based on what might be best for a specific conflict.

> *The key to handling conflict effectively is to be able to choose and use the best method for a particular situation.*

Avoiding

We use the avoidance style when we ignore or flat-out deny that a conflict exists. Avoiding does not always have to be a bad thing. If a conflict is minor, it may not be worth investing in, but both parties would have to agree that it is not worth pursuing. Just because a conflict is minor to one person does not mean it is minor to another. But even a person who initially thinks a conflict worth pursuing may find that as his or her own anger and frustration subside, it no longer seems important.

Avoiding can be very negative, however, because often a conflict is important enough—at least to one party—that all those involved should try to resolve it. If, however, our tendency is to avoid, even when another person takes the conflict seriously, we may want to think about the possible harm we are doing to that person by not dealing with the situation (not to mention the harm it might do to us). People cannot restore harmony in relationships when a conflict is ignored or trivialized. Nor does disagreement just go away when someone continues to see the conflict as serious. Instead, increasing hostility is more often the result of continued avoidance.

When conflict is not trivial, avoidance is most effectively used only as a *temporary* strategy. It can be a good idea to temporarily avoid a conflict if one or both parties

- Are angry and a cooling off time is needed
- Are not feeling well
- Are sleep deprived
- Are in a bad mood
- Do not have enough time to deal with the conflict right then
- Have other drama temporarily going on

A note on drama. If a person we are in conflict with lives with some form of drama most of the time rather than as a temporary state, then we will have to set a time to deal with the conflict anyway. Some people live in such constant states of drama that we would have trouble finding a time when they are drama free.

Accommodating

Accommodators are pleasers. Instead of voicing their own views, accommodators want to know what others want. Their motto is "peace at any price." Given that we were created to live in harmony, this style may seem noble. It often is, especially if we sacrifice something we want, like time or money, to serve someone else. It can also be good to accommodate if we do not have a strong preference for a particular situation but the other person does. Many accommodators, however, have not developed a solid sense of who they are, and instead they become like whomever they are with at the time. In the romantic comedy *Runaway Bride*, Ike, a reporter, is assigned to write a story on a woman, Maggie, who bails at her own weddings. As Ike follows Maggie around, he notices that she seems to like whatever the man she is currently dating likes, including his hobbies and how he likes his eggs. When Ike asks Maggie how she likes her eggs, she realizes that she doesn't know. In a scene toward the end of the movie, we find Maggie making a variety of recipes to discover how she likes her eggs (which, for what it's worth, ends up being Eggs Benedict).

Acting as if we like what someone else likes can be very unhealthy. It can indicate a lack of conviction and backbone. It can even result in our eventually feeling hostility toward the other person—even though our hostility is most likely due to frustration toward ourselves for living inauthentically. In addition, too much accommodating can result in a lack of the kind of give-and-take that leads to mutual respect and more authentic connections with others. That's why it is important to be aware of why we accommodate when we do, and to work toward more intentionality in choosing to accommodate when it is to the benefit of the relationship. When the Apostle Paul wrote in 1 Corinthians 9:22, "I become all things to all people," he said that it was "*so that* I might by any means save some" (emphasis mine). Paul had a reason for accommodating—to lead people to Jesus. That's a good reason for any accommodating we do.

Competing

Our older son, David, has had a competitive spirit for as long as my husband and I can remember. One weekend I watched our younger son, Michael, then three, carry on a conversation with his teenage cousin as they both sat in the hot tub at a hotel. It was such a cute scene between a preschooler and a teenager that I later said to David, then five, "Katie and Michael had a really nice talk in the hot tub!" David's response was "Who won?"

If we usually look at life as a competition, we already know our predominant style. As much as competition is necessary on the sports field, it is often not helpful in connecting like Jesus, as this style involves winners and losers. It involves preserving the interests of some to the detriment of others. Yet many of us continue to use competition as our predominant conflict style. I once had a student tell me that if during a conflict he realized he was wrong, he would still argue a position he no longer believed because he had to win. That is so sad. Whenever our desire to be right overshadows our desire for another person's well-being, we are not living for Kingdom purposes. As Oswald Chambers wrote in *My Utmost for His Highest*, "Every time I insist on my own rights it hurts the Son of God."[9]

There are, however, times when good *can* come from competition. This style may be just

> *Whenever our desire to be right overshadows our desire for another person's well-being, we are not living for Kingdom purposes.*

what the situation calls for when there is an issue of the rights of others who cannot defend themselves. As Christians we may need to compete against those who make decisions that oppress people whom Jesus called "the least of these"—those who are poor, sick, or in prison (Matthew 25:31–46). Competing for the rights of others in God-honoring ways also relates to how we treat our competitors. We can "fight fairly" by engaging in dialogue, listening, asking questions, and avoiding defensiveness while we continue to work for what we believe is just.

A note on fairness. As much as fairness can be a biblical value as related to working for justice, having an intense sense of fairness regarding certain issues may also be indicative of a negative competitive style—meaning that what we may really want is for a situation to be fair to *us*, even if that means it may not be fair to anyone else involved. Real, God-honoring fairness is about looking at a situation from differing perspectives, especially the perspective of the underdog. Then, those involved come together to discuss their perceptions and try to reach an agreement that is better for everyone, especially the underdog, which will most likely mean making use of one of the next two styles.

Compromising

Being willing to give up something to help manage a conflict is what we do when we compromise. It is the conflict style used most in negotiations and mediation. Compromising can be very effective when both parties give up something either to reach an acceptable agreement or to create an environment for continuing conversations. Sometimes the giving up is on both sides, sometimes on one side only. In our interview, Shane Claiborne talked about one of the times his community had to compromise to come to an agreement:

We had such a hard decision to make in our community when there was a journalist who wanted to come and do a story on us. We were leery of whether or not our story would be told right. But one person in the community said we should do it because we needed to get our message out. Then someone else countered, "That's the problem—it's our message, and it's going to be very distorted." So the community felt divided. We decided to have a "conversation in the middle" that everybody was a part of, and we ended up compromising. We decided to have the journalist come to the community and see if enough trust could be developed with him to have him do the story. The journalist came and ended up doing the story on one of the homeless women in our neighborhood as well as the elderly people who make our blankets by hand. It was a great story, and it actually ended up not having anything to do with us.

Because we can't always resolve conflicts in the way we want, "conversations in the middle" may be our best choice. We must, however, be careful when it comes to compromising our beliefs. We don't want to go too far and compromise ourselves right out of the Kingdom. We can give up so much of what we believe that we are no longing living the way Jesus calls us to live. That is why it is important to understand and live out our beliefs through prayer and the study of scripture, combined with an understanding of church tradition, reason and research, and experience—all in the context of a community of believers committed to living out God's Kingdom on earth. This kind of Kingdom living takes much time and energy, two key components of the next and final conflict style.

Collaborating

Coming up with a solution that is better than either party could have found alone is the goal of collaboration. This style is often referred to as the win-win approach to dealing with conflict. It takes the most time and energy of any of the styles because it involves

- ○ Brainstorming possible outcomes
- ○ Evaluating and ranking those outcomes
- ○ Seeing how the top-ranked outcome works
- ○ Moving to the second-ranked outcome if the first one did not work well, and so on through the remaining outcomes

Collaboration at its best takes a commitment to work out differences in a spirit of self-giving love so as to discover the best possible solutions for both parties. Although collaboration might sound like the best style overall, again, the most effective style to use depends on the situation. We cannot always afford the time and energy involved in collaboration; sometimes a quicker decision needs to be made, for which compromising or accommodating may be best.

A note on stirring up conflict. Some people either create or escalate conflict. They may be hard to live with (literally), like the students I mentioned in Chapter Three who insist they've had several bad roommates but who can't seem to see who the bad roommate might really be. Those who stir up conflict take situations or decisions that others may have accepted without too much thought and turn them into conflicts that need to be resolved. They are sometimes seen as either hard to please or unable to choose their battles well. Those who escalate conflict may see others as avoiders who are too complacent and uncaring about certain issues. Although people can be too complacent when it comes to conflict, escalators typically are not very good at discerning complacency in others because they seem to find more conflicts than most. If you feel that you are someone who has an inordinate amount of conflict in your life, you may want to consider whether you possibly create more conflict than necessary. Observing how you deal with conflict compared to how several others outside your family handle conflict can help you discern whether or not you stir up unnecessary conflict. The spiritual practices discussed later in this chapter can also help you in this discernment process.

Choosing and using the best conflict style for the situation, as well as being alert to whether or not we stir up conflict, are good ways to help us connect instead of disconnect with others through conflict. But following all the best conflict advice may still fall flat when certain emotions come into play during conflict, which they will—especially anger.

The Anger Factor

Anger is one of the most volatile feelings a person can have. In fact, some people rarely engage in conflict without accessing their anger fairly quickly, even when the situation does not

Anger, more than any other emotion, can escalate conflict and damage souls.

seem to warrant such a response. Because anger, more than any other emotion, can escalate conflict and damage souls, it is of vital importance to learn how to handle our anger and that of others in more redemptive ways.

In his most famous sermon, the Sermon on the Mount (Matthew 5:21–24), Jesus told the multitudes,

> You have heard that it was said to those of ancient times, "You shall not murder"; and "whoever murders shall be liable to judgment." But I say to you that if you are angry with a brother or sister, you will be liable to judgment; and if you insult a brother or sister, you will be liable to the council; and if you say, "You fool," you will be liable to the hell of fire. So when you are offering your gift at the altar, if you remember that your brother or sister has something against you, leave your gift there before the altar and go; first be reconciled to your brother or sister, and then come and offer your gift.

Brian McLaren spoke to these verses in our interview:

> I think what Jesus is saying is if we want to have a less violent world—a world without murder—we've got to start by dealing with anger. We've got to back up and deal with the process so much earlier, before we even get angry. To me this is where meditating on the cross—which was God's way of demonstrating an alternative to vengeance and anger by absorbing and feeling pain—is a powerful spiritual discipline. Then every time we celebrate the Eucharist, our previous reflections on the cross can bring us to a potentially trans-forming experience so that we become less prone to anger and violence.

What About Righteous Anger?

The argument often used to justify our own anger (but typically not others' anger) during conflict is that Jesus got angry. The account in John 2:13–22 of Jesus' overturning the money changers' tables and driving the animals out of the temple appears to indicate intense anger (although John refers to it as "zeal"). It would also seem reasonable to assume that Jesus was angry more than once with the religious leaders of his day, calling the Pharisees "white-washed tombs" and then saying, "So you also on the outside look righteous to others, but inside you are full of hypocrisy and lawlessness" (Matthew 23:28).

Although Jesus may have responded at times with anger, we must be careful using any examples involving Jesus to justify our own anger. Any anger Jesus displayed would have been toward those who were interfering with his mission to advance God's harmonious Kingdom on earth. As social activist Dorothy Day said so well, "Even the most ardent revolutionist, seeking to change the world, to overturn the tables of the money changers, is trying to make a world where it is easier for people to love, to stand in that relationship to each other."[10]

But we cannot always say the same, *especially* when we are angry, because our anger may be about something else, including pride. Kathleen Norris, author of the book *Amazing Grace*, wrote, "Now that I appreciate God's anger more, I find that I trust my own much less."[11] It's a good idea to be extremely careful in justifying any use of anger, as anger can quickly escalate within ourselves and others, causing a conflict to spiral out of control. Does this mean we are never to be angry? Not necessarily. Benedictine nun Joan Chittister contends that "Anger can be a very positive thing, the thing that moves us beyond the acceptance of evil."[12] Our anger is to flow out of a sense of God's righteousness and not because we get a charge out of being angry—which some people do. As followers of Christ, everything we do, including how we handle our anger, is to be done out of love (1 Corinthians 16:14). Even what we see as righteous anger may not be God's righteousness. Dallas Willard, who writes extensively on the spiritual life, believes that "All anger is 'righteous' in the moment it arises. That is because of its close association with will and with pride. A little time usually dissipates the 'righteousness,' and that is why habits of 'counting to ten' and so forth are really so important in dealing with anger. Such good habits allow us not to live at the mercy of our own anger: not to 'make room for the devil.' Then we can soon step out of it, and 'not let the sun go down on your anger'" [Ephesians 4:26–27].[13]

> *What we see as righteous anger may not be God's righteousness.*

Responding to Another's Anger

We may not have any control over someone else's anger in a conflict, but we can have control over how we respond to that anger. In our interview, Brian McLaren talked about how he deals with another person's anger.

In a conflict, even though I don't have control over the other person's anger, I ought to have control over my own. If I'm out of control, then the conflict can go out of control. I don't think there's any way to get good at this without practice. . . . [T]he first time somebody gets angry at you, chances are you're not going to respond that well. Even if your response isn't that bad, probably by the tenth time you go through something you might learn how to respond a little bit better. When Jesus says in Matthew 5 not to be angry, he puts the pressure on me to focus on my response rather than on the other person's, no matter what the other person is saying. The challenge to me is how I am going to respond. I have to try to maintain the awareness that the issue here isn't whether I win or lose the conflict. The issue is, can I respond in a Christlike way? If so, then I'm not interested in winning over the other person; I'm interested in winning over all of my own really unhealthy reactions.

We read in Proverbs 29:11 that "A fool gives full vent to anger, but the wise quietly holds it back." Self-control is one of the fruits of the spirit found in Galatians 5:22–23. Anger is not. Instead, in Galatians 5:20 (NIV), "fits of rage" is listed as one of the desires of the sinful nature, which is contrary to the Spirit (Galatians 5:17) and therefore contrary to the healing of souls.

What If We Are at an Impasse?

What if after numerous discussions and debates there is still serious disagreement on how to handle differing beliefs on issues? Often, even with fellow Christians, we won't come to agreement, but that does not mean our relationships have to suffer. Handling conflict in a God-honoring manner includes learning to live together in love even when we find ourselves at what seems to be an impasse. The key to dealing with any perceived irreconcilable difference lies in discovering redemptive ways of agreeing to disagree.

> *Handling conflict in a God-honoring manner includes learning to live together in love even when we find ourselves at what seems to be an impasse.*

Consensus Minus One

One redemptive way to deal with a possible impasse comes from Shane Claiborne. Because he's had lots of experience living in community, he's had lots of experience dealing with conflict. In our interview, he talked about an idea that has worked well in his community:

> One of the things that we've experimented with in a very practical and concrete way is an idea called "consensus minus one." Basically it's a consensus because we all agree that we would never be the one person who would stand in the way of the community's energy to move toward something, so no one person can roadblock a decision that other people feel is a good one. And it's not about disrespecting that person because we all submit to the idea, and we say that if what I want is in the best interest of everyone, at least one other person should agree with me. If no one does, then I submit to what the rest of the community decides.
>
> We were dealing with the issue of the Internet in our community. We had one person who did not want us to have the Internet because it was just another way that the rich are exponentially more efficient and the poor are left further behind. Because a lot of people in our neighborhood didn't have the Internet yet, she said she thought we should reject having it. But then someone else in the community said that he actually wanted to help try to change that. He wanted to wire our whole block with the wireless signal so that people could get the Internet and we could get computers to kids so they can have access to what other kids have.
>
> The issue wasn't just an ideology. There was a sense of wanting to respect where we live and why we live here, but either solution could be one of respect, so as a community we ended up being able to say yes to both of those ideas. Even though the one person still didn't agree with having the Internet, she submitted to the idea of consensus minus one for the sake of the community. So now some people may never use the Internet, and other people helped their whole neighborhood use the Internet. One of the gifts of community is that we can celebrate different people's visions and still have a common vision.

Consensus minus one may seem similar to compromise or even collaboration, but there are important differences. The reason it is not compromise is that the one person who does not agree with the decision does not give up something but instead concedes (or "surrenders") his or her own views for the good of the community. It is also not collaboration because the person doesn't see the decision in consensus minus one as better than what both parties could have come up with on their own—he or she still isn't in agreement with the decision, but chooses to go along with it anyway, again for the sake of the community.

Keeping the Door of Dialogue Open

Two of the best role models for staying committed to their relationship despite conflicting beliefs are Tony and Peggy Campolo. They lovingly live together while also seriously disagreeing about one of the most divisive issues among Christians today: gay marriage. Here is their story in Tony's words:

> My wife and I have gained some degree of notoriety because of our very public differences on the matter of gay and lesbian marriages. I hold a somewhat conservative view in accord with what I believe to be the teachings of scripture in the first chapter of Romans, while my wife, growing out of her extensive experiences in counseling gays and lesbians, has a more liberal position. She believes marriages for gays and lesbians can provide them with relationships that can enhance their spirituality and make them into much more fulfilled people.
>
> We have been called to publicly debate with each other before church groups and denominational gatherings on the matter of gay and lesbian marriages. Denominational leaders are especially prone to have us do our debate (which Peggy calls a dialogue) because we are able to demonstrate that it is possible to have strong differences of opinion without getting a divorce. They want their people to learn that there is no necessity for divorce within the church even though there are strong differences of opinion on this issue within their denominational constituencies. They want them to see that people can love each other and remain in relationship with each other, even when strong differences of opinion exist.
>
> When asked to explain how it is possible for us to carry on such a dialogue when our points of view are so different and how we are able to maintain a loving relationship given the conflict on this issue, we have a standard answer. We tell the inquirer, "We are able to maintain the dialogue in a loving relationship because each of us entertains the possibility, 'I could be wrong!'"
>
> We then go on to explain that unless each party entertains that possibility, they end up challenging each other and shouting at each other, which is too often the case among Christians. If each party acts and believes as though he or she is a proclaimer of absolute truth on the controversial issue, then dialogue is impossible, but civil dialogue is what is needed, given the tense topics that are before God's people these days.
>
> Peggy and I are both ready to admit that we are learning things from each other. We each entertain the possibility that our minds

could be changed on this topic. Without that kind of attitude, there is no way that there will be anything constructive emerging out of verbal exchanges on controversial subjects.

In any disagreement, it can be easy to assume we are right. It could be that we *are* right, but we could also have a limited understanding of an issue—or wrong information, even about core beliefs. Growing in Christ is a process, and we aren't perfect. As the Apostle Paul said, sometimes we "see through a glass darkly" (1 Corinthians 13:12, KJV). Admitting that we may not see clearly concerning a belief or issue keeps the door of dialogue open, which is essential if we want to fulfill our calling as Christ followers to live in unity with one another, especially amid conflict.

> *Admitting that we may not see clearly concerning a belief or issue keeps the door of dialogue open.*

Still, it might be very difficult for some of us to entertain the possibility of changing our minds on a certain belief or stance we hold, especially if our conviction is strong. If the idea of our minds being changed does feel uncomfortable or wrong, we may want to remember how a core belief of Peter's was drastically changed. Although he believed and strictly followed the Jewish law that said a Jew could not associate in any way with a Gentile, Peter accepted through a vision from God that he was to reach even the Gentiles with the good news (Acts 10 and 11). Peter did not let his strong conviction prevent him from accepting a new revelation regarding the Kingdom of God.

Becoming more aware of how we deal with conflict, and trying ways to be more redemptive during conflict, go a long way in helping us connect through conflict. But because dealing with conflict is often emotionally and physically draining, it may be difficult to keep up the energy required to handle conflict in loving ways. Truth be told, we may not even want to do what is best for others with whom we are in conflict, especially when dealing with people we find hard to tolerate, much less love. Still, we know that's what God calls us to do. The spiritual practices in the next chapter can empower us to more consistently live out the conflict practices in this chapter. Committing to both kinds of practices will enable us to experience conflict as a redeeming endeavor for every person involved, thereby honoring God and others in the way we handle conflict.

8

Redeeming Conflict

Prayers and Other Practices for Oneness

So far as it depends on you, live peaceably with all.
—Romans 12:18

The ultimate measure of a man is not where he stands in moments of comfort and convenience, but where he stands at times of challenge and controversy.
—Martin Luther King Jr.

STEPHEN WAS A DEVOUT FOLLOWER OF JESUS in the early church who found himself in serious conflict with some powerful religious leaders. After Stephen "did great wonders and miraculous signs among the people" (Acts 6:8), these religious leaders argued with Stephen. We are told in Acts 6 that "they could not withstand the wisdom and the Spirit with which he spoke (v. 10). They decided to frame Stephen by telling lies about him, which "stirred up the people as well as the elders and the scribes" (v. 12). Stephen was brought before the Sanhedrin, where false witnesses testified against him. He replied to the charges by giving a speech in which he told how the Israelites refused to obey Moses' words from God. He concluded the speech with these words, "You stiff-necked people, uncircumcised in heart and ears, you are forever opposing the Holy Spirit, just as your ancestors used to do. Which of the prophets did your ancestors not persecute? They killed those who foretold the coming of the Righteous One, and now you have become his betrayers and murderers. You are the ones that received the law as ordained by angels, and yet you have not kept it" (Acts 7:51–53).

His accusers were furious. We are told in Acts 7 that "they covered their ears, and with a loud shout all rushed together against him. Then they dragged him out of the city and began to stone him" (vv. 7:57b–58a). As they were stoning him, Stephen prayed "Lord Jesus, receive my spirit" (v. 59). Then just before he "fell asleep," he fell on his knees and cried out, "Lord, do not hold this sin against them" (v. 60).

I don't know about you, but I think it might be hard for a lot of us to imagine saying, "Lord, do not hold this sin against them" to a group of people who did to us what they did to Stephen. When Stephen was dying, he spoke the same words Jesus did as he was dying on the cross: "Father, forgive them; for they do not know what they are doing" and "Father, into your hands I commend my spirit" (Luke 23:34, 46). Stephen took literally what it means to imitate Jesus and follow in his steps. But he could never have responded that way on his own. Earlier in the story, we are told that Stephen was a man "full of faith and the Holy Spirit" (Acts 6:5). It was the power of the Holy Spirit that fueled Stephen to imitate Jesus' ultimate redemptive act. Stephen's Christ-like response is what led to the spreading of the Gospel beyond Jerusalem (Acts 8:4).

As bad as conflict can get in our lives, most of us will never be involved in a conflict as serious as Stephen's. But what does it say about me if I am involved in trivial conflicts compared to Stephen's and don't come even remotely close to responding as he did? What if I want someone to pay for hurting my feelings? The best communication practices won't produce in us the kind of love and forgiveness that Stephen was able to demonstrate, even when we are in much less dire circumstances. But there's good news. We really can learn to respond like Stephen—that is, if we are empowered by the Holy Spirit as Stephen was. The following practices can help create space for us to be open vessels for God's love to be "poured into our hearts through the Holy Spirit" (Romans 5:5). Combining these kinds of practices with other communication practices like those highlighted in the previous chapter can create in us a spiritually charged communication that will empower us to handle any conflict, big or small, in redeeming and unifying ways.

Practicing Love

The best starting point for redeeming a conflict is to ask ourselves, "What is the most loving thing to do?" Then we do it, even if we don't feel like it. It's called "acting *as if*." I act *as if* I want God's best for the other person even if that's not how I actually feel. Acting as if is not hypocritical if our motive is to be more loving; instead, it is the way to actually

The best starting point for redeeming a conflict is to ask ourselves, "What is the most loving thing to do?"

become more loving by acting ourselves into a different way of responding.

In his book *The Myth of the Greener Grass*, J. Allan Peterson tells the story of a minister, Dr. George Crane, who counseled a woman who wanted to divorce her husband. The woman told Dr. Crane that her hatred was so intense for her husband because of all the pain he had caused her that she wanted not only a divorce but also to hurt him as much as she could. Dr. Crane suggested that to really hurt him, she was to go home and act as if she really loved her husband. She was to tell him how much he meant to her, to compliment all his good qualities, to make sure she was as kind and generous as possible, and to do anything else that would make her husband believe that she loved him. Then after she had convinced him how much she loved him, she was to "drop the bomb" and tell her husband she wanted a divorce. That, Dr. Crane told her, is what would really hurt him. She loved the plan and faithfully carried it out. For two months she acted as if she loved her husband by treating him with kindness, talking with him, listening intently to him, and serving him. When she didn't go back to Dr. Crane's office, he called her and asked if she was ready to go through with the divorce. She responded, "Divorce? Never! I discovered I really do love him."[1] The woman's loving actions changed her feelings, resulting in a renewed love for her husband.

We too can act as if. Think of a conflict situation you have recently been involved in or are involved in now. What might it look like to react to that situation for the sake of the other person or persons involved? What are ways in which your words, attitude, and behavior could be more loving? How could you be more supportive rather than defensive, even if you don't feel like it? If you are tempted to deal with the conflict with anger, instead of angrily asking, "How could you do such a thing?" try saying in a calm tone, "Tell me what happened here." When listening, if you are tempted to roll your eyes, use defensive or sarcastic tones, interrupt, or fold your arms in a stern posture, you could instead look the person in the eyes, use noncynical tones, listen intently, and have an open posture. Another concrete way to deal more redemptively with conflict is to use "I" language. Saying "*I* felt frustrated when . . ." instead of "*You* made me feel frustrated" shows that you are trying to own the feeling. "I" statements can result in less defensiveness on the other person's part and therefore more openness to resolve the conflict.

Asking the Holy Spirit to make you willing to respond in these more loving ways when you don't feel inclined to do so opens the door for caring for the other person's soul. That is our goal—even in conflict—if we want to connect like Jesus.

Praying About the Conflict

How you pray about a conflict is a good indication of where your heart is in relation to both the situation and the specific people involved. If you are able to pray for God's best for *all* involved, and even to pray that way *with* those involved, that's a good sign that your heart is in the right place. If you are not willing to pray for God's best for the others involved, you may want to consider praying a prayer that Brian McLaren recommended.

> How you pray about a conflict is a good indication of where your heart is in relation to both the situation and the specific people involved.

In our interview, Brian shared the following story to illustrate the powerful effects of this prayer that focuses on blessing our enemies.

> There was a Serbian Orthodox bishop named Nicolai Viliberavich who was in Yugoslavia and spoke against the Nazis. When the Nazis took over Yugoslavia, he was immediately arrested. The only people he had spoken against the Nazis to were the priests under his care, so he knew that one of his priests had betrayed him. Viliberavich was taken away to Daval, and there he was with his life in danger, but all he could think about was his fury toward whoever betrayed him. While he was in prison, instead of nursing the hatred and fury toward his betrayer, he decided to focus on "How can I have this fury removed from my heart?" He wrote a prayer called "Prayer Regarding Critics and Enemies." There's a line in the refrain that says "Bless my enemies, O Lord." This thought is so common in the Bible—bless your enemies—but we never *really* think about it. That's why I think his prayer is one of the most beautiful and important pieces of literature I have ever read—you watch a Godly saint processing his anger and turning it into compassion. It's very, very powerful.

Here is a shortened version of the prayer:

Bless my enemies, O Lord. Even I bless them and do not curse them. Enemies have driven me into your embrace more than friends have. Friends have bound me to earth; enemies have loosed me from earth and have demolished all my aspirations in the world.

Just as a hunted animal finds safer shelter than an unhunted animal does, so have I, persecuted by enemies, found the safest sanctuary, having ensconced myself beneath Your tabernacle, where neither friends nor enemies can slay my soul.

Bless my enemies, O Lord. Even I bless and do not curse them.

Bless them and multiply them; multiply them and make them even more bitterly against me:

So that my fleeing will have no return; So that all my hope in men may be scattered like cobwebs; So that absolute serenity may begin to reign in my soul; So that my heart may become the grave of my two evil twins: arrogance and anger;

So that I might amass all my treasure in heaven; Ah, so that I may for once be freed from self-deception, which has entangled me in the dreadful web of illusory life.

It is truly difficult for me to say who has done me more good and who has done me more evil in the world: friends or enemies. Therefore bless, O Lord, both my friends and my enemies. A slave curses enemies, for he does not understand. But a son blesses them, for he understands.

For a son knows that his enemies cannot touch his life. Therefore he freely steps among them and prays to God for them. Bless my enemies, O Lord. Even I bless them and do not curse them. Amen.[2]

If we ask the Holy Spirit to help us willingly pray this prayer, while we think of people with whom we have serious conflict, our anger and resentment can truly be transformed into the kind of love Jesus calls us to have for our enemies.

Speaking the Truth in Love

Perhaps one of the most used and misused verses in the Bible is Ephesians 4:15–16, where Paul writes, "But speaking the truth in love, we must grow up in every way into him who is the head, into Christ, from whom the whole body, joined and knitted together by every ligament with which it is equipped, as each part is working properly, promotes the body's growth in building itself up in love." This verse has been used all too often to justify saying hurtful things to others in the name of love. Brian McLaren also spoke to this issue in our interview:

> Whenever people tell me "I'm saying this in love," I always brace myself to be brutalized. I think religious people are at their worst in religious conflict. If I'm a long-standing churchgoer with a lot of pew time and someone cuts me off on the road, I'm not so likely to gesticulate and treat them to a bunch of four-letter words. But if the preacher says something in a sermon that I don't like, I might send an e-mail later that day filled with pious profanity.
>
> Recently I was thinking about Jesus' words about turning the other cheek and how that applies to religious conflict. There's so much going on with that story, but one thing that helps me clarify "turn the other cheek" is when you see what it doesn't mean. It doesn't mean lie down on the ground and start crying and pleading never to be hit again, making promises like "I'll do whatever you want." It doesn't mean run away and hide, and it doesn't mean take out your sword and strike them back. What it means is get back up and take it again. There are certainly conflicts that I get into that are just due to my own stupidity, but there are times when I may actually be speaking the truth in love and people don't like it. To turn the other cheek then means that if they attack me, I don't attack them back and I don't run away. It means I have the courage to get up and speak the truth in love again. That, to me, is a very powerful dimension of how Christians are to communicate in conflict.

As Brian said, when speaking the truth in love, our words may not be met with a positive response. Even when people tell us to be totally honest, our honesty can be met with resentment. Or we may be the one who invites honesty and then feels bitterness toward the person for telling us something we didn't want to hear. If we decide to speak the truth in love, we must be prepared for the other person not to receive the truth in love and accept the consequences of their possible bitterness toward us. In the Communication Department at Spring Arbor University, if one of our majors consistently communicates in ineffective ways, one of our professors will talk with him or her about the behavior. More than once, when told of an off-putting communication habit, students have focused on resenting the professor who told them instead of on changing the behavior.

Speaking the truth in love may require a firm, even "tough" love in the way we respond to others. Firmness, however, does not mean coming across in rough and ruffled ways. François Fénelon advised that we remember that "True firmness is gentle, humble, and calm. A sharp tongue, a proud heart, and an iron hand have no place in God's work." If we find ourselves acting in these negative ways, Fénelon said to "Humble yourself immediately. Uphold a godly standard, but admit when you uphold it in an ungodly way."[3] In his sermon "On Love," John Wesley preached these words on how we are to demonstrate loving patience with others whom we find "in error":

> If thou love thy neighbour for God's sake, thou wilt bear long with his infirmities. . . . If he be in error, thou wilt mildly endeavour to recover him, without any sharpness or reproach: If he be overtaken in a fault, thou wilt labour to restore him in the spirit of meekness: And if that cannot be done soon, thou wilt have patience with him. . . . In all provocations, either from the weakness or malice of men, thou wilt show thyself a pattern of gentleness and meekness; and, be they ever so often repeated, wilt not be overcome of evil, but overcome evil with good. Let no man deceive you with vain words: He who is not thus long-suffering, hath not love.[4]

Not Defending Ourselves

Not defending ourselves can be one of the hardest things to do in conflict; yet there are times it may be what is best for the situation. Remember Jesus standing before Pilate, remaining silent when Pilate asked him, "'Are you the King of the Jews?' He answered him, 'You say so.' Then the chief priests accused him of many things. Pilate asked him again, 'Have you no answer? See how many charges they bring against you.' But Jesus made no further reply, so that Pilate was amazed" (Mark 15:2–5). Jesus did not state his case. No matter how much we may want to "make things right" for ourselves in a conflict situation, that may not be what is best for the good of the community. As the Apostle Paul wrote to the body of believers in Corinth, "The very fact that you have lawsuits among you means you have been completely defeated already. Why not rather be wronged? Why not rather be cheated?" (1 Corinthians 6:7, NIV). Fénelon advised us to "Let everything that bothers you flow like water under a bridge. Live in the presence of God."[7] Not always having to prove we are right is good not only for the community but for ourselves as well. As counterintuitive as it may seem, there is tremendous freedom in letting go of our need to defend ourselves.

Practicing Forgiveness

Obeying Jesus' command to love our enemies and pray for those who persecute us (Matthew 5:44) may require us to forgive others or to ask for forgiveness ourselves. There is tremendous soul-healing power in forgiving ourselves and others. Practicing forgiveness can actually be an easier habit to develop than we thought, or it can be the hardest thing we have ever done.

> *There is tremendous soul-healing power in forgiving ourselves and others.*

Forgiving Others

We hope that forgiveness comes easily when someone takes "our" parking place after we have been waiting to turn into it. If it doesn't, we may have more anger issues to deal with than we thought. But forgiveness doesn't come easily when we or someone we love is treated badly. In certain situations, we may even feel that there is no way we could ever forgive someone for what he or she has done. We could be right. Remember my friend Jacob, the lost boy, whose parents were killed? He found he could forgive only through the power of the Holy Spirit in his life.

Trusting God to work in us to forgive means yielding to the Holy Spirit instead of to our own wounded spirits. The conscious act alone of yielding to the Spirit will result in some people's being able to say, "I forgive you." Others will need to ask the Spirit to make them willing to forgive. Some of us do not want to forgive. It may be because of the nature of the conflict, or it may be that forgiving someone will mean accepting a person back into our lives in ways we want to avoid. If you aren't in a place where you can even ask God to make you willing to forgive, perhaps you can ask the Spirit to make you willing to be made willing. Regularly praying even a tiny form of a willing prayer can help you begin to trust the Spirit to transform how you feel.

Practicing Forgiveness Through the Lord's Prayer and the Prayer of Examen

When it comes to forgiving others, we often forget how Jesus taught us to pray: "Forgive us our sins *as* we forgive others" (emphasis mine). What scary implications for those of us who have trouble forgiving! The prayer of examen, discussed at the end of Chapter Three, can greatly help us here. The second part of the prayer, in which we ask the Spirit to show us areas where we have acted in disharmony with others, ends with our talking to Jesus about what the Spirit has revealed to us and asking God to forgive us. Thinking of the less than loving ways you have treated others, combined with the realization that God loves you and offers you total forgiveness, can help you be more forgiving toward others—no matter the seriousness of the issue. Here's what Brian McLaren said about praying "forgive us our sins as we forgive others":

> I can say those words on auto-pilot without thinking, but if I mean them and other people insult or attack me, I realize that they don't know anything bad about me compared to what I know and have admitted to God, so why *should* I get defensive about the things they are criticizing me for? I know there's a lot worse that I've shared with God. There's just so much about the practice of confession that helps our relationships with others.
>
> That prayer also acknowledges our hurts at the hands of others, but we don't allow ourselves to do that. We want to just focus on our sins against God or our sins against others which are ultimately our sins against God, but that prayer gives 50 percent of the attention to how others have hurt us, so again, it becomes another reason why we ignore the fact that to be a human being means we are going to be hurt by others, so we need spiritual practices that deal with being hurt. But if we're obsessed with being forgiven and we don't go much further beyond being forgiven by God, we aren't even noticing what it means to forgive others.
>
> There is almost nowhere in the New Testament where we celebrate God's forgiveness of us without immediately dealing with our forgiveness of others. This concept is so strong in the New Testament and it is so invisible in most evangelical preaching and singing. But once you start noticing it, you just can't get away from it. Ephesians 4 says, "Be kind and compassionate to one another, forgiving each other just as in Christ God forgave you" [Ephesians 4:32, NIV]. In the Sermon on the Mount, Jesus tells us, "If you forgive men when they sin against you, your heavenly Father will also forgive you. But if you do not forgive men their sins, your Father will not forgive your sins" [Matthew 6:14–15, NIV].You almost get the feeling in the New Testament that the purpose of forgiveness is to turn you into a more forgiving person. But for many of us, the only purpose of forgiveness is to get into heaven.

Saying "Forgive Me"

For some of us, "Please forgive me" may be the most difficult phrase to say in the English language. As hard as it is to forgive others, asking for forgiveness can be even harder. Pride can too easily get in our way, blocking soul connections that we could make if we admitted we were wrong and then refrained from making excuses for what we had said or done. One of the greatest acts of humility comes in being able to say at least one of these three-word combinations: "Please forgive me," "I am sorry," or "I was wrong." As Shane Claiborne said in our interview, "There's something healing that happens when we confess things that we've done. There are ways that we've hurt each other, and there's something contagious about the humility that comes from saying we are sorry. Great revivals have started by people saying 'I'm sorry.'"

> For some of us, "Please forgive me" may be the most difficult phrase to say in the English language.

Trappist monk Thomas Merton knew the value of saying "I am sorry." In his book *Faith and Violence*, Merton has a chapter called "Apologies to an Unbeliever" in which he apologizes for what he and the Christian community have "inflicted . . . in the name of religion" on those who do not believe in God.[5]

What Thomas Merton and Shane are referring to, however, is not a cheap confession. As much as the popular phrase "My bad" has helped us more easily admit some of our wrongs, it also carries a flippant tone that may mean that we really aren't being sincere. We also have to examine whether or not saying we are sorry is truly an apology. Saying "I'm sorry if you misunderstood what I meant" is not what it means to ask for forgiveness. Framing an apology that way may instead be an attempt merely to "technically" apologize and thereby satisfy someone who told us we had to, or to relieve us of any personal responsibility for our role in the conflict. In his letter of apology, Merton wrote, "If you distrust the word 'apologies' and if you think that I am trying to afflict you with apologetics, please set your mind at rest. By 'apologies' I mean simply what the word says."[6] He then goes on to apologize for several negative ways in which Christians have harmed those who don't share their particular beliefs.

What If You're Not Sure You Did Anything Wrong?

There may be times when someone believes you have wronged him or her, but you don't think you did anything wrong, or at least you aren't sure you did. Either way, it's important to be willing to ask God to show you if you have wronged the person in any way. If time permits, taking a few days to see if your attitude changes can be very helpful, especially if you are one who wants to take care of a conflict immediately. In addition, talking with a spiritual mentor or another trusted, neutral person can help you discern if you might be at fault. Being open to the possibility of having wronged the other person is vitally important in connecting through conflict. If after prayer and talking with others you believe you did not wrong the other person, then engaging in an honest, loving conversation with the person may be the best route to take.

Can Someone Be Selfishly Sorry?

There are some people who may seem to be apologizing profusely when confronted with how they have wronged another, but the apology is actually more self-centered than other-centered. These people "fall on their sword" and say something like, "I feel awful. I'm a lousy person. Why do you put up with me?" The "wronged" person can then feel so sympathetic that he or she ends up comforting the "wrongdoer"—who then, instead of changing, will most likely perpetuate the same cycle in the future. If someone you know responds like this to being confronted, you may want to lovingly tell the person how he or she is coming across. That way neither one of you is cheated out of the healing that comes when someone can genuinely focus on the wrong he or she has done.

Praying an Empathy Prayer

Praying for someone with whom you are in conflict, while at the same time trying to put yourself in the person's shoes, is what the empathy prayer is all about. As you begin to pray, take some time to think about that person and how Jesus loves him or her too. Then picture Jesus, you, and the person talking together. Stay with the scene until the Holy Spirit empowers you to have empathy for the person and for his or her side of the conflict. Finally, ask the Holy Spirit to change both of your hearts so as to honor and glorify God in the ways that you relate to one another. Try to avoid the temptation to pray for God to do more changing in that person than in you. If you find it difficult to pray this generously for the person the first time, don't worry. The empathy prayer is not a one-time prayer; it is a spiritual practice that you can come back to regularly.

Fruits of Connecting Through Conflict

Engaging in practices like those suggested in this chapter and in Chapter Seven can help you experience God's Spirit powerfully at work in your spirit, producing in you a transforming love that changes the way you see and deal with conflict. These practices can help you experience increased freedom from the need to defend yourself, as well as increased freedom from your own and others' anger and resentment. Loving others with whom you have serious disagreement can become less difficult as you experience the love of God empowering you to connect with others in redeeming, and even unifying, ways. The Holy Spirit truly can enable you *in the midst of conflict* to respond with love and forgiveness, just like Stephen, who through the power of the Spirit followed in Jesus' steps.

9

When Stories Tell the Story

The Power to Shape a Narrative

Mary Albert Darling and Tony Campolo

Story re-orders, sifts through experience, and allows others . . .
to hear what we think truly matters. It is, in fact, a way
we can begin to define what we mean when we use
the term "spirituality."
—Barbara Kimes Myers, *Young Children and Spirituality*

IT MAY SEEM ODD THAT Danish philosopher Søren Kierkegaard loved
stories and loved to communicate philosophy through stories. After all,
philosophers are often considered heady, analytical thinkers. But
Kierkegaard believed that storytelling was the best method for philoso-
phizing. He was not so much interested in developing propositional
truths that could be logically validated (a typical approach of philosophers) as he was committed to driving his readers to explore the subjective depths of who they are. His desire was to provide not only stories
that his readers could interpret but stories that would help his readers
interpret *themselves*. One such story is Kierkegaard's parable of the
ducks, in which he describes a town where only ducks live:

> Every Sunday the ducks waddle out of their houses and waddle down
> Main Street to their church. They waddle into the sanctuary and
> squat in their proper pews. The duck choir waddles in and takes its
> place, then the duck minister comes forward and opens the duck
> Bible. He reads to them: "Ducks! God has given you wings! With
> wings you can fly! With wings you can mount up and soar like eagles.
> No walls can confine you! No fences can hold you! You have wings.
> God has given you wings and you can fly like birds!"
> All the ducks shouted, "Amen!" *And they all waddled home.*[1]

Kierkegaard believed stories like this one would "indirectly" (his word) cause listeners or readers to let down their defenses and then face up to truths about themselves that they had been avoiding or had sought to conceal.

The best examples of how stories can be used to indirectly confront readers or listeners with truths about themselves can be found in scripture. One such story is that of King David, a dynamic leader who united the people of Israel. In 1 Samuel 13:14, we are told that God even called David "a man after his own heart." But David was not without serious fault. While he was king, David had an affair with Bathsheba, the wife of Uriah the Hittite, one of David's faithful warriors. Bathsheba became pregnant, and David arranged for Uriah to come back from war to sleep with his wife to hide that David was the real father. Uriah, out of loyalty to King David and the men in his army, instead slept outside the palace. Because David could not get Uriah to sleep with Bathsheba while on leave, David arranged to have Uriah put in the front line "so he will be struck down and die" (2 Samuel 11:15). Uriah was killed in battle, and soon after David made Bathsheba his wife. Then one day God sent the prophet Nathan to David to tell him this story:

> "There were two men in a certain town, one rich and the other poor. The rich man had a very large number of sheep and cattle, but the poor man had nothing except one little ewe lamb he had bought. He raised it, and it grew up with him and his children. It shared his food, drank from his cup and even slept in his arms. It was like a daughter to him.
>
> "Now a traveler came to the rich man, but the rich man refrained from taking one of his own sheep or cattle to prepare a meal for the traveler who had come to him. Instead, he took the ewe lamb that belonged to the poor man and prepared it for the one who had come to him."
>
> David burned with anger against the man and said to Nathan, "As surely as the Lord lives, the man who did this deserves to die! He must pay for that lamb four times over, because he did such a thing and had no pity."
>
> Then Nathan said to David, "You are the man!" . . . Then David said to Nathan, "I have sinned against the Lord." [2 Samuel 12:1–7a, 13a]

Why did Nathan use a story to confront David about his sin? Had Nathan confronted him directly, David could have been quick to justify his actions, thereby fortifying his defensiveness and hardening his heart even more. Instead, Nathan drew David in with a story, which opened David's heart to hear the truth.

The Bible is full of stories, from "In the beginning" (Genesis 1:1) to John's stories in Revelation of how God's Kingdom will be actualized in history. Scripture is God's story of creation, the fall, and redemption. Because God chooses to use stories as a primary means for connecting with us, we would do well to follow God's lead and use stories to connect with one another.

> *God chooses to use stories as a primary means for connecting with us.*

The Power of Stories

God created us to respond to stories, and that is why few speaking techniques engage an audience better than a good story. Stories not only catch and keep our attention but also create memorable, challenging, and convicting visual images. A well-told story can powerfully connect with us emotionally, bypass our defenses, and find a clear path to our souls. As we saw with the story of David and Nathan, stories reach those parts of us that may not typically be open to change. As Barbara Kimes Myers wrote in *Young Children and Spirituality*, "Story connects us with that which lies beyond ourselves and this process makes us ask questions about the meanings of our lives."[2] Because stories are such powerful influencers, it is important for us to learn when and how to tell stories in our everyday communication with others as well as in public speaking situations. What better place to start than with the master storyteller himself.

Jesus and Storytelling

Scripture indicates that while on earth, Jesus used storytelling more than any other means of communication to teach what it means to be a part of the Kingdom of God. More specifically, he used a form of storytelling called parables (Matthew 13:34). Screenwriter Dudley Nichols explained the significance of Jesus' use of parables when he wrote, "Jesus of Nazareth could have chosen simply to express Himself in moral precepts; but like a great poet He chose the form of the parable, wonderful short stories that entertained and clothed the moral precept in an eternal form.

It is not sufficient to catch man's mind, you must also catch the imaginative faculties of his mind."[3]

Jesus used parables to invite, challenge, and convict his listeners in matters related to the Kingdom of God. In fact, many of his parables started with the words "The Kingdom of God is like . . ." Here are some examples:

THE KINGDOM OF GOD IS LIKE . . .

A man who sowed good seed in his field (Matthew 13:24)

A mustard seed (Matthew 13:31)

Treasure hidden in a field (Matthew 13:44)

A net that was let down into the lake and caught an abundance of fish (Matthew 13:47)

A landowner who went out early in the morning to hire men to work in his vineyard (Matthew 20:1)

A king who prepared a wedding banquet for his son (Matthew 22:2)

As you can see, Jesus connected to his audience by comparing the idea of the Kingdom of God to what was familiar to them, such as farming and fishing. By using comparisons, Jesus caught and kept his audiences' attention, even though they did not always understand the point he was making.

If you read Jesus' parables in their entirety, you too might find that some are hard to interpret. In Mark 4:10, we are told that when Jesus finished telling the parable of the farmer who sowed seed, the disciples asked Jesus what the parable meant (see also Luke 8:9). Their difficulty in understanding may seem to contradict our previous point that Jesus used illustrations and comparisons to teach crucial concepts and thereby heal souls. Yet when telling his disciples why he spoke to the crowds in parables, Jesus said, "To you has been given the secret of the kingdom of God, but for those outside, everything comes in parables; in order that 'they may indeed look, but not perceive, and may indeed listen, but not understand'" (Mark 4:11–12). Why would Jesus say this? Why would he expect his disciples to understand his parables, but then speak in parables to the crowds so that they would *not* understand?

While Mary was in graduate school, one of her professors offered an interesting explanation for why Jesus spoke this way. He said that Jesus had three kinds of people in his audiences, and compared each of the three to a typical college classroom audience. First, he said, there were those who listened with the intent of criticizing and confronting, in order to catch Jesus in a contradiction—they were the Pharisees, not unlike some students who have it as their goal to be confrontational and antagonistic toward a teacher. Next were those who were genuinely interested in listening to Jesus and wanted to be with him and learn more from him—these were the disciples. The professor compared this type of audience member to students who want to talk with the teacher outside of class because they are eager to learn more. Finally, there were those who came to hear Jesus out of curiosity. Even though he held their attention, they walked away without a commitment to act on anything they heard—they were the multitudes, the ones who Jesus said were "ever hearing but never understanding" (Mark 4:12, NIV). The professor compared them to the majority in class who are there not for the purpose of learning and understanding the material but only for the grade.

This professor's comparison helps make sense of Jesus' assertion that he spoke in parables so that his listeners would not understand. Why Jesus did this can also be understood in the context of certain storytelling techniques of the ancient Hebraic world in which he was raised.

Storytelling in Jesus' World

Because we know that Jesus came to save the whole world, we can rest assured that he was not out to deliberately conceal the truth from any person. Instead, he was using a technique he most likely had been taught. Rabbis would often tell a story to help people who *thought* they knew the truth come to the awareness that they really did not know the truth at all. This rabbinical technique was used to prod those who did not understand the story to ask for clarification and, in the process, to come to grips with the truth that the story was meant to convey. Consistent with the explanation from Mary's professor, this technique could draw out those who truly wanted to follow Jesus.

We too can use Jesus' parables to prod others (and also prod ourselves) to seek clarification of certain Kingdom truths. Those who want clarification can then reflect on the parables during quiet times with God, as well as discuss them in groups or with spiritual mentors—all with the goal of discovering more and more what the Kingdom of God is like, so that we can learn how to live more consistently in that Kingdom.

As an old Turkish proverb states, "To speak is to sow; to listen is to reap."[4] Telling stories that sow seeds to help the Kingdom of God grow will be our goal if we want to use stories the way Jesus did. This means that before we tell a story, we'll want to check our motives to see if they are in sync with advancing the Kingdom. Thinking about *why* we want to tell a certain story can help us decide whether or not it really is best to tell it. Stories that make others laugh, that help others get to know us better, or that show how we connect to others' joys or struggles can all be in line with Kingdom purposes. But if we are using our stories to make someone look bad or make ourselves look good, we probably need to tell a different story—or none at all.

Connecting Through Spiritually Charged Storytelling

So far, with the exception of the story of David and Nathan, our focus has been on storytelling to larger groups of people. Although storytelling by itself can be effective in front of an audience, if we were to try to communicate solely through stories in our everyday lives, our ability to connect would be limited (not to mention that we'd be very annoying, as you might know if you have ever been around someone who has a story for everything). We hope it is evident throughout this book that connecting with others means drawing from a variety of communication practices. As important as storytelling is, we still need to determine when it might be most appropriate. Then we need to decide what story may be best to use and make sure we are prepared to tell it—not only in terms of learning good storytelling techniques but in terms of being spiritually prepared as well. Storytelling is not only an art but a spiritual practice for those who want to tell stories for the glory of God.

> *Storytelling is not only an art but a spiritual practice for those who want to tell stories for the glory of God.*

No matter your skill (or lack thereof) with storytelling, you can learn to tell stories more effectively. We hope you will find the following suggestions on storytelling, presented in question-and-answer form, useful in your quest to be storytellers for the Kingdom of God.

Where Do I Start?

If your goal is to connect like Jesus through storytelling, then the best answer to this first question is to pray. You can ask God to help you be more attentive to how stories affect lives and to alert you to stories you can use.

People have told Tony that they are envious that storytelling (as well as speaking in general) comes so easily to him. But Tony actually takes great care in how he prepares to tell a story. He puts much spiritual and emotional energy into telling stories in ways he hopes will best connect with his audiences. Once he has found a potential story, he is careful not to use it until he feels he "has it down." For Tony that means prayerfully reflecting on or, even more specifically, "praying" potential stories. Before telling a story, Tony will ask the Holy Spirit to help him endeavor to relive the story in his mind and heart over and over again, and with his imagination, he tries to enter into the feelings of each of the persons involved in the story. This takes a great deal of reflection, and he doesn't use the story unless he thinks he has a good sense of what each person in the story is experiencing. If the story is from scripture, Tony often enters into it by "praying the story" through lectio divina (a spiritual practice highlighted in Chapter Four and in Tony's chapters on teaching and preaching in Part Three). Here is how Tony describes this practice:

> I enter into a state of quietude, and I try to imagine myself back in the time of the setting of the story. Then I silently yield to the work of the Holy Spirit by waiting for the Spirit to teach me things from the scriptural story. I try to be open to what the Spirit wills to reveal to me. Jesus said that when he ascended to his Father, he would send the Holy Spirit to reveal truth to those who seek it (John 16:13). Because God often relates truth through stories, we can seek truth through prayerfully reflecting on stories. Someone once suggested that I use stories instead of theology as a basis for preaching. My stories do not illustrate my theology—they *are* my theology.

People often approach Tony to tell him that they heard him speak many years before, and although they couldn't remember other things he said, they remembered the stories he told. Certain of Tony's stories have become his trademarks. His stories not only are remembered but have often prompted listeners to make life changes for the Kingdom of God. That's the power of bathing stories in prayer, and that's the power of God working through stories and storytellers.

When Might It Be Best to Tell a Story Instead of Communicate in Another Way?

If you find that you are not connecting with someone using your typical communication style, then it may be time for a story. In their book *The*

Language of Love, Gary Smalley and John Trent write about a powerful type of story called an "emotional word picture." They define emotional word pictures as a type of story that simultaneously activates both the emotions and the intellect of a listener, causing the person "to experience our words, not just hear them."[5] It is what the prophet Nathan used with King David. But you don't have to be a prophet to use them. Anyone can use emotional word pictures, especially when nothing else seems to work. Smalley and Trent tell the story of a teenage girl who was devastated when her father left her, her mom, and her little brother. She wrote her dad a long letter, comparing the impact of his leaving to a fictitious car accident in which the three of them were all badly battered and bruised. Here are excerpts from her letter:

> It was nighttime, and we had just turned the corner near our house. Suddenly, we all looked up and saw another car, out of control, heading straight for us. Mom tried to swerve out of the way, but the other car still smashed into us.
>
> The thing is, Dad, just before being hit, we could see that you were driving the other car. Sitting next to you was another woman.
>
> There have been times since that night when I wondered if any of us would make it. Even though we're getting a little better, we're all still in the hospital. The doctors say I'll need a lot of therapy on my leg, and I know they can help me get better. But I wish it was you who was helping me, instead of them.
>
> The pain is so bad, but what's even worse is that we all miss you so much. Every day we wait to see if you're going to visit us in the hospital, and every day you don't come. I know it's over. But my heart would explode with joy if somehow I could look up and see you walk into my room.
>
> Are you all right? Are you hurting from the wreck? Do you need us like we need you? If you need me, I'm here and I love you.

The daughter's analogy so potently conveyed the effects of her dad's leaving that a week after she sent the letter, he came to the house. He said the letter made him "face the fact" that he had caused much pain to his family. Two days later, he went for counseling with his wife; not long after that, he moved back home. His wife and daughter had tried pleading with him before he ever left, but it had not worked. It was his daughter's use of an emotional word picture that changed his heart and brought him home.

Stories with this kind of emotional impact may take a lot of time and energy to craft, but as this example illustrates, the results can be life changing. If you want to try creating an emotional word picture, we suggest you set aside time for reflection and ask God to help you formulate just the right images. You could also enlist the help of people you know who have good imaginations. If you still have trouble coming up with just the right story, then it may be time to use someone else's.

Where Can I Find Other Stories?

Stories are everywhere—in books, music, films, speeches, the news, and in everyday life. All we have to do is pay attention. Our lives are full of stories we have personally experienced, observed, or heard from others. Tony often listens to recordings of great sermons while he's driving, and pays careful attention to the stories preachers use to make their points. He will also often ask people if they have any new stories he might be able to use.

Unfortunately, many stories we hear are forgotten. That's why you may want to consider filing certain things you read, watch, hear, or experience that could possibly make a good story, even if you have no idea at the time how you might use it. Then when you want to make a point come to life and no story comes to mind, you may find just the right one in your files. It should be noted, however, that when it comes to finding a good story, we often need look no further than the Bible.

THE POWER OF BIBLICAL STORIES We are told in 2 Timothy 3:16 that "All scripture is inspired by God and is useful for teaching, for reproof, for correction, and for training in righteousness." If you believe in the power of stories to heal souls and you believe these words from 2 Timothy, then becoming more familiar with stories from the Bible is essential. Since most of the Bible is a series of stories about peoples' struggles to connect with God and others, it is an invaluable source from which we can draw lessons about God and the meaning of our lives. Besides becoming more familiar with these stories, you could also commit to regularly reflecting on them, perhaps starting with Jesus' story and the stories he told. As we have both described in previous examples, you could put yourself in the stories as you read them. Picture yourself as a major character or even a bystander: what are the sights, sounds, smells? What is happening, and how are you responding? What happens in the scene may speak so deeply to your soul that when you share the story with others, they may be moved by the story in ways that inspire them to want to experience scripture through this kind of prayerful reflection too.

THE POWER OF PERSONAL STORIES Since we often connect best with others when they sense we can relate to their life experiences, our own stories can be the most powerful stories we tell. We can also connect others to God through our own stories. Mary finds that people listen much more readily to what the Bible says about dealing with fear and anxiety when she shares her own struggles and victories with fears and anxieties. Taking time to bring to mind events in your life that have helped shape you (even funny or embarrassing moments) can help you gather a variety of personal stories to draw on when relating to others.

> *Our own stories can be the most powerful stories we tell.*

But just because a story is your own, that doesn't mean you will automatically remember or tell it well. It's easy to forget crucial details, put events in the wrong order, or even fail to make sense if you do not intentionally think about *how* you are telling the story. Mary's pastor encourages those in their church to write out their salvation story so as to be prepared to share it. He is not advising that they then pull out a piece of paper and read their story if the time seems right. Instead, he is encouraging people to know their story well enough to be ready at any moment to share how Jesus has changed their lives.

Tony tells the story of being on airplane one day, exhausted and not feeling like talking to the man sitting next to him, although the man seemed agitated and acted as though he wanted to talk. Tony pretended he was sleeping, and then said to God, "God, if you want me to talk to this man, you are going to have to give me a SIGN." Just as they were about to land, the man looked at Tony and said, "I need GOD." It's a good thing Tony was prepared to share how Jesus changed his life! He walked off the plane with the man, talked to him for two hours about Jesus, and the man left the airport with a commitment to live for the Kingdom of God.

Because signs of when to share stories of what Jesus has done and continues to do in your life won't usually be that clear, you can ask the Holy Spirit to alert you to any time a person is open to hearing about Jesus, whether it's during a conversation in a coffee shop or at a sporting event. The Holy Spirit can make us sensitive as to when the time is ripe for someone to hear parts of our stories and when we should wait. If you are not sure but you decide to share anyway, then noticing how the other person is responding may be a good clue as to whether or not it's the right time.

An important by-product of intentionally reflecting on and sharing stories of Jesus at work in your life is that you will become more aware of what part you are currently playing in God's Story. Whether it's a leading or supporting role doesn't matter, as long as you are being obedient to how God wants you to participate in the Story. Determining your role is a matter of discernment through prayer, scripture reading, and feedback from other trusted lovers of Jesus. If you find you are only making guest appearances in God's Story, you can ask the Holy Spirit to empower you to expand your part in the way you serve behind the scenes or in more public roles like those of the Apostles. We read in Acts 4:20 that they could not "keep from speaking about what [they] have seen and heard."

With the emphasis we are putting on personal stories, we do not mean to imply that sharing intellectually developed concepts and sound theology is not important for a good proclamation of the Gospel, because we do believe that this kind of sharing is important too. Yet there is no substitute for the power of a personal story in the healing of souls. Several years ago, when Tony was teaching at the University of Pennsylvania, he had two undergraduate students who wanted to go on and earn advanced degrees in sociology. The two of them went on to Cornell University and decided to room together. This deeply concerned Tony because one student was the most brilliant he had ever had and the other was a young Christian. He worried that the brilliant student, who was also an agnostic, would overwhelm the other with arguments against Christianity and gradually lead him away from the Lord.

To Tony's surprise, a couple of years later when he happened to meet up with the two students again, he found that the agnostic student had become a Christian. Tony was both elated and intrigued, and asked him how it had happened. The student explained that night after night, the two of them would go back and forth as to why the Gospel story might be true or not. Over and over again, he said he would overwhelm his Christian friend with arguments and win every debate. But his friend would end every debate by saying how real Jesus was to him—that he sensed Jesus' presence every day, that Jesus made a difference in his life. It was the constant reference to his personal experience with Jesus that wore the brilliant student down.

As we can see with this student's personal story, stories of how God changes our lives go a long way in the healing of souls—often further than any logical argument ever could.

How Can I Know Which Kind of Story Might Be Best to Use, Based on My Audience?

Because there are so many places you can get stories, how do you choose the best? You can start by praying for the Spirit to alert you to stories God may want you to use, whether in conversations with individuals or in a larger, more formal setting.

If you need to talk to someone about a serious matter, then you may want to consider asking God to help you come up with an appropriate emotional word picture, as we discussed earlier. If you are planning a speaking engagement, you can ask God to bring to mind stories that might best illustrate your points, and then sit in silence from a few to several minutes to see if any ideas emerge. A story may come to your mind during this time; it may come later; or you may have to search for a story in your memory, at the library, on your bookshelf, or in your own files of stories. We believe that the more you become in tune with God's Spirit, the more you can trust the Spirit to bring stories to mind, during both specific times of prayer and other times in your planning as well.

Tony remembers his seminary professor of evangelism, Dr. Albert Williams, telling his class these three points about storytelling:

o You have a story to tell.

o It is supremely worth telling.

o Love will get the story told.

Tony has never forgotten these three points. He knows that being connected to Jesus means you have a story to tell, that stories of lives changed through knowing Jesus are definitely worth telling, and that love *will* get the story told. This last point is why Tony believes that one of the most important ways to connect to audiences is to love them, as Jesus loved his. For Tony this means he prays in advance that God will help him love his listeners, no matter who they are and what their attitude might be toward him or the stories he chooses to tell.

> *Being connected to Jesus means you have a story to tell.*

Praying for God to help you love your listeners includes praying that you will be sensitive to what God may want to say through you to your specific audience, whether that is one person or many. Being sensitive to your listeners includes thinking ahead about what stories might best fit them based on their age, gender, sense of spirituality, level of education, social status, or ethnic background. If your listeners are children, you may want to use your imagination even more than you would with adults, because children respond so well to creative images. If you have a hard time thinking of creative images, becoming familiar with a variety of children's stories can help prime the pump of your imagination. If your audience is mainly adults, you may want to appeal more to moral reasoning and critical thinking, although that doesn't mean adults don't appreciate childlike imagination. Oftentimes the same story can touch young and old alike, appealing to our hearts and our minds—for example, C. S. Lewis's *Chronicles of Narnia*. Many adults love reading these seven books to their children, not only because their children love the imagery of Narnia with its castles and talking animals but also because of the profound theology that emerges in each volume. That's the beauty of a good story.

You can also ask yourself listener-centered questions, such as "What might be a good way to connect with this particular person, given what I know about him or her?" or "What story could I use to show what we have in common so that listeners can see that I relate to their experiences?" Borrowing from what Tony said about putting himself *in* a story to learn the story, you can try imagining yourself in another person's story to discover, at least in part, what it might be like to experience life as he or she does. Coming up with stories related to what is familiar to an audience will help you establish common ground with them and connect in soul-healing ways.

What Do I Need to Know When Using a Story That's Not My Own?

If a story isn't your own, it is important to get permission to use it. If the story is of a private nature and has not been told publically, you'll need to check with the person to make sure it's OK to tell. If it's a published or recorded story, it is important to give credit where credit is due. Not citing the origins of a story is called verbal plagiarism and is as ethically serious as written plagiarism. Besides, citing the source lends greater credibility to what you have to say, unless of course you have a source that is not credible, and then it's a bad idea to tell the story anyway.

If you can't find the origins of a story, be careful. Sometimes a story has been told so many times that it is no longer even the original story. It's always a good idea to research the origins of a story and to fact-check its details in their current form to see if it is still being told authentically and accurately. Our credibility can be compromised when we inadvertently tell a story with inaccuracies, not to mention if we intentionally make up or embellish parts of a story. If a story isn't good enough to stand on its own, there are enough good stories out there to replace it—all you have to do is look and listen, and continue to watch out for stories that may be embellished or not true at all.

Years ago a student told Mary a story about her grandma getting her purse mixed up at the airport with someone else's purse and how embarrassing it was because her grandma started eating someone else's candy bar from what she thought was her purse. Halfway through the story Mary said, "Oh yeah, I've heard this one before." The student seemed genuinely surprised. She told Mary that she couldn't have heard it before because it had just recently happened to her grandma. Mary told her that it was a kind of story called an urban legend, and that more than once she has heard a person tell the same story someone else did, with the exact same details, as if it had happened to that person instead. If you do not want to be fooled the way Mary's student was, there are lots of Internet sites that can help you find out whether or not a story is true.[6]

Although some people think it's ethically OK to tell a story "for the truth," we do not agree, unless the storyteller makes it clear at some point in the conversation or public speaking event either that it is not a true story or that it is true, but that it didn't actually happen to him or her. Even if you are sure you are telling a story in a way others couldn't possibly believe as happening to you, you'd be surprised how it can still be heard as the truth. Even if you don't see this as an ethical issue, it's still a credibility issue. If someone discovers that what you said wasn't true, he or she could discredit other important truths you want to communicate. Tony, on more than one occasion, has had a minister ask him *not* to use a particular story because the minister sheepishly said, "I used that story and told them it happened to me."

On the other end of the spectrum are those who think a story is fiction when it really is true. Mary recently heard someone tell a story she didn't think could possibly be true, but at the end the person said "true story." That can be a helpful phrase if our story seems hard to believe (as long as the story is, in fact, true!). It can also help us not to exaggerate our stories. In our interview, Shane Claiborne said that one of the reasons he doesn't travel alone to speaking engagements is that "Having someone travel with me affects how I tell stories. Another person makes sure I don't tell them 'too big.'"

How Might I Best Organize a Talk Using Stories?

Tony often organizes his talks around stories because he believes they are one of the best ways to connect more abstract ideas to audiences' hearts and minds. He tries to come up with at least one good story for each of the major points he wants to make in a talk. More than one illustration per point can work, but he tries to be careful so as not to overload one point with illustrations to the detriment of the other points he wants to make. As a general rule, there should be symmetry in a talk, with fairly equal weight given to each of the points. Using too many stories on any one point can make the other points seem less important. Tony also thinks we should be careful not to use too many stories, lest people forget the actual points we are making. His professor of preaching in seminary said of himself, "My sermons are a lot like the Empire State Building—just one story on top of another."

In many cases Tony uses the same illustration to make entirely different points in different talks. He has used his talk on Good Friday and Easter, called "It's Friday, but Sunday's Coming," to lift the spirits of those who have suffered a great emotional loss, such as the death of a loved one, and also to encourage those who are depressed to believe that better things lay in the future. People have often come to Tony and said that "It's Friday, but Sunday's Coming" gave them optimism in the face of a difficult situation. Tony has also used this story to declare his beliefs about what will happen when Jesus returns.

How Can We Best Structure the Story?

If you have ever heard a story that was boring or too detailed, or that didn't make sense as a whole or in parts—and not because it was one of Jesus' confounding parables—then you know the importance of structuring a story for maximum effectiveness. Quentin Schultze, professor of communication at Calvin College, sees the following as essential elements of a well-told story:

- o Setting: describe vividly where and when it takes place.
- o Characters: paint visual images with your words and body to illustrate how people look and act.
- o Motivation: explain what the characters are trying to accomplish or overcome.

○ Timing: keep the story moving, delivering key lines at the right places and concluding the story before it wears thin or dominates the entire speech.

○ Relevance: make sure the story is relevant to the point of the speech.[7]

In addition, reflecting on the varying points of view of significant characters, as Tony mentioned, can help you determine what engages different emotions in your audience, and brings different perspectives to light. Depending on the point you are illustrating and where you want the story to end, you might consider focusing on only one aspect of the story and developing that aspect. You can do this by picking one character, one specific scene, or maybe one overarching emotion to focus on.

Including dialogue among characters is another good rule of thumb for making stories come alive. Finally, being intentional about letting the drama, humor, excitement, intensity, or mystery build throughout the story to its climax will make your story even more engaging and memorable.

Here's an example from Tony's book *Let Me Tell You a Story* that illustrates some of these important elements:

A young man was working his way among the people in the gate area of an airport. As the people waited for the boarding announcement to be made, he was handing out copies of that little booklet *The Four Spiritual Laws*, doing a faithful work of evangelism.

There was an elderly African-American man slumped in a seat in the waiting area, sound asleep. He was a dignified figure with white curly hair and a fashionable tailored suit. This old man was as sound asleep as a man could get, but the young evangelist was not about to be deterred by that. He tapped the man on the knee. When the old man woke, he was extremely startled. He blurted out, "Where am I? What's going on? What's happening?" The persistent young man simply and sternly asked, "Sir! Are you saved?"

"Yeah," said the old man. "I guess I'm saved! I suppose I'm saved! Yes! I'm probably saved!"

"That's not good enough!" the young man responded. "Can you tell me exactly when you were saved?"

"Not exactly," the old man answered. "It was almost two thousand years ago!"[8]

This story shows how we can structure a story with compelling details and dialogue that build to a climactic ending.

How Long Should a Story Be, Given Attention Spans and Settings?

If you have ever heard a story that dragged on too long, you know the importance of being intentional with the length of a story. No matter how much you are convinced that certain details or tangents are important, running your story by others and trusting their advice can help you edit your stories so that they best engage your listeners. So can remembering that more isn't necessarily better. Your listeners may lose interest or at least lose the point if your story has a sea of descriptions and details. Jesus knew this—his stories were never very long, yet they were powerful enough not only to change individual lives but to transform all of history. That's why it is important not to lose focus on the message you are trying to convey. Once you have made your point, being careful not to overextend it will give your listeners enough time to think about the story without losing attention altogether. Remember that storytelling is an art. Carefully crafting your words into shorter stories will often have greater impact and will keep your listener's interest far better than lengthy stories—no matter how good you think they are.

Taking into account *where* you are telling a story is also crucial to its length. If it is ninety degrees and you are outdoors, if your listeners are in a hurry, or if the seating is uncomfortable, you'll need to be sensitive to these conditions and either streamline your stories or wait until another time to tell them.

When and How Is Humor Best Used in Storytelling?

As the saying goes, laughter is good for the soul, so humor is something to consider using in your storytelling. Humor can be a powerful way to connect with others. It can grab attention, draw listeners into a serious topic, and help them be more receptive to it.

Humor that uses dialogue and the element of surprise can be especially effective in storytelling. In addition, stories in which you make fun of yourself can help you connect with listeners in ways that other forms of humor rarely do. When talking about the topic of fear, Mary will, at times, introduce the subject with this story, in the hope that it connects her to her listeners right away:

Several years ago, while on a road trip out west, our family took a scenic ride on a ski lift in Sundance, Utah. My husband and sons claim that while they were enjoying the scenery, I was white-knuckling the bar (which I made them put down so we wouldn't fall out) and ruining their time by telling them not to rock the lift car. Out of the blue, Michael, our younger son asked me, "Are we staying in a hotel tonight with a pool?" David, then nine years old, immediately turned toward me, looked me straight in the eyes, and said slowly, "If there *is* a tonight."

Although humor can be a very effective element in storytelling, you have to be careful not to offend listeners or irritate them by overdoing it. Humor can be especially offensive if it makes fun of a certain gender, race, or sex or uses language inappropriate for the particular audience. If you aren't sure if the humor in your story might be offensive, we suggest you ask a few people who are a different gender, race, sex, or age than you. You'll also want to watch how many humorous stories you tell. Some people tell too many, whether while speaking in public or during informal conversations. If you are a stand-up comic, then using a lot of humor is appropriate in that context. But when you are no longer standing up in front of an audience, it is not appropriate to use humor as your primary way to communicate. Although laughter *is* good for the soul, too much of it can be irritating. It can also hinder soul healing if it is used as a substitute for authentic connecting with others. If you are wondering if you use too much humor, you may want to make that a matter of reflection, perhaps during the prayer of examen. If after reflection you still aren't sure, you can ask others for their honest opinion (but only if you are ready to accept their response). Humor is something to be savored and enjoyed in small bites, not in big chunks. Drawing out any humor for too long risks losing soul-healing moments that come from balancing laughter with more serious dialogue and reflection.

How Can I Best Practice My Stories?

The best place to start is to ask the Holy Spirit to help you tell a story in a way that will glorify God. Then you need to commit to practicing your story. Even the best stories can fall flat if you don't practice them ahead of time. Working on timing, volume, tone, rate, pauses, facial expressions, eye contact, gestures, and other body movements are all important for telling stories well. Practicing these delivery techniques is not about producing a fake, canned delivery but about telling stories in conversational ways that are not "all over the place" and that best engage your listeners.

Because in preparation Tony "prays his stories," as well as practices them ahead of time, his listeners report that they often feel he is telling a story for the first time. Even though he has told the stories many times before, they say his stories appear fresh and spontaneous to them. When Tony is telling a story in front of an audience, he often senses that the Holy Spirit is infusing his stories with power from "on high." Although he knows that the Holy Spirit can speak through anyone at anytime (even a donkey—Numbers 22:22–25), Tony believes that his times of surrendering to God before he speaks makes him a more open vessel for the work of the Spirit.

What Channel of Delivery Might Be Best?

Jesus told his stories face-to-face, whether one-on-one or to larger groups because that was the primary channel of delivery for his time and audience. With today's technology, our options are, of course, much more numerous, meaning we have to decide what channel is best: the spoken word face-to-face; through a podcast or other means of broadcasting; or through the written word. With no intention of trivializing the message of Jesus in any fashion, imagine Jesus using today's technology. Maybe he would choose to blog some of his stories. This form of storytelling would allow certain audiences to send comments and ask questions about his material at their leisure. Or perhaps his disciples would podcast his parables. Although these examples might seem extreme, we do live in a computerized world that allows us to connect in myriad ways. So if connecting is what you are after, then it's important to carefully choose and use the channels at your disposal in ways that honor God in how they minister to others.

After I Tell the Story, Should I Explain My Specific Reason for Telling It or Leave the Meaning up to the Listener(s)?

Storytelling "purists" will say a good story stands on its own—that any explanation only taints it. Others are believers in giving the moral of a story so that the listener doesn't miss the point. Discernment is needed when determining whether or not we follow up a story. The danger in explaining the point or moral of a story is that listeners may have connected to the story in other ways that touch their souls; our explanation could derail that connection. Often it is best to give listeners time to think without their having to hear any explanations or opinions. That way they aren't tempted into adopting another person's bias. Besides, explaining a story can make your communication seem didactic. A good general rule is to follow Mary's professor's earlier description of Jesus' three different kinds of listeners and see if anyone has questions or wants to engage in dialogue about the story. In addition, it's best to avoid basing assumptions about listeners' reactions on their immediate verbal or nonverbal response to your story. It's good to remember these words from storyteller Jack Maguire: "When you tell a story, you are giving your listener something to think about, so you may as well give him or her the time to think about it as well."[9]

Discernment is needed when determining whether or not we follow up a story.

Other Types of Illustrations

Although we have been focusing on storytelling in this chapter, it's important to note that in connecting with others, Jesus frequently used shorter illustrations, often in the form of metaphors, similes, and analogies (types of comparisons). Here are two examples from Jesus' Sermon on the Mount (Matthew 5–7):

> "Enter through the narrow gate; for the gate is wide and the road is easy that leads to destruction, and there are many who take it. For the gate is narrow and the road is hard that leads to life, and there are few who find it" (Matthew 7:13–14).

> "Beware of false prophets, who come to you in sheep's clothing but inwardly are ravenous wolves. You will know them by their fruits. Are grapes gathered from thorns, or figs from thistles? In the same way, every good tree bears good fruit, but the bad tree bears bad fruit. A good tree cannot bear bad fruit, nor can a bad tree bear good fruit. Every tree that does not bear good fruit is cut down and thrown into the fire. Thus you will know them by their fruits" (Matthew 7:15–20).

Jesus used metaphors like "the narrow gate" and "bad fruit" to create potent visuals that made his points come alive to his listeners in ways that plainly stating them would not.

Jesus used metaphors to create potent visuals that made his points come alive.

Great communicators throughout history have followed Jesus' use of comparison to powerfully illustrate a point. When Martin Luther King Jr. wanted to express in his "I Have a Dream" speech how America had not treated black citizens fairly, he used the metaphor of a promissory note. King said that America "has given the Negro people a bad check" and that they were sending it back, marked "insufficient funds."[10] King's comparison made the point so much stronger and more memorable than had he said, "the Negro people have not been treated right, and we aren't going to take it anymore."

You don't have to be a master communicator to find metaphors and other types of illustrations. Like stories, they are everywhere. Because Jesus used the familiar, if he were walking the earth today we believe some of his illustrations would involve cell phones, cars, television, film, video games, and computers—including social networking tools, such as Facebook and Twitter. If Jesus' audience were familiar with Facebook, he might ask them how they would respond if they received a friend request on Facebook from him—would they click "confirm" or "ignore"? He might ask his audience, "Did you know that accepting my friendship means you are to do what I command [John 15:14]? Are you willing to do that?"

When we pay attention to what is familiar to our audiences, we can find illustrations that connect us to them, just as Jesus did to connect to his audiences.

The principles and practices we have been focusing on in this chapter can make our stories and other illustrations "pop," not only with purpose but with passion. They can cause listeners to rethink established assumptions and reexamine personal beliefs, and can even motivate them to change their lives. If you want to go to the highest level of storytelling and connect to others through stories the way Jesus did, then asking the Holy Spirit to empower your storytelling is essential. Jesus' storytelling changed lives not simply because he knew how to tell a story well but because he was empowered by the Spirit. We believe engaging in practices like those we have been highlighting can help your stories change lives too, whether they are told to individuals or in the context of teaching and preaching, which is the focus of the rest of this book.

PART THREE

PRACTICES FOR TEACHING AND PREACHING

TONY CAMPOLO

10

Preparing the Soil

Laying the Groundwork for Spiritually Dynamic Speaking

In the presence of God and of Christ Jesus . . . I give you this charge: Preach the Word; be prepared in season and out of season; correct, rebuke and encourage—with great patience and careful instruction.
—2 Timothy 4:1–2 (NIV)

BEFORE WE BEGIN EXPLORING the dynamics of teaching and preaching in the context of connecting like Jesus, I want to point out that when Jesus spoke, he did so to a variety of audiences and in a variety of settings. Because we are following Jesus' model for connecting, it's important that we not limit the scope of teaching and preaching to classrooms and congregations. In this and the following chapters, my intent is to demonstrate how dynamic teaching and preaching can be carried out in a variety of contexts, including small groups, classrooms, workshops, and main stages at conferences. That is why you will often notice me referring to teaching and preaching as "speaking" or "giving a talk."

Why I Am Combining Teaching and Preaching

When Jesus delivered what is called his Sermon on the Mount (Matthew 5–7), he did a combination of teaching and preaching. He instructed as well as proclaimed, and in so doing Jesus inspired and challenged his listeners. He taught them how to pray (Matthew 6:5–13), he told them they were blessed (Matthew 5:3–12), and he warned them what would happen if they heard his words and didn't put them into practice

(Matthew 7:24–27). Although it says in Matthew 5:2 and 5:28 that Jesus was teaching when he told the crowd these things, he was preaching too—hence the same *Sermon* on the Mount.

The difference between teaching and preaching is a matter of emphasis. In the context of connecting like Jesus, there should be some instruction in our preaching, and in our teaching there should be some of the proclaiming that happens in preaching. And both should inspire. The main goal of teaching is to help others gain an understanding of a specific body of knowledge. In relation to connecting like Jesus, the purpose of teaching is to help others learn what it means to live for God by imparting specific knowledge about the Kingdom of God. The main goal of a preacher is to proclaim the truth of the Gospel either by calling people to make initial decisions to live for Christ or by calling those who already claim to follow Christ to live more radically for the Kingdom of God.[1]

> *The difference between teaching and preaching is a matter of emphasis.*

Whereas preaching inspires listeners to decision making, teaching is an ongoing process of instruction in how to live out those decisions. That's why preaching and teaching go hand in hand. As important as preaching is, we need sound teaching in how to daily live for God. Through Christian teaching, those who have made decisions to live for Christ are nurtured into ways of thinking and acting that enable them to become conformed more and more into Christlike persons.

Although I will continue to make certain distinctions between teaching and preaching, it must be said that they have so much in common that most of what I write about one will apply to the other. Consequently, you will find in what you read a constant movement between the two.

Jesus' Purpose in Preaching and Teaching

There is no doubt when it comes to defining the purpose of Jesus' teaching and preaching: it was to recruit disciples who would become colaborers with him as he carried out his plan to transform this messed-up world into the Kingdom of God. Jesus was very clear about what he was motivating his listeners to do in response to his teaching and preaching. A critic recently said of me, "He's just a glorified motivational speaker." When I was told about this criticism, I responded, "That's not a criticism. That's a compliment! Of course I'm a motivational speaker. The important thing is *what* I'm trying to motivate people to do. I am trying to motivate them to surrender their lives to the transforming work of the Holy Spirit, and to accept the challenge to give themselves over to the will of God. Wasn't Jesus a motivational speaker? Wasn't he trying to motivate people to repent and become disciples who would 'turn the world upside down'?" If Jesus is our model, then modern-day teachers and preachers should zealously endeavor to follow his example.

Jesus was very clear about what he was motivating his listeners to do in response to his teaching and preaching.

Although we emphasized Jesus' purpose for connecting with others in Chapter One, I want to reiterate the magnitude of its importance in the context of teaching and preaching. When Jesus preached, his sermons were a call for his listeners to become special agents of God who would join the struggle to bring the Kingdom of God into being. Jesus' teaching and preaching resulted in others becoming aware of deep spiritual truths about this Kingdom. Whether or not people chose to accept what they heard Jesus say depended on their own openness to those truths. As we have been stating throughout the book, what was required of those who would preach and teach about God's Kingdom was a kind of connecting with others, spelled out in Jesus' many directives identified throughout the Gospels and reiterated in numerous verses in the epistles. These requisites were, and continue to be, extremely difficult to live out. Although many have heeded Jesus' call and have become part of his revolution, there are still too few who are willing to live out the radical discipleship he required.

Jesus was well aware that what he was asking of those who wanted to be his disciples would be so difficult that most who might volunteer would find what was expected of them humanly impossible. In the midst of a society that serves materialistic goals, Jesus asked would-be followers to be disciples who would not even think about pressing toward the consumerist goals of life prescribed by the dominant culture. Instead, he wanted them to seek a lifestyle that did not take into consideration what they would eat and drink (Matthew 6:31–34). The cost of discipleship, Jesus said, would be high. If anyone would join his radical movement, such a person must be ready to give up everything in order to help those who are poor (Mark 10:21), and be ready to suffer, if need be, for membership in God's Kingdom. Other radical requisites he taught and preached included such new commandments as having his followers abandon the time-honored tradition of the "an eye for an eye and a tooth for a tooth" kind of justice, and contrary-wise would return good for whatever evil might be done to them (Matthew 5:38–42).

There can be no Kingdom of God without Kingdom people. A transformed society requires citizens who are themselves transformed. There are those, like the Marxists, who have concentrated only on transforming the institutions of society, believing that a just and equitable political-economic order inevitably would produce good people—that if social justice and economic equality pervaded society's institutions, something like the Kingdom of God would gradually emerge. These activists, however, usually ignored the need for introducing individuals to the converting work of Christ and the power of the Holy Spirit. They failed to recognize that unconverted persons can make a hell out of any imagined societal heaven, and that only spiritual transformations through the power of the Holy Spirit can create men and women fit to live in God's Kingdom. Jesus declared that with the Holy Spirit at work in their lives, his followers could live the radically countercultural lifestyle that he required (Mark 10:27) and be a model for others (John 17:21). Jesus had this dynamic power in his own life. The reason the crowds were amazed at Jesus' teaching and preaching was that he was empowered by God through being filled with the God's Spirit (Luke 4:1, 14).

> *There can be no Kingdom of God without Kingdom people. A transformed society requires citizens who are themselves transformed.*

There are also many who think that all that is needed for the transformation of the world is to proclaim and propagate the Gospel. Ignoring the pleas of those who emphasize programs for social justice, these believers, who embrace an exaggerated belief in individualism, assume that the church should only seek to win converts to Christ. This latter group of Christians assumes that the Kingdom of God will somehow emerge naturally or, as social scientists say, *sui generis* if just enough persons "get saved."

In reality, both personal evangelism *and* social justice efforts are required, because the Kingdom of God is composed of transformed people living in a transformed society. Consequently, the Kingdom of God requires both personal and social transformations. This is the holistic Gospel that Jesus lived, taught, and preached. Today, he calls his

Any of us who attempt to speak on behalf of Jesus are to teach and preach the holistic message of Jesus.

followers to do the same. That is why any of us who attempt to speak on behalf of Jesus are to teach and preach the holistic message of Jesus.

Up to this point I have only briefly mentioned the major defining differences between teaching and preaching. Before I get into further considerations that apply to both teachers and preachers, there are some distinguishing characteristics of each that need to be highlighted.

Teachers: Characteristics and Considerations

In Ephesians 4:14, we read how Paul made it clear that sound teaching is essential if Christians are to mature in their faith so as not to be swayed from sound doctrine. Whether we choose to be or not, all of us are teachers in one way or another, if only informally, in the course of life. Therefore, what we have to say about teaching should have relevance for everyone. Mothers and fathers teach their children. Coworkers in offices and factories teach each other. The young learn from the old, and the old learn from the young. Some of us formally teach, and some of us teach from example—whether we intend to or not. There are, nevertheless, some who appear especially suited to make teaching a more professional vocation. Within the church, there is even reason to believe that becoming a teacher is a special calling from God. The Bible states that God gives a unique *gift* to those who have this calling (Ephesians 4:11).

Highly effective teachers have certain characteristics in common. Good teachers know that there are certain facts and skills that students need to learn and, therefore, that a specific body of knowledge must be covered. They know that effective teaching requires adapting to different learning styles and that asking good questions for reflection and discussion is an essential teaching technique. But highly effective teachers also know that they have to do more. They know that even the best teaching tools do not always inspire students to learn. The best teachers can so mesmerize their students that their students can, at times, even forget to take notes—and still recall what the teacher said. There are some teachers who have such charisma as part of their DNA, but there are others who gain such a capacity to spiritually connect with others as a result of being infused by the Holy Spirit. The Apostle Paul made a point that in his teaching, it was the Holy Spirit who enabled him to establish intense connections with those whom he taught. He wrote, "When I came to you, brothers and sisters, I did not come proclaiming the mystery of God to you in lofty words or wisdom. For I decided to know nothing among you except Jesus Christ, and him crucified. And I came to you in weakness and in fear and in much trembling. My speech and my proclamation were not with plausible words of wisdom, but with a demonstration of the Spirit and of power, so that your faith might rest not on human wisdom but on the power of God" (1 Corinthians 2:1–5).

Paul claimed that his spiritual dynamism came through prayerfully surrendering to an infilling of the Holy Spirit. Many teachers would love to have the impact that Paul had, but I wonder how many of them, like Paul, are willing to spend extensive time in quiet, as he did. How many teachers are willing to take the time to go through spiritual practices that can lead to the infilling of the Holy Spirit before trying to teach? To those who long to possess Paul's kind of spiritual connectedness with their students, I say, with biblical backing, prepare yourselves for teaching as he did, with spiritual practices like the ones we propose in this book.

I suggest that those who would be teachers in a classroom set aside time as part of their class preparation to go to what the Celtic Christians called "a thin place" and, in surrender of self, plead with God to be filled with the Holy Spirit. You could go, as the Bible says, "into a closet," if not literally at least figuratively, to pray. Before teaching, spend a few minutes in spiritual solitude, simply praying, "Spirit of the Living God, fall afresh on me." Then *wait* in silence for an infilling of the Spirit that can offer the kind of spiritual renewal that, at times, can send you into a teaching situation *soaring like an eagle* (Isaiah 40:31). I also suggest you pray for students by name, whether by naming them as a group or by focusing in on a few. Through praying for your students, you can become a channel of blessing for them. I guarantee that such praying will help you feel more connected to them.

There are some teachers who serve in one particular Pentecostal college I know of who go into their classrooms hours before the students arrive, and pray that the Holy Spirit permeate the rooms. When the students arrive, these teachers want them to enter sacred space. They hope that their students will feel the presence of God even before the lessons of the day begin.

If you are a schoolteacher, a college professor, or a trainer in a business seminar, you ought to realize that there will be those "sitting under you" at times who really don't want to be there. If getting them to learn is really important to you (and it should be), then being spiritually empowered to enliven them should be a primary concern. Whether the topic is overtly Christian or not, if you are a follower of Christ, then what you teach should be worthy of spiritual empowerment, no matter the subject. If it is not, you may want to reconsider what you are teaching and why. Teaching is not only a matter of covering a certain amount of material. If we want to connect like Jesus, then any teaching we do will not only convey information but also contribute to helping others gain an understanding of the meaning of their lives. This requires that we be so spiritually alive that there will be an enlivening power flowing over and under the words we speak, making learning a spiritual experience.

> *If we want to connect like Jesus, then any teaching we do will contribute to helping others gain an understanding of the meaning of their lives.*

Preachers: Characteristics and Considerations

These days there are some who fail to recognize the miraculous effects that preaching can have. They are reluctant to acknowledge the validity of the declaration of the Apostle Paul, who said, "For since, in the wisdom of God, the world did not know God through wisdom, God decided, through the foolishness of our proclamation, to save those who believe" (1 Corinthians 1:21). When empowered by the Holy Spirit, preaching becomes a force that can bring about historically significant societal changes as well as initiate radical alterations in the lives of individuals.

Jesus' preaching was of two types: pastoral and prophetic. He used both of these distinct kinds of preaching to bring about individual as well as societal change. It has been said that the pastor comforts the troubled, whereas the prophet troubles the comfortable. As pastor, Jesus shepherded his followers, caring for them and deeply ministering to their hurting souls. As such he was a reconciling agent, gently bringing people into a sense of being comforted and in harmony with God and others. In contrast, as a prophet in the tradition of the ancient Hebrew prophets and his forerunner, John the Baptist, Jesus preached against those who hindered the advancement of the Kingdom of God. I hold up both kinds of Jesus' preaching as models to be imitated, and in this chapter and the next suggest how your preaching can incorporate both of these ways of helping bring God's will to earth as it is in heaven.

The Preacher as Pastor

There are preachers who believe that most, if not all, preaching is to be of the pastoral kind. Harry Emerson Fosdick, the avowed liberal preacher at the great Riverside Church in New York City, was one such preacher. He believed that a sermon should address "every kind of personal difficulty and problem flesh is heir to"; that "A sermon was meant to meet such needs; it should be personal counseling on a group scale."[2]

There *is* a time for pastoral preaching, and I hope that the suggestions toward the end of the chapter can help you connect with your audience in the vein of a caring and compassionate pastoral preacher—when that is how the Holy Spirit wants you to speak. I also hope that you will be alert to the possibility that there may be times when you are called to be prophetic in your preaching. Because much of the kind of preaching that goes on today already is pastoral, I will spend more time in this chapter focusing on the second kind of preaching Jesus did: prophetic.

The Preacher as Prophet

Jesus said, "A prophet is not without honor, except in his own country" (Luke 4:24). His words certainly ring true for many, if not most, preachers who try to be prophetic. It is especially difficult for those who have congregations that prefer only to be shepherded. It is, however, possible to be both pastoral and prophetic—if we can establish personal connections with our listeners.

During the height of the Vietnam War, Rev. William Sloan Coffin, the well-known chaplain at Yale University, preached a sermon denouncing the war, utilizing scathing language. In the congregation was a military officer who writhed in anger during the entire sermon. On the way out of church, the officer, with great intensity, said to Coffin, "It was all that I could do to keep my seat while you preached. I wanted to get up and stomp out, march up the center aisle, and turn back simply to shout at the top of my lungs, 'bull***t!' "

Coffin responded, "Why didn't you?"

The officer answered, "Because the night my wife died, you sat at her bedside all night long, holding her hand and praying with her up until the moment of her death."

I tell this story to emphasize that when possible, the work of a prophet should be connected to pastoral care. People are much more willing to listen to those who listen, and show compassion, to them. Prophets who are given a "fair hearing" are most often those who prophesy with tears in their eyes because they know the hurts of the people to whom they are delivering their prophetic messages.

Even when prophets speak with compassion, that does not guarantee a fair hearing. During the 1950s and 1960s, preachers who spoke against the racism inherent in members of their congregations could quickly be without pulpits, or worse. In today's troubled world, even suggesting that loving justice be extended to certain people, such as gays and lesbians, is likely to elicit strong negative reactions, if not a movement to remove the pastor from the pulpit. But being fired might not be the worst that can happen to prophetic preachers.

In some oppressive totalitarian states, preachers who preach prophetically are put to death. Such was the fate of Archbishop Oscar Romero (1917–1980) of El Salvador, who dared to speak out against the ruling dictator of his country whose oppression tyrannized those who are poor. As long as he talked about the importance of charity in his pastoral sermons, he was safe and even praised. But when he spoke out on behalf of justice for those who live in poverty and against those who oppress them, he was persecuted by his nation's political leaders. Romero knew that as important as charity is, when people are oppressed, justice is also needed. He also knew that message was not easy to hear and certainly wasn't popular with the political leaders. Brazilian Archbishop Dom Helder Camara (1909–1999) once said, "If I give food to the poor they call me a saint. If I ask why the poor have no food, they call me a communist." The same could be said of Romero. Because of his prophetic voice regarding justice, he was shot in the back one Sunday morning as he faced the altar while celebrating mass.

John Perkins, one of the prophetic voices of the African American community and the convener and organizer of the large and significant Christian Community Development Association, tells about a white preacher friend of his who, during the 1950s, endeavored to preach for social justice for black people. They didn't kill his white friend. Instead, they so humiliated, harassed, and persecuted him that he ended up taking his own life. There's more than one way to destroy a prophet! Such reactions to the prophetic preacher should not surprise us, considering that Jesus said, "They will arrest you and persecute you; they will hand you over to synagogues and prisons, and you will be brought before kings and governors because of my name" (Luke 21:12). He also warned his followers that their fate might be the same as his, because "the servant is not greater than the master" (John 15:18).

Sometimes, when a pastor feels an urgent need to have a prophetic word given to the congregation, he or she will invite in some "outside" speaker to do the job. That way, if people respond negatively over being challenged to change, the pastor can say, "Well, you'll have to aim your complaints at that outside speaker. I would never talk to you that way!" Sometimes, as Shakespeare once said, "discretion is the better part of valor." But then what is sometimes called discretion just might be another name for cowardice.

At a recent clergy conference, I delivered a prophetic message condemning the affluent consumerist lifestyles of some Christians. I came on strong against those who live with relative indifference toward people who live in poverty. Following my sermon, several of the pastors who were present said to me, "I could never get away with talking that way in my church." It's likely that they were telling the truth.

The Integrity of a Prophet

Walter Brueggemann, in his book *The Prophetic Imagination*, provides important insights into what integrity requires of anyone who would speak like a prophet. Among his or her primary attributes, according to Brueggemann, is that the prophet identifies with the people. The true prophet does not simply point an accusing finger and declare, "*You* have violated God's will!" Rather, the godly prophet recognizes his or her solidarity with the people and makes it clear that he or she stands with them as together they face up to the judgments of God.[3] For example, in scripture we read how the prophet Jeremiah, like all true prophets, wept over the people of Israel because he knew that their fate would be his fate as well. He knew that if they, as a result of their unfaithfulness, were defeated by their enemies and carried into captivity, he too would share in their destiny and be carried into captivity with them. The prophet always empathizes with the sufferings that the people will endure because of their unfaithfulness. Not to weep with people is to fail to be the kind of prophet God calls us to be.

The story is told of a church that secured a new preacher, and the word spread around town about how well he preached. The church members were abuzz about what an improvement he was over their former preacher, and how much more attention they gave to his sermons. When the town cynic asked what made this new preacher so much better than his predecessor, he was told, "The old preacher told us that we're all sinners, and that if we didn't repent, we'd burn in hell forever!"

This cynic then asked, "And what does this new one say?"

The answer was, "That we're all sinners, and that if we don't repent, we'll burn in hell forever!"

When the cynic responded that he didn't see any difference between the two of them, he was told, "This new preacher says it with tears in his eyes." The true prophet weeps!

If you are going to be prophetic, be sure to include yourself among those who are under God's judgment. Be sure to talk about *our* sin rather than *your* sin, and what is wrong with *us* instead of what is wrong with *you*. Pointing a finger at the congregation and declaring, "You're sinning!" or "You're failing God!" suggests that you are above their faults. It implies that somehow you are vastly superior. Such finger pointing might drive people to despair and get them to the altar, but a prophet who identifies with those to whom he or she is speaking is likely to do things differently. Let it be known that you yourself have flaws and that even if you have not fallen short and failed God in the same way as those in your audience, you too are in need of God's mercy because of failures in your own life. At best, you should make it clear that you are not holding yourself up as an example of what it means to be all that God expects a Christian to be, but rather that you are inviting them to join you as you travel on the path of repentance. Weeping with them about shared unfaithfulness is a practice that comes from imitating biblical prophets, and it in no way will diminish your credibility.

> *If you are going to be prophetic, be sure to include yourself among those who are under God's judgment.*

When speaking to the failure of Christians to embrace the radical lifestyle that Jesus spelled out, I have used myself as an example of that failure. Explaining how Jesus called his disciples to respond to the needs of those who live in poverty without worrying about their own financial security, I have described how I myself have failed to live out Christ's directives. I admit how I have put away far too much money in 401(k)s for my retirement. As the stock market fell and my retirement nest egg showed signs of disappearing, I have confessed that this caused me to panic because I had put my trust in Mammon and not been completely willing to live by faith. I let it be known that although I have claimed to have trust in God, I haven't been willing to go along with Jesus, who said, "Therefore do not worry, saying, 'What will we eat?' or 'What will we drink?' or 'What will we wear?' For it is the Gentiles who strive for all these things; and indeed your heavenly Father knows that you need all these things" (Matthew 6:31–32).

In my prophetic sermon, I go on to hold myself up as a foolish man, likening myself to the man whom Jesus described in Luke 12:16–20:

> The land of a rich man produced abundantly. And he thought to himself, "What should I do, for I have no place to store my crops?" Then he said, "I will do this: I will pull down my barns and build larger ones, and there I will store all my grain and my goods. And I will say to my soul, 'Soul, you have ample goods laid up for many years; relax, eat, drink, be merry.'" But God said to him, "You fool! This very night your life is being demanded of you. And the things you have prepared, whose will they be?"

"I feel like I'm that man," I say. "I'm not saying that I failed to tithe. What I am saying is that I have had too much left over after my tithe was paid up. I could have done so much more as a steward of God's wealth, rather than put so much away to secure my well-being in my old age."

Because the audience can identify with me, rather than becoming defensive (as we can tend to do when under condemnation), they are more open to examining themselves in the light of Jesus' teachings in the Sermon on the Mount.

This kind of prophetic preaching doesn't always have a happy ending. Sometimes there are hardened people out there who are just waiting for the preacher to show some vulnerability so that they can justify their attacks. There is evil in everyone, and sometimes that evil will express itself in efforts to destroy the preacher. Jesus warned his followers that there would be religious people who would think that they were doing God's will as they set out to destroy the servant of God.

There is also warning when it comes to listening to prophets: be on guard against "pretend prophets"! They are the preachers who can be harsh in what they say, without fear of recrimination, because their condemnation is aimed at people who aren't "assumed" to be present in the congregation. A case in point is the preacher who makes strong declarations against gays and lesbians, assuming either that they aren't present or, if they are, that they're "in the closet" and won't protest. Such a preacher is a pretend prophet. Pretend prophets want to sound as though they are taking risks in what they are saying, when in reality there are no risks being taken at all, at least not by them.

In the end, a true prophet passionately and compassionately declares God's truth about the Kingdom of God, no matter the consequence. Better the consequences than compromising his or her message to avoid conflicts.

Offering Hope and a Future Vision

The prophet, according to Walter Brueggemann, has still another sacred responsibility in addition to weeping with the people as confessions are made of unfaithfulness to God's will. The prophet must also clearly provide a new vision of the future. A prophetic message should be marked with hope, promising that with repentance comes new possibilities because "where there is no vision, the people perish" (Proverbs 29:18, KJV). When Zechariah pronounced God's judgment on the people of Israel for not showing "true justice, mercy and compassion to one another," he then went on to give the people a vision of the way things would be when they allowed their hearts to be broken by the things that break the heart of God. He described to them a peaceful and joyful vision of the future that gave them hope. He wrote, "Thus says the Lord of hosts: Old men and old women shall again sit in the streets of Jerusalem, each with staff in hand because of their great age. And the streets of the city shall be full of boys and girls playing in its streets" (Zechariah 8:4–5).

There is little question that prophetic preaching will, at times, offend people. But as William Brosend, of the School of Theology in Sewanee, Tennessee, says, "Worry less about offending the people and more about offending the Gospel."[4] May we never be accused of offending the Gospel. And may we do all we can to care for our audiences in ways that help them see that we truly want God's best for their lives and for the world. To that end, the following section focuses on three crucial elements that help us connect with our audiences whether we are teaching, pastoring, or prophesying.

Three Essential Elements for Teaching and Preaching

The ancient Greek philosopher Aristotle is considered an expert in principles for effectively connecting with an audience. Aristotle had much to say on the topic of rhetoric, which he defined as the "faculty of observing in any given case the available means of persuasion."[5] Because so much of teaching and preaching involves persuasion, it's a good idea to look at what Aristotle considered to be three essential elements of rhetoric: *ethos, pathos,* and *logos.*

Ethos: Appealing Through Character

Aristotle's first prescription for good speaking is *ethos* (Greek for "character"). By *ethos* he meant that the credibility of the communicator is a prime factor in whether or not what is said will persuade an audience to believe or act differently. In Acts 11:22–24, we read about Barnabas, of whom it was said, "for he was a good man, full of the Holy Spirit and of faith. And a great many people were brought to the Lord." That Barnabas was effective as a preacher was highly contingent, as these verses suggest, on the kind of person he was. People want to know about the character of the preacher or teacher who asks that his or her spoken words be taken as credible. There are preachers and teachers who protest that they don't want their personal lives to be constantly under surveillance. They complain that they resent living in a "fishbowl." If you don't want to live in a fishbowl, you shouldn't try to be a communicator of Gospel truth. We must always be aware that there is potential to live contrary to what we teach and preach. Without a lifestyle that evidences the values and principles we advocate, however, we will have little hope of having in-depth connections with others. Every listener, whether in a church congregation or in a classroom, is always asking, "Why should I listen to what that person has to say?" If no one in your audience cares about your character, then you are not talking to those who are ready to be changed by what you have to say.

We are told in Matthew 7:28 that after Jesus finished speaking, "the crowds were amazed at his teaching because he taught as one who had *authority,* and not as their teachers of the law" (emphasis mine). Pilate, Herod, and the Pharisees all had power, but they did not have authority. Authority has to be earned through a life lived with authenticity and integrity. In teaching the things of God, there must be, according to one master teacher, *the hermeneutics of testimony.* What you *are* must be an incarnation of what you say. This was so with Jesus, and it must be so for anyone who seeks to connect in any way that comes near to approximating the way Jesus connected.

> *What you are must be an incarnation of what you say.*

A young Dominican doctor I knew, who had all the credentials to set up a lucrative medical practice, chose to forgo the "good life" American style and return to his homeland to serve the poor. Two days each week he would earn money by practicing medicine and doing surgical work for rich people. He would make a lot of money that way. Then he would take the money that he earned serving the rich and use it to buy medicines. At least three days a week he would take that medicine to the slums of Santo Domingo and give care to those in poverty who could not afford proper care. He would serve them without pay and give away medicine to those who had no means to buy it.

Each day, when this talented young doctor finished his work in the slums of Santo Domingo, he would climb on top of his pickup truck and call people to gather around to hear him preach the Gospel. People came, listened, and even responded to his invitation to accept Christ—because he spoke as one having authority.

Consider that when Mother Teresa spoke, people listened to her, even though her actual delivery was anything but dynamic. She spoke as one having authority—even more authority than the pope! It was authority she earned on the streets of Calcutta by serving the poor.

Closer to the here and now is the rise to international fame of my friend and former student, Shane Claiborne. This young advocate of radical Christianity asks his listeners to do nothing more and nothing less than what Jesus asked of them. Shane calls a generation of young people to a simple life of sacrifice on behalf of those who live in poverty and other forms of oppression. But lots of people teach and preach that message, so why does he draw such huge crowds when he is speaking? The answer lies in his credibility. Shane lives out the lifestyle prescribed by Jesus in the Sermon on the Mount. He actually *does* give away his money to others who need it more. He lives in a rundown neighborhood in house that was purchased for next to nothing. His clothing amounts to little more than what is on his back, and they are clothes that he made himself with the help of his mother. It is no secret that he earns what some would call "big bucks" as a speaker, then turns that money over to the intentional community with whom he lives, called the Simple Way. This community then uses that money to meet the needs of the people who live around them in their marginalized neighborhood. It is no wonder that one young Christian told me, "I listen to him because he's the real thing. He doesn't just talk the talk; he walks the walk." The consistency between what Shane says and what he does earns him credibility, and that's what makes him into somebody who connects with his listeners. T. S. Eliot once wrote that "between the idea and the reality falls the shadow." May we strive to live so close to the idea that there is little to no room for a shadow.

Pathos: Appealing to Emotions

Have you ever been convinced of something not by fact but by hearing a gut-wrenching story? As we saw in the previous chapter, stories can do much to convince others to change how they believe and act.

That's the power of *pathos* (Greek for "suffering" or "experience"), which is what Aristotle saw as appealing to the emotions or sympathies of the audience. Many people respond to messages by feeling the pain of what a speaker is describing and making decisions based on those feelings. Because stories that generate pathos are included in the previous and next chapters, what I want to mention here is the importance of speakers' bringing a radiant spiritual vitality to their emotional appeals that will help these appeals more deeply connect to their audience. Without such a personal dynamic, any speaking, no matter how good the emotional appeal is, can fall flat.

The most important way to gain inspiration for pathos is to ask the Holy Spirit to infuse you with the kind of spiritual energy that will cause you to be an open vessel for the Spirit's work in your life. To be open to the Spirit, you need to become a "cleansed lens," through which the Spirit can flow to others undeterred. If you are a "dirty lens," then the power of the Spirit flowing through you will have diminished effectiveness. One of the best ways to become a cleansed lens for the Holy Spirit is to commit to praying the prayer of examen in the manner Mary described in Chapter Three.

Another way speakers can become infused with spiritual vitality is to join a support group of three or four persons who meet regularly for intimate sharing of life's experiences and for prayer. In Matthew 18:20, you read that where two or three come together in the name of Christ, the Holy Spirit will be there, connecting them with each other and making them one. Something quite wonderful can happen in such a gathering. Jesus himself, in his humanity, gained spiritual sustenance through such a support group composed of Peter, James, and John. He regularly met with the three of them and found in them energy for the tasks that were part of his mission. I believe that any teacher or preacher should seek to be so energized from intimate friends.

It's important to note that even though pathos is an important element in speaking, not everyone is persuaded by emotions. Although almost everyone responds to certain stories, there are some people who would prefer being spoken to more directly. It may be because they have a learning style conducive to more direct, logical reasoning, or are leery, for whatever reason, of being emotionally manipulated (or both). It's important, however, to remember that we can't know the personality or learning styles of each person in our audiences. If we do know something about the preferences of the majority of our audience, then it's a good idea to tailor most of our appeals to those preferences. But because we won't always know, appealing to both emotions and logic is a good rule of thumb.

Logos: Appealing Through Logic

Finally, there is *logos,* which according to Aristotle is persuading through the use of reason. Good teaching requires that both preacher and teacher have rational points and insights. If what you say does not make sense, you will lose credibility fast, even if you make strong emotional appeals. Study is essential if you are to offer reasonable insights for those who listen to you. There are credible sources available for almost any subject matter you present. When researching those sources, you may want to know that as valid as common rationales or explanations may be, novel or fresh ways of looking at issues are known to be especially convincing. If you can say something in a way that makes sense *and* causes your listeners to say, "I've never thought of it like that before," you have gone a long way in influencing your audience. Lectio divina, the practice of praying the scriptures that both Mary and I have been highlighting throughout the book, can give you compelling new insights into Jesus' life that you can share with others.

LECTIO DIVINA AS A SOURCE OF LOGOS Over the past few decades, there has been a growing appreciation of lectio divina as a source of logos. Brilliant insights into the meanings of scripture and revelatory perspectives on the Gospel are forthcoming from listening to what the usually uneducated people who live in poverty and oppression have to say from their experiences with lectio divina. For those of us who have been socialized to listen to and read brilliant scholars as means of gaining an understanding of theological truths, this idea is strange and perhaps difficult to accept because we have been acculturated to assume that truth always comes from the "top down." We have come to believe that there are academics in seminaries and universities with earned degrees in biblical studies, philosophy, and theology whose job it is to teach the clergy. The clergy, in turn, are to take what they learned from academic scholars back to their people, who are waiting to be taught.

But God's truth also comes from the bottom up. People whom the world might consider to be "nothing" when it comes to being sources of truth may be those through whom God chooses to reveal some of the deepest and most relevant truths of scripture. As the Apostle Paul wrote in 1 Corinthians 1:19 and 21, "For it is written, 'I will destroy the wisdom of the wise, and the discernment of the discerning I will thwart.'

For since, in the wisdom of God, the world did not know God through wisdom, God decided, through the foolishness of our proclamation, to save those who believe."

Some people working in our mission organization, the Evangelical Association for the Promotion of Education, have seen truth come from the bottom up through a program that utilizes lectio divina in their missionary work in Haiti. Although this program has been going on

People whom the world might consider to be "nothing" when it comes to being sources of truth may be those through whom God chooses to reveal some of the deepest and most relevant truths of scripture.

for awhile, you'll see why it is now even more crucial, as Haitians work to rebuild their country after the devastating earthquake in January 2010. The program, developed by Kent Annan, a staff member of Haiti Partners, one of our core ministries, makes lectio divina an integral part of the education processes among the Haitian people they work with in churches and communities throughout the country.[6] Kent works with a Haitian team to arrange for small groups to gather together and reflect on scripture read aloud. It sounds simple, but it's powerful. One of the places this happens is in literacy centers, where people are eager to use their new reading skills. Often the first book the newly literate want to read is the Bible.

Kent invites someone to read a few verses of scripture in the Creole language out loud. Then the group members are instructed to close their eyes and bow their heads, and in silence wait for the Spirit of God to speak to them. As the moments pass, the stillness often becomes electrified with the presence of the Holy Spirit. On more occasions than can be cited, something of God moves among the participants. Those present become aware of the biblical truth that wherever two or three are gathered together in God's name, God is there in the midst of them.

After a period of silence, the participants are invited to lift their heads, open their eyes, and one by one explain what the Spirit told them about what those verses mean for their lives. From peasants with no formal education, wonderful truths are often articulated. Messages that are relevant to the participants are heard. Blessings of God fall upon everyone, and they know that God has been with them. It is a simple process in which many profound things can take place: some develop their new reading skills; children and adults become more confident speaking in a group; church leaders experience the value of mutual learning in a community of faith; church gardens and community development projects, as well as new collaborations among different denominations, have been started out of the bond formed in these groups; and most important, at the root of it all, people learn in silence how to listen to what the Spirit would teach them from the scripture that they have just read.

What is most wonderful in the practice of lectio divina is that you can go back to the same passage of scripture time and time again and it will always be fresh. What is more, the Holy Spirit might teach you new things about the same passage of scripture. The Bible becomes a vehicle through which God speaks to the particular situation in which those who practice lectio divina find themselves. The best kind of teaching and preaching often comes out of practicing lectio divina. Here in the United States, professional Bible scholars have been increasingly making it a practice to meet regularly with deeply committed Christian laypersons with the express purpose of learning what these ordinary people have learned from scripture. Also, there are some preachers who, before delivering their sermons on Sunday, will meet with members of their congregation in order to glean from them perspectives on the messages that they are preparing.

We believe, from our own observations and from what we read in scripture, that Christian communicators can have access, through the inspiration of the Holy Spirit, to deep insights that will aid them in connecting with others. The Holy Spirit, who Jesus promised would lead us into truth (John 16:13), blows unpredictably on persons irrespective of educational status or intellectual capability. In short, because the Holy Spirit is a teacher, Christian communicators have a unique source for the logos of their messages.

THE ROLE OF APOLOGETICS IN LOGOS Providing rational arguments that intellectually legitimate Christian doctrine is something that can help Christians who want to connect with those whom Friedrich Schleiermacher, the nineteenth-century theological apologist, called Christianity's "cultured despisers."[7] There are, however, those who say that people cannot be argued into the Kingdom of God, and that apologetics is a waste of time and energy. There might be some truth in that assertion, but I believe that if the Holy Spirit has prepared a person to hear and accept the Gospel, an apologetic presentation of Christian doctrine can be quite effective. At the same time, any intellectual presentation of Christian truth without the Holy Spirit's creating spiritual connections with those being addressed will fail to win converts. As has been accomplished by the likes of Ravi Zacharias through his book *Can Man Live Without God?* and Josh McDowell through his book *Evidence That Demands a Verdict,* when the Holy Spirit is at work in and through an apologetic presentation of the Gospel, many can be led to accept Christ. When rational argument, bolstered by scientific evidence, is mobilized to make a case for the validity of the Gospel, and the Holy Spirit is operative, connections can be made that result in transformed lives. *A Case for Christianity,* written by the famous literary genius C. S. Lewis, is an apologetic that many claim led them into the Christian faith.

Rational arguments can help those who have intellectual qualms regarding the truths of scripture to become more open to messages of the Gospel. In this sense, they can be very much a part of what has been called "pre-evangelism." It is the work of the Holy Spirit to convert persons to Christ, but there is little questioning of the fact that good apologetics can lead some people to be more open to the work of the Holy Spirit in their lives.

There is a second purpose for apologetics that deserves consideration by those of us who try to justify the use of rational and scientific arguments as part of logos. That second purpose is that such arguments can bolster the faith of those who already believe the Gospel.

Recently, Francis Collins, the scientist who led the team that decoded the genome, wrote a book titled *The Language of God.* That book, given the prestige of the author and the soundness of his arguments, has provided great encouragement to students of biology who have too often been ridiculed by antitheists as being naïve believers who hold to their convictions in spite of scientific evidence to the contrary. Collins, while not overwhelming the ideologies of agnostics and atheists, certainly demonstrated that there is solid scientific ground on which Christians could stand in making their case. Collins's apologetics have increased the boldness of many Christians who had been seriously challenged by aggressive atheists such as Richard Dawkins, who makes the case against God in his book *The God Delusion.*

The Templeton Foundation, established by Sir John Templeton, the billionaire Christian philanthropist, has published a massive array of books with apologetic themes. Many of these books show that the discoveries of cosmologists since Albert Einstein often harmonize with biblical descriptions of creation and, at the very least, make theism a respectable intellectual option. These books, produced by some of the most reputable scientists of our day, demonstrate that although theism cannot be proven, science certainly makes room for believers within the context of the contemporary marketplace of ideas and scientific findings. Like all good apologetics, although not necessarily proving the existence of God and the validity of the Gospel, the Templeton publications certainly make it easier for those enmeshed in a scientific worldview to maintain their convictions and to ward off the attacks of Christianity's opponents.

These are just a few examples of how apologetics can be used to make believers more secure in their faith. In short, rational and scientific knowledge can add much to the logos of those who preach and teach the truths of scripture.

Understanding the role that logos, as well as ethos and pathos, plays in effective speaking is foundational for our teaching and preaching. The foundation will crack and crumble, however, if we don't recognize that it is the Holy Spirit who infuses those elements with power from "on high." It is our job, then, to build on that foundation by incorporating certain skills into our teaching and preaching, which is the subject of the next two chapters. As you will see, it is the work of the Holy Spirit, combined with effective speaking skills, that can empower us to speak with authority as Jesus did. Without that dynamic combination, you and I cannot connect with people the way God wants us to.

11

Planning Your Message

Crafting the Shape of Your Talk

Then I said, "Ah, Lord God! Truly I do not know how
to speak, for I am only a boy." But the Lord said to me,
"Do not say, 'I am only a boy'; for you shall go to all to whom
I send you, and you shall speak whatever I command you. Do
not be afraid of them, for I am with you to deliver you,
says the Lord."
—Jeremiah 1:6

TEACHING AND PREACHING are art forms. Like all art forms, they can appear effortless when being executed, but behind that execution are careful planning, prayer, and practice (as well as possibly dealing with fear, as Mary addressed in Chapter Four). Over the years, I have found that preaching and teaching require much more than the application of important knowledge and skills learned in theology, public speaking, or preaching courses. As I hope was apparent in the previous chapter, preaching and teaching require that we be connected to God in prayer so that we can attempt to connect like Jesus in all of our speaking.

Throughout this chapter, I will try to convey how I attempt to "know" my audiences when I speak so that I am not only delivering a message but connecting with them. In addition, I will share several mechanics of planning and delivering a message, based on what I have observed and experienced in my own speaking.

The Importance of Rest

This may seem like a strange place to start, but if you want to connect like Jesus in your speaking, rest is essential. Rest may not *seem* very spiritual, but it is a very important part of preaching and teaching. You can assume that Jesus rested: he obeyed God's commands, and the idea of Sabbath, one of the Ten Commandments, is about taking time to rest. To lack the physical energy that a good message requires is to speak in such a way as to cheat your listeners of the best that you have to offer. There is an interactive relationship between the body and your spiritual condition. When the body is weak, so is the soul. The most prominent Pentecostal preacher in New Zealand told me that his ability to exercise his spiritual gifts of healing are diminished greatly when he is tired. He went on to say that this was also true of his preaching. Physical exhaustion, he claimed, "quenches" the Holy Spirit. Rest is always an important consideration if you want to speak to the best of your ability.

> *Rest may not seem very spiritual, but it is a very important part of preaching and teaching.*

Along with being rested, thinking about our audience is another crucial consideration for our teaching and preaching.

Knowing and Loving Our Audience

The story is told of a man who was asked to speak at a civic club but was not given a specific topic. After some thought, he decided to show slides from his recent travels. That idea would have been acceptable for many clubs, but not this one. It was not until he arrived to speak that he discovered that his audience was blind.

This man obviously failed to conduct good audience analysis. He apparently did not ask any questions in advance about his audience so that he could tailor what he would talk about during his time with them. Instead he made assumptions. Admittedly, he was also more than a little unlucky. In most cases this man's presentation would have been safe. But why chance it? Every public speaking textbook will tell you that audience analysis is essential for any public presentation. It is even more essential if you are to connect in your teaching and preaching of the Gospel.

Jesus was a master at understanding who he was encountering, and then choosing a specifically relevant way to communicate with his audience. Jesus related differently to different people, meeting them where they were, no matter who they were. He would speak pastorally to people living in poverty and oppression and prophetically to the religious leaders of the day. There have been some, such as Karl Barth, who say that such relevancy is not necessary. Barth said, "Pastors must aim their guns beyond the hills of relevance."[1] In terms of preaching, Barth taught that relevance was the work of the Holy Spirit and that a preacher should be confined to making his or her sermons nothing more or less than expounding scripture. I disagree.

> *Jesus related differently to different people, meeting them where they were, no matter who they were.*

Most examples of how the teachers and preachers described in the New Testament endeavored to connect with their listeners will reveal that they brilliantly, though at times subtly, did what great speakers do: establish common ground with their audiences. For instance, the way in which the Apostle Paul spoke to a Jewish audience was different from the way he spoke to a Greek audience. When talking to Jews, Paul connected with his audience by explaining how Jesus was the fulfillment of all that the Hebrew prophets had predicted about the Messiah. When he taught the Jews, he spoke in Hebrew—their own language—and when he did so they quieted down and listened (Acts 13 and 22). But when talking to the Greek intellectuals on Mars Hill, he spoke in Greek and connected Jesus to the teachings of Greek philosophers and poets with whom his audience would be familiar (Acts 17). In another setting, when Paul was making his case before King Agrippa, he talked like a lawyer, using argument and reason (Acts 26:2–29).

A careful reading of the synoptic Gospels will provide ample evidence that the three writers of these books adapted what they said to their different audiences. Consider the slightly different ways that each of them described the instructions that Jesus gave his disciples concerning money. Mark, addressing an audience of a lower socioeconomic level, has Jesus telling them, as recorded in the original Greek language, to take no *copper* coins with them, copper being the common medium of exchange employed by those who were poor. Luke, telling the same story but writing to a different audience, has Jesus telling his disciples to take no *silver* coins. Matthew's audience was somewhat mixed and was likely to have included people who were rich. It is not surprising, then, that he has Jesus telling the disciples (again, as stated in the original Greek) to take no copper, silver, or *gold*.

To the casual reader of the Gospels, these differences might seem inconsequential, but to experts in rhetoric, they are evidence that these apostles knew what coinage their readers would consider relevant to their lives.

Getting to Know Your Listeners

When you are asked to speak, if your goal is to connect with your audience the way that Jesus and his disciples connected with theirs, the following questions will help you tailor your message to that goal. The first you must ask is *What is the purpose of this specific speaking situation?* The answer to this question should determine how you communicate your message. Does the situation call for you mainly to teach? preach? be pastoral? prophetic? In other words, are you to instruct, comfort, or challenge, or do you need to communicate in a way that combines all of these? If you are regularly speaking to a certain group, and think you know what your purpose is, it still might be wise to reflect on whether or not that purpose may need revisiting. If you are invited somewhere to speak, it would be wise to ask those who invited you what they want or are expecting. Then I suggest you take some time in prayer and ask the Holy Spirit to reveal to you the direction God wants you to go with what you say. Sit in silence and "wait upon the Lord" to see if God reveals anything to you. If something comes to you, start putting your message together, continuing in prayer throughout the process (the next chapter includes specific ideas for the planning process).

After you determine the specific purpose of your message, you are ready for several other important questions:

○ How many might be in your anticipated audience—a small group, several, hundreds, or even perhaps thousands?

○ Where are you meeting? Having a feel for the setting of he event, whether it's in a large auditorium or in a smaller, more intimate room, will affect how you speak and whether or not you need a microphone.

○ What time of day will it be? How will that fit in with your energy level and the energy level of your audience? If you are to speak in the early morning, after lunch, or in the late evening, you and your audience may be tired, so you ought to anticipate that.

○ Will your audience be doing an activity before you are to speak? This may tire them. Will they be listening to someone else before you? If so, what will that person be talking about?

○ Do you know your audience well, somewhat, or not at all?

   ○ Are they young, old, male, female?

   ○ What ethnicity are they?

   ○ What is their educational level?

   ○ What is their social class?

   ○ Will they be disposed to being favorable, unfavorable, or neutral to you or your purpose in speaking?

   ○ What kinds of response(s) might you anticipate?

If you don't know the answers to some of these questions, then you could ask the organizers of the event or anyone you know who might be in the audience. What is assumed in conducting any good audience analysis is that you will take your carefully researched responses to the questions that are relevant to your audience and then figure out the best ways to design your talk given that information.

Knowing Beyond the Questions

As important as good audience analysis questions are, they are not enough to really *know* your audience if you answer those questions without a sense of the spiritual condition of your listeners. "To know" in the biblical sense means to enter intimately into the minds and hearts of people in a way that goes beyond demographics. To know our listeners requires a spiritual awareness that they are more than the sum of the parts of what even the best audience analysis can provide. Again, I offer Jesus as our model. Jesus knew his audiences in the deepest sense of the word. That's because when he interacted with others, he looked not only at outward appearances but also at people's hearts (1 Samuel 16:7). Jesus saw others both with his natural eyes and with his spiritual eyes. Jesus' spiritual awareness led him to see past surface matters to issues of the soul. Jesus, as the scriptures say, "knew what was in men" (John 2:25). Undoubtedly that is what made him the ultimate communicator. As a speaker, you should try to imitate Jesus as much as possible and try to know what is "in" your audience, whether that audience is one person or a thousand persons. What are they feeling? What are they thinking? What issues are looming high in their consciousness? Most important, you should try to imitate Jesus in how he loved his audience.

Loving Your Listeners

The best way to deeply connect with your audiences is to love them. Jesus loved his audiences and was "moved with compassion" for them (Matthew 9:36, 14:14, KJV). You too are to love your audiences and be moved with compassion toward them. In this sense, crucial questions to ask before speaking are, "Do I feel love for the people to whom I am going to talk? Do I really care about them? Does my heart go out to them?" I cannot tell you how important it is to love your listeners; people will feel your care and concern—or not, depending on how you answer these questions. They will instinctively feel how you feel about them. They will feel the emotion flowing from you to them. This is all the more essential in our postmodern world where truth is often understood to transcend what is rational. Love goes beyond reason, yet it is love for your listeners that makes any reasonable presentation of the Gospel effective.

Love goes beyond reason, yet it is love for your listeners that makes any reasonable presentation of the Gospel effective.

Remember that the Apostle Paul said we can speak "with the tongues of men and of angels," but if you do not have love, either for the individual or the audience to which you are speaking, your words do not amount to anything (1 Corinthians 13:1). Love is a prerequisite for effective speaking. In your preparation for speaking, I urge you to pray to be imbued with the Spirit of love. Love is one of the "fruits of the Spirit" (Galatians 5:22), and whoever loves is born of God and communicates the love of God (1 John 4:7).

Being empowered to connect with people in love takes the kind of empathic understanding referred to in Chapter Five. There is no way to overemphasize how essential empathy is for connecting with your listeners. In order to have empathy, you could learn much from the sociologist George Herbert Mead, who would say that for effective communication to occur, it is necessary for the speaker to take the role of "the significant other."[2] This means that, just as Jesus did, you should try to put yourself in the place of the person or persons to whom you are speaking, feel what they are feeling and think what they are thinking, and become aware of how they are taking what is being said.

It is God who prepares both the audience and you for what needs to be said and heard. And it is God's Spirit that can enable you to "feel your way" into people's hearts and minds and souls. A way to do this is to ask the Holy Spirit to enable you to imagine yourself as a typical member of the congregation, and then try to reflect on what needs to change in the life of such a person as a result of what he or she hears. Pray that God will help you connect with that person so that you can gain some understanding as to what is going on in his or her heart and mind. Ask God to help you relate what you have to say to the struggles and concerns in that person's life. In an effective talk, you will have "felt" your way into the listener's soul.

The Holy Spirit must also prepare the listener if your message is to have convincing and convicting effectiveness. You should pray that the listener is made ready to hear what you have to say. When what is preached relates to what the Spirit of God has prepared a listener to hear, the message gains something that far transcends anything that eloquence alone could possibly generate. Given that reality, you can understand how crucial it is that in your prayer time before you speak, you ask God to connect your thoughts to the thoughts and concerns already stirring within the souls of the listeners, and ask that the Spirit will give you just the right words to say.

Seeing Who God Wants Us to See

You can think you know and even love your audience when you have prayed and have asked and answered all the "right" questions, but make sure you don't forget this final question: Are you looking at those in your audience whom the Holy Spirit yearns for you to see? When Jesus looked at a crowd, he didn't merely *see* those whom others might consider the undesirables of society and look past: he focused in on them. One day in particular, when a large crowd followed Jesus, he went up a mountainside and sat down to teach them. The first ones he addressed were outcasts whom so many chose (and still choose today) not to see. Jesus not only saw them but knew the deep needs of their souls and spoke to them with revolutionary words of blessing (see the Beatitudes in Matthew 5:1–12). We also need to see beyond

If you do not currently speak to the kinds of audiences to whom Jesus often spoke, then you may need to consider "enlarging your territory" in ways that expand your audiences.

those whom we may be accustomed to seeing, to those Jesus wants us to see. If you do not currently speak to the kinds of audiences to whom Jesus often spoke, then you may need to consider "enlarging your territory" in ways that expand your audiences.

Getting Good Material

Once you feel that you have a handle on who your audience is and you have prayed for them, it's time to prepare your message. Although preparing specifically for individual talks is essential when your goal is to connect, overall preparation for teaching and preaching starts long before you ever sit down to think through a specific talk. A good speaker is always collecting possible topics and supporting materials. Ideas, stories, quotes, testimonials, statistics, and research are often right in front of us. We just need to stop, look, and listen. Mary recently told me that she finds new illustrations whenever she asks her brother and sister-in-law about the vineyard they recently planted. The ins and outs of growing grapes can easily be related to our spiritual lives. For instance, she learned that although you can't see Lake Michigan from their vineyard, it is this "Great Unseen Lake" that moderates the climate and allows grapes to grow to their full potential. Now that will preach!

When you use someone else's illustration, don't forget to cite the source. I never mind it when someone tells me that his or her minister quoted me and told one of my stories in a sermon. To be frank, I'm flattered. And if you have ever heard me speak, you know I don't hesitate to use and credit someone else's story in my speaking.

Fred Craddock is a well-known preacher and seminary professor, and I have often used his sermon illustrations. I always make sure that I acknowledge him as the source of those illustrations. One of his best made-up stories I like to use, as best as I can recall it, is one in which he tells about an uncle who made it his mission to rescue greyhound racing dogs from racetracks after their racing days were over. Explaining that these retired dogs make great pets and are particularly good with children, Fred goes on to tell about one day visiting this uncle of his:

> There were a couple of kids playing with this big greyhound dog right in the middle of the living room floor. That dog and those kids were romping and rolling around with each other and having a great old time. I asked, "Dog! Why aren't you racing anymore? Did you stop winning?"

"Nope!" said the dog. "I was still winning. That's not why I'm not racing anymore."

"Well, maybe you just got tired of racing, and that's why you're not racing anymore," I said.

"That's not it at all!" answered the dog.

"Then tell me, why did you stop racing?"

"Well," answered that greyhound dog, "One day I realized that that rabbit I was chasing just wasn't real."

That fictitious story is a perfect takeoff point or illustration for a talk to college or university students, who can easily make decisions about life that have them chasing after that which is meaningless and disappointing. That "rabbit" they may be thinking about chasing may not be real.

In addition to using other speakers' stories, I will often pick up from the media stories that are potential illustrations. One morning in a motel room in suburban St. Louis, I happened to turn the TV on for the morning news. The anchorman's tone of voice immediately caught my attention. With an air of grave seriousness, he announced that something he considered disturbing, sad, and infuriating had occurred in one of the city's parks during the early morning hours. I can remember his opening words because they were so startling: "Someone has stolen Jesus," he declared.

It was Christmastime and, evidently, someone had stolen the plastic baby Jesus from the manger scene set up by the local Rotary Club on the lawn of the city hall. According to the TV anchorman, sometime around three in the morning someone had taken the plastic Jesus and run off with it. The anchorman then made a plea that went something like this: "If anyone has any information as to the whereabouts of the stolen Jesus, please call this station as soon as possible. We very much want to recover the Baby Jesus during this Christmas season and return him to where he belongs. There's a reward for anyone who can help us in this search."

I wondered whether or not the anchorman was saying all this with his tongue in cheek or if he was as dead serious as he appeared to be. Regardless, I rushed to get a pen and wrote in my notebook what he had said to the best of my memory. What I had just heard would make a great introduction for a variety of talks. My mind soared as I thought of just how that story could be used to decry the ways in which those with commercial interests had stolen Jesus and transformed him into an icon for marketing.

Another train of thinking I had was that there are some who have stolen the Jesus as revealed in scripture and put in his place another Jesus who is nothing more than the incarnation of their own traits and values. Being uncomfortable with the hard sayings of Jesus as set forth in the Sermon on the Mount (Matthew 5–7), they have removed him and put in his place a watered-down version of Jesus that did not make the kind of demands that would disrupt their comfortable, American, middle-class lifestyles.

For still another way of using this story, I considered how often the Jesus who transcends partisan politics has been stolen for political purposes and replaced by another Jesus who is either a Democrat or a Republican, depending on whether it is the religious right or the religious left that wants to use Jesus to endorse their policies.

It has been said that God created us in God's image and that we have returned the favor. All too often the Jesus who is taught and preached is recast in the image of whoever is telling the story. The news report that morning provided me with a story to start a variety of different talks that could take aim at each of these idolatries.

When choosing to use resources from other preachers and great thinkers, I take time to reflect on different meanings of the material and then decide if and how I might want to use it.

You would do well to write up good stories and other supporting material on index cards or make computer files so that you can access them when creating a talk. I have hundreds of such index cards and regularly go through them so that they are fresh in my mind and available for easy recall.

Preaching the Good News

There has to be good news in every message. *Gospel* means "good news." As you prepare to speak, think carefully as to how you will give people the good news they long to hear. To this end, in every talk there should be some kind of declaration of what God is doing and can do in the personal lives of those who surrender themselves to Christ and also the good news of what God is doing in the world. Every time I speak, I do my best to incorporate this good news into the message. I say to the

There has to be good news in every message.

Lord when the talk is finished, "I could have been more eloquent, and I could have been more profound; but Lord, I did the best I could to hold up the

Gospel of Jesus Christ and let people know who you are and what you can do in and through them."

Choosing and Using Scripture

When preparing a talk, you have to ask the obvious question as to what biblical text you are going to employ and how you will interpret that text. The Bible can speak to just about every subject imaginable, and the effective use of scripture is dependent on having a passage from the Bible that speaks to the topic you have chosen to address. There are certain advantages to those who belong to churches that conduct worship services according to the liturgical year. In such cases, the scripture to be preached is prescribed. The advantage of this approach is obvious in that it keeps speakers from being "Johnny One-note" teachers and preachers. It is all too easy for a speaker to become preoccupied with one particular theme and ride on the same message over and over again, week after week. It is easy to become riveted on one subject to the neglect of others. Those who have to preach according to the requisites of the liturgical year are usually delivered from that temptation.

PREPARATION THROUGH EXEGETICAL RESEARCH In anticipation of expounding on a particular biblical text in a particular message, it is vital that you conduct scholarly research so as to prepare properly. You need to learn, through careful study, the makeup of the first-century audience for whom the message was originally intended. Your having a grasp of the social, economic, and political setting of the passage can give you great insight into what the writer of the scripture had in mind for that particular audience. Also, when you can, try to get at the meanings and implications of the words used in the designated text as given in the original biblical languages. All of this can help you relate what the passage might have meant for the audience back then to your present-day audience.

PREPARATION THROUGH REFLECTING ON SCRIPTURE Matching the best scriptural passage to the topic you have chosen requires not only extensive knowledge of scripture but reflection on scripture as well. For example, while I was developing a sermon on love, what came to my mind was a passage that might not relate to love when first read. The passage is John 14:12: "Very truly, I tell you, the one who believes in me will also do the works that I do and, in fact, will do greater works than these, because I am going to the Father."

When I first read that verse, I thought that it was a promise from Jesus that his followers would be performing the same kind of miracles that he had performed—and then would do even "greater works." But as I reflected on the verse, I realized that this could not be what Jesus was telling his disciples. Matching what Jesus did—walking on water, raising the dead, turning water into wine—is not thinkable, even for the most faith-filled persons. Then it occurred to me—I believe it was the Holy Spirit teaching me—that Jesus wasn't talking about doing miracles; he was talking about *loving*. This is especially clear when we read this verse in context. (See what comes before this verse in John 13:34–35.) Let me explain.

When the eternal Christ was incarnated in the body of Jesus, he was limited to connecting in an intensive "I-Thou" intimate loving relationship—face-to-face—with just one person at a time. However, if that same Christ that was in Jesus is incarnated in each one of us—in other words, if *each* of us becomes the body of Christ through the Holy Spirit dwelling in each of us, then Christ could connect in love with a host of persons throughout the world, *because* there are so many of us. That, I came to believe, is why he could say that we would be able to do even greater works than he did.

It is not only academic knowledge of what John 14:12 says that is important in this use of scripture, but also what can come through teachings from the Holy Spirit (John 14:26). Here, once again, is where lectio divina becomes essential. Lectio divina allows the Holy Spirit to teach you things that you need to learn at the particular place and time you find yourself (John 16:12–13). It is a crucial spiritual practice when preparing a talk in which you use scripture.

When I engage in lectio divina, I choose a few verses of scripture, read them slowly, and then close my eyes and wait for at least ten minutes for the Holy Spirit to bring to mind divinely inspired insights that address the topic I've chosen. But don't be upset if no special insights come from this kind of spiritual meditating. Sometimes the meaning of a text is obvious. Or it may not be the right time for further insight. If no insight comes, I encourage you to do lectio divina on the passage again later; in the meantime you could continue to reflect on the verse as you go throughout your day and see if the Holy Spirit reveals anything to you. Staying open to hearing from the Spirit is an important aspect of developing a habit of soaking in God's Word.

The practice of lectio divina does not in any way preclude a scholarly approach to understanding the passage of scripture that you plan to use for your talk. Knowing what great biblical scholars have had to say about the verses you plan to use is extremely important, lest your imagination carry you into interpretations that run contrary to what is the consensus of Christian saints down through the ages. Whenever I have what I believe are divinely inspired interpretations of scripture, I check what I have received to see if it is of God (1 John 4:1). If there is a contradiction in what I think the Spirit taught me from the chosen verses and what the saints of the church and scholars I trust say about the same passage of scripture, a red flag goes up in my mind. When that happens, I talk it over with other mature Christians and get their reading of my interpretation. In checking commentaries by noted scholars (such as Anders Nygren's *Commentary on Romans* or Williams Temple's *Reading in St. John's Gospel*), I have not only gained many further insights that have added much to my messages but sometimes I discover ways I might have misinterpreted a given scriptural text. Also, I find that when respected authorities have the same interpretations of the passage that I was planning to talk about, citing them in my talk often gives more credibility to any unusual insights I've discovered through lectio divina.

Studying and Reflecting on Ideas from Great Thinkers

When it comes to topics and ideas for your talks, it is important to read the writings of the great thinkers. I suggest going to notable Bible scholars and theologians, especially those who have defined the thinking of Christians in our contemporary society. However, do not avoid reading those secular philosophers and social scientists whose ideas and writings have challenged much of what traditional Christianity has held to over the centuries. In my experience, the critics of our faith, and even those who have been outright enemies of the church, have had many insights and perspectives that we Christians must take seriously. I often find that our enemies have scrutinized our beliefs and critiqued our thinking in ways that are seldom evident in what our friends and colleagues have to offer.

Friedrich Nietzsche, one of Christianity's most severe opponents, has provided more insights into the pressing religious issues relevant to our present situation than most of the theological and biblical scholars who support my views. For instance, Nietzsche's insights into human nature—apart from the transforming effects of the Holy Spirit—are more profound than any contemporary Christian philosopher or theologian whom I have read. Nietzsche declared that the primary drive governing human behavior is "the will to power." As I reflected on this assertion by Nietzsche, what first came to mind was the biblical story of the fall of humankind. What motivated Adam in his rebellion against God was *his* will to power. Adam wanted the power that was the exclusive prerogative of God.

What I recognized next was that resorting to power, even to do good, is extremely tempting, but can have dire consequences. When Jesus was tempted by Satan in the wilderness, the three temptations were attempts to get Jesus to give in to the powers that the world respects. Turning the stones into bread was the temptation to win the world through the use of economic power. Leaping from the highest pinnacle of the temple and floating gently to the ground was the temptation to gain a following through miracles that could earn him religious power. And finally, Satan offered Jesus political power by offering him dominion over all the kingdoms of the world. Needless to say, to each of these temptations, Jesus said, "No!" Jesus came into the world to save the world through sacrificial love. Rather than coercing us into accepting him as our Lord, he chose to draw us to himself through the cross (John 12:31–32).

Power and sacrificial love are difficult, if not impossible, to express at the same time. In any relationship, whoever is expressing the most worldly power is expressing the least love. Nietzsche saw this. Love requires giving up power and becoming vulnerable. What he said about power made clear to me what Paul stated in Philippians 2, where he declared that in Jesus, God "emptied" God's self of power and took the form of a slave (*dulos*, the Greek word for "slave," is incorrectly translated in some versions of the Bible as "servant"). After reading Nietzsche, there was no doubt in my mind that only by giving up power could Jesus fully express his love for us. This is just one of a host of examples that I could give to illustrate how a non-Christian philosopher can provide profound insights for the preacher.

Paul Tillich, one of the most famous theologians of the twentieth century, talked about what he called "the theological circle." In describing this concept, Tillich proposed that in any age it is the philosophers who pose the questions that the theologians are called upon to answer.[3] If we take Tillich seriously, we must read the secular philosophers if we are to grapple with the most profound questions of our present age.

Tillich, however, did not give enough consideration to the reality that philosophy in the twentieth century had shifted away from the kind of profound existential questions that trouble people today. Theories that dominate contemporary philosophy do not address such concerns as the meaning of our lives, the essence of our humanity, and our ultimate destiny. In reality, social scientists are now the ones who provide us with the questions that we are required to answer in our contemporary setting, and they are the ones who raise the concerns that now trouble us. The questions that preachers must address about abortion, sexual identity, euthanasia, stem-cell research, and the variety of political and economic issues that dominate the news are questions posed by social scientists. Consequently, reading up-to-date literature in the social sciences is essential if you are going to be able to connect with your listeners' most pressing social concerns. Books such as Christopher Lasch's *The Culture of Narcissism*, Robert Bellah's *City on the Hill*, and Thomas L. Friedman's *The World Is Flat* will provide gold mines for preaching prospectors who want intriguing and essential insights into the motivations of the typical American churchgoer. Samuel Hunnington's *The Clash of Civilizations* is must reading for anyone who wants to understand the geopolitical threats generated in the struggles between Islam and Christianity; and Ernest Becker's *Denial of Death* will provide you with some of the most profound psychological insights into the fears and anxieties that eat away at the psyches of those who are in our audiences.

Whenever young students ask me what college major they should choose for the best preparation for the preaching ministry, I tell them to major in sociology (as I am a sociologist, this shouldn't surprise you). In my opinion, sociology is a discipline that encompasses insights from all the other social sciences. Those who major in sociology will learn just enough about other academic disciplines to know how to use them as source materials to ensure that their talks are meaningful to those who are struggling to make sense of their lives in this confusing modern world.

An ongoing commitment to study great thinkers and reflect on their writing can greatly enhance the way our preaching and teaching connects with our listeners. We must store knowledge in our memories; preparation cannot be a cram job. In most cases, great messages are creations that come from ongoing study and reflection.

> *Great messages are creations that come from ongoing study and reflection.*

When Your Topic Is Chosen for You

Sometimes you may not be free to choose your own topic; for example, you might be asked to speak at a conference for which the planning committee has established a theme and is expecting you to have a message that fits specifically with their theme. This is another time when yielding to the Holy Spirit in preparation will prove to be crucial. Sit alone in stillness and ask the Spirit to direct your thinking so that what comes to mind to speak about is what the Spirit wants the audience to hear. You will often discover that what comes to you from the Spirit fits very well within the parameters of the conference's theme. I have never had the Spirit fail me in such circumstances. Sometimes as I "wait upon the Lord" over an extended period of time—usually I give this kind of meditation at least half an hour—I not only get a sense of what I should say but also often feel directed as to what scripture to use and which illustrations to employ. When I am aware of the presence of the Holy Spirit encompassing me and saturating my personhood, it becomes abundantly clear what Jesus was talking about when he said that at such times he would put words in our mouths (Mark 13:11).

When I am spiritually enlivened, it is not unusual for the Holy Spirit to bring to my mind words that are especially relevant to the congregation *even while I am in the act of delivering the sermon.* When I am in such a "zone" spiritually, and feel that the Spirit is in control, I sense that I have gone beyond my own thinking and preparation and have yielded to a transcendent messenger. I never know when this "special anointing"—a name given to such experiences in African American churches—is going to happen. Nobody can control the Holy Spirit. Jesus said the Spirit blows where it "chooses. We do not know where it comes from or where it goes" (John 3:8). Somehow, in ways that are impossible for me to understand, results that come from such special times of anointing usually prove harmonious with the theme or topic that had been prescribed for that particular message.

Narrowing Your Topic

You can't explain everything about the Gospel in one presentation. Indeed, Jesus never told the whole story of the Kingdom of God at once. He always spoke only what people were ready to hear, and he sometimes announced that there were deeper things and more complex things that he wanted to tell them, but that they were not ready to hear them at that given time (John 16:12). Following Jesus' example in preparing what you are going to say, you need some spiritual discernment not only as to what your listeners are ready to hear but also as to how much to cover in one talk so that people don't get overwhelmed with too many points. Mary told me that one time after she spoke in chapel at Spring Arbor

University, a religion professor came up to her and said, "Wow, you had about four sermons in that talk." Mary took that as a compliment of the depth of her material until she realized that what he was really saying was that she had way too much material for one twenty-five-minute talk.

Discerning the appropriate depth and breadth of what you have to say requires that you spend time in prayer, asking the Holy Spirit to help you say what God wants you to say for your particular audience and for the time allowed. There is a kind of "sixth sense" that you can develop over time and through an ever-deepening relationship with Christ that enables you to know even *in the midst of speaking* just how far you can or should take the listeners in a given message. It comes from developing the habit of empathizing with audiences so that you know when you've reached a good stopping point. One time when I asked my wife, Peggy, to tell me how she thought my sermon went, she said, "You went on far too long after you were finished."

Organizing Your Talk

A listener should be able to easily discern in a message an intentionally defined structure that outlines the major points and that flows effortlessly as it is delivered. A good talk is clearly "going someplace." Essential to a message is the clear definition of both the beginning and ending. If a talk doesn't begin well, you may lose your audience right off the bat. You can still get them back, but it will most likely take great effort and exceptional material.

Ways to start strong include a good opening story, question, or quote that relates specifically to where you are going with your message. Concerning the ending, I believe that if you don't end with a call to some change in attitude or behavior, none of your prior words matter much anyway. Listeners may gain some interesting insights into the scriptures or learn some good theological lessons, but unless your message encourages your listeners to make some kind of change, I contend that it has fallen short. Because I believe that how a talk is ended is the most important part of the message, I will devote much space to that topic in the next chapter. Between the beginning and the end, there must of course be a carefully worked out progression of thought.

> *Unless your message encourages your listeners to make some kind of change, I contend that it has fallen short.*

When I was a seminary student, the professor who taught me homiletics made the claim that it is best for a sermon to have three points. He
said that having three points not only gives symmetry to a sermon but
is easiest for listeners to remember. I know of no empirical research to
support these assertions, but his advice has served me well. Consequently,
I try to develop my message with three points.

You may also want to use a common oratorical device I've heard
preachers use throughout my life—alliteration—which means having the
main points of a message start with the same letter. For instance, one
sermon I remember hearing had as its three points

1. Finding the truth

2. Feasting on the truth

3. Fulfilling the truth

I remembered this sermon because of the alliteration, and that's why
I try to use alliteration whenever possible. If I find that I'm stretching
it—meaning that I can only come up with words that are too corny or
that don't fit my meaning just right—then I don't use alliteration: I don't
want to undermine my message. If you aren't sure if your alliteration
will work well with your audience, try asking a few people ahead of time
how it sounds to them—just make sure they fit the profile of your audience members, because what works for one audience may not work for
another.

One more thing: if you find you are spending more time trying to come
up with clever alliteration than you are developing your actual points, I
suggest giving up the idea of using alliteration for that talk.

Of course there's more to a good outline and a memorable message
than three points and good alliteration. For example, the scripture you
use in and of itself can suggest an outline for your message. Once when
preparing a sermon for the funeral of an outstanding Christian, who had
also been a personal friend, I used a description of Barnabas as given in
Acts 11:24. The phrases in this verse seemed to jump out at me, suggesting the following points:

1. He was a good man.

2. He was full of the Holy Spirit and faith.

3. Because of him, many were added to the Lord.

In designing another message that addressed the need for college students to make commitments and make sacrifices for the Kingdom of
God, what came to mind was the story of Jesus' encounter with the rich

young ruler (Mark 10:17–22). Then, while doing lectio divina, three parallel points came to me. The young man in this story

1. Came to the right person
2. Asked the right question
3. Made the wrong decision

When I gave my talk, I asked the students whether they would make the same mistake the rich young ruler had made, or whether they would make the sacrifices that accompany becoming a true disciple of Christ.

Along with your well-structured points, it is crucial to have enough good supporting material. Although statistics and other research can lend great credibility to your words, stories are what people are most likely to remember. Listeners may have a hard time recalling the various truths you tried to communicate unless they were given stories to hang them on. When preparing what I plan to say, I carefully outline the major points I want to convey, and I then work hard to come up with stories that can illustrate each of these points. As was mentioned in Chapter Nine, I also try to make sure I'm not overloading one point with too many stories while giving little story support to the other points. If you find you have a hard time coming up with stories, I encourage you to refer back to that chapter for ideas.

In summary, the old adage "Tell 'em what you're going to tell them; tell 'em; tell 'em what you told 'em" is still one of the best pieces of advice for organizing a talk.

Using Humor

Humor can often be used in presentations with great effectiveness, but the best use of humor is to relieve tension. If I have been especially forceful in bringing people under conviction and the intensity of the situation may be such that I sense that the listeners cannot handle any more confrontations with their failures or shortcomings, it may be necessary to interject something humorous to relieve the tension. I find that if I build people up with declarations and stories that generate emotional intensity, I need to relieve some of their tension with humor; then I can build up the tension again. Thus the presentation becomes a matter of crescendos followed by releases, building ultimately to a climax in which I ask for decisions to be made.

As a case in point, I have often preached on the failure of Christians to set aside time for being alone and silent with God. Jesus had strong words against those whose prayers are little more than a public display of piety. He taught his disciples that if they really want to encounter God in prayer, they should seclude themselves; in quietude and aloneness they would experience that blessing (Matthew 6:5–8). Following my pointing out what Jesus said, I ask those in the congregation when the last time was that any of them had done what Jesus told his disciples to do when they pray. "How many of you," I ask, "have waited in stillness for God's Spirit to flow into your personhood?" I usually can feel the congregation tense up as I cite the scripture where we are instructed to "wait patiently for the Lord." I go on to make the claim that what is often the case is that their prayers are seldom more than giving God a wish list of what they want from God, as though God were waiting to be informed as to what they need.

That kind of preaching makes people defensive, and I know that it's time for some relief through humor. So I say, "Your prayers are too often like that of my son's when he was just seven years old. He came into the living room one evening and said, 'I'm going to bed! I'm going to be praying! Anybody want anything?'" That little bit of humor breaks the tension and gets those in the congregation to let down their guards and become open to more of what I have to say.

Humor also comes in handy when dealing with the flaws and short-comings in our lives, as it is generally a better idea to make fun of those shortcomings than to declare harsh condemnation. For instance, in dealing with our failures to really commit to the transforming effects of full surrender of all that we are and *all* that we have to Christ, I jokingly recite (or sometimes sing) a modified form of a familiar hymn:

> One-tenth to Jesus I surrender,
> One-tenth to Him I freely give.
> I surrender—one-tenth!
> I surrender—one tenth!
> One-tenth to Jesus I surrender,
> I surrender one-tenth!

The congregation quickly gets the point that tithing is not enough. Then it is easy to follow that up by declaring the words of Dietrich Bonhoeffer, "When Jesus calls a man, He bids him come and die."[4] This might be followed up by another line that conveys truth in the context of jest. I say, "Too often when the invitation for total surrender to Christ's service is given, it becomes one of those invitations wherein you sing twenty verses of 'Just as I Am,' and you come down the aisle just as you are . . . and then go out just as you *were*."

I can count on laughs, but the point has been made, and the humor helps the audience accept the hard call of Christ.

Admittedly this is only my opinion, but I find telling jokes to get people's attention, or using humor that has no viable role to play in driving home an essential point in a talk a "turnoff," and perhaps in an objective evaluation, such humor cheapens both the message and the messenger.

In the end, teaching and preaching are serious business and require serious dedication. You should be saying to yourself, "Woe is me if I preach not the Gospel of Jesus Christ—prayerfully, carefully, and thoughtfully."

I hope the suggestions in these chapters help you do just that.

12

Presenting Your Message

Why It All Leads Up to the Finale

They were astounded at his teaching, for he taught them as one
having authority, and not as the scribes.
—Mark 1:22

WHEN I WAS IN SEMINARY, I took a course in homiletics. During that semester, each of the students was required to preach a sermon to the rest of the class. When it was my turn, I was ready! My points were clearly defined, and I thought I gave good expression to the meaning of the biblical text from which I had developed the sermon. I had given careful attention to the choosing of illustrations that would clarify what I was trying to say. Even my humor was timed as it should have been to relieve any distracting tension that might have built up in my listeners. In preaching that sermon, I thought I gave it my best.

Later, when I received a written evaluation from my professor, I was stunned by what he had written across the top of the report sheet. In bold, red letters under the grade were the words, "Tony. You can't convince people that you are wonderful and that Jesus is wonderful in the same sermon." I have never forgotten those words. Before I prepare a talk, I ask myself how Jesus can be lifted up through what I say.

Little more than a century ago, the British Isles were blessed with one of the best communicators of all time, the great Charles Spurgeon. So extensive was Spurgeon's fame that those who lived in and around London made hearing him preach a "must-do" event. Even Herbert Spencer, the prominent sociologist and somewhat infamous agnostic, took time one evening to go and hear Spurgeon preach at his famous Metropolitan Baptist Tabernacle. Following the sermon, Spencer's assistant asked him, "Well? What did you think of him?"

As though coming out of a hypnotic trance, Spencer responded, "About whom?"

"About the preacher—Charles Spurgeon," his assistant replied.

Still awed by the way in which Spurgeon had connected with him, Spencer answered, "Oh, Spurgeon! I haven't been thinking about him. I've been occupied thinking about Spurgeon's Jesus!"[1]

Oh, that all preachers could connect with their congregations like that, so that when the sermons end, people would say, "I can't tell you much about the preacher. I was too preoccupied with thinking about Jesus."

Then there is the story of a man who, after hearing one of the other great Christian orators of the day, was overheard saying to a friend, "What a preacher! What a preacher!" The following week, this same man, having heard Charles Spurgeon, was overheard to say, "What a Saviour! What a Saviour!"

> *It is not until I have spent time in prayer asking God to help me point people to Jesus instead of myself that I focus on how I will actually deliver my message.*

In my own case, it is not until I have spent time in prayer asking God to help me point people to Jesus instead of myself that I focus on *how* I will actually deliver my message.

Doing what makes you Christ centered in your speaking does not render unnecessary the use of all the best delivery techniques that Jesus and other master communicators have used to stir pathos in the hearts and minds of listeners. That's why it is important for you to intentionally consider and also practice key aspects of delivering a talk. The best material can get lost in bad delivery.

The Importance of Practice *and* Passion

The great Greek orator Demosthenes once said that the three most important aspects of speaking are "delivery, delivery, delivery." At its best, a good message comes across as being spontaneous, even when it has been carefully prepared. By *spontaneous* I mean a conversational or "extemporaneous" style, but not in the sense of not practicing how you will deliver your message. You can create a conversational effect with or without notes, as long as you thoroughly prepare and practice.

A conversational tone, however, isn't enough if you want to really connect with your audience. Passion is also essential. There is a much greater probability that your audience will connect with you and care about your topic if they perceive that *you* deeply care about what you are saying. That's the starting point for communicating passion. Without passion, a message might provide some thoughtful reflections on theological and biblical truths, but it won't have the sense of urgency that motivates listeners to respond. If the talk is supposed to be evangelistic, then for you to communicate the urgency of what you have to say, there must be an intensity in how you make your plea for listeners to give themselves to Christ. Should you be calling for social justice, there must be sorrow or moral indignation in what you decry. And if you are calling your listeners to commit to missionary service, you must get them to feel the desperate needs you are asking them to meet in the lives of others. Messages to draw people to the Kingdom of God must be marked by passion lest they be little more than religious lectures.

> *Messages to draw people to the Kingdom of God must be marked by passion lest they be little more than religious lectures.*

If you do not feel passionately about your topic, I suggest you spend some serious time with God in prayer, asking the Holy Spirit to fill you with passion. Sometimes, however, it's not the topic you lack passion for; it's the supporting material you have gathered to talk about your topic. If that's the case, I encourage you to go back and do more digging, including looking for good stories as well as engaging in lectio divina on some scripture passages that relate to your topic.

How you actually deliver your message will greatly affect whether or not the audience senses that you are passionate about your topic. That doesn't mean you have to shout or cry or run around the platform; rather, you need to be intentional about how you use your voice, eye contact, gestures, and any other body movement crucial to communicating passion. Although I am not going to elaborate on each of these delivery techniques—there are numerous writings on effective delivery already out there—I do want to expand on what I've learned about the speed and volume of delivery, as I believe these are two of the most important considerations for showing passion. I have found that if you speak too slowly, you will lose your listeners. The human brain is able to take in words in a fairly rapid fashion, and if you speak too slowly, your listeners will become frustrated waiting for you to catch up with their train of thought. But then you must also realize that in speaking too quickly you will sometimes leave your listeners behind, unable to follow where you are going in your talk.

What I have just stated about the speed of your delivery should not discourage you from speeding up and slowing down for special effect. For example, in certain instances when you are hoping to have your listeners deeply meditate on what you are saying, you might find that speaking not only slowly but softly will help to that end. In contrast, if you want to stir them to zealous action, increasing the cadence of your words along with increasing your volume can work quite well. One of the best ways to perfect the rhythm and volume of your talk is to ask others to listen to you practice ahead of time.

You can learn about effective speed and tone as well as other important delivery techniques by listening to speakers who have earned reputations as outstanding communicators. In this day when CDs, DVDs, and podcasts of great speakers are available, there is no excuse for missing out on what you can learn from them, but be sure to develop a style that fits your personality. Having a style of your own is essential for effectiveness. Learning from the practices of others is never for the purpose of becoming just like them in your speaking. You are to be who God wants *you* to be in your speaking, with your own unique style and personality emerging, expressed through effective speaking techniques. Preparation and practice combined with passion and prayer are what will get you there.

When you've done all the prep you can, if it occurs to you that "this isn't very good," you could do what I do. I say, "Look, God, this is not my thing; it's yours. If you have something to say to these people, please, please, please put the words in my mouth." I often say this to God about twenty minutes before I speak.

As essential as it is to prepare ahead of time to speak, it is just as essential to be in a state of spiritual preparedness in the minutes before you speak. In the prayer time immediately prior to speaking, I ask God to fill me with *passion*. I've mentioned the importance of communicating passion in terms of how we practice our delivery, but there is no substitute for the passion that the Holy Spirit can provide while we are speaking.

When it's time for me to speak and I first get to the microphone, I try to take a good look at the audience and really connect with them. In an empathic way, I try to put myself in their place and try to have them love me in return. This is a very serious, spiritual process that helps me connect. As I hope I have already made clear, I believe that to connect like Jesus, a speaker has to fall in love with his or her audience. If all you are doing is delivering words, it's like sitting in an empty room all by yourself and saying, "I love you," as opposed to sitting with someone you really love and saying, "I love you." Every message should be a love story. That's why my prayer just before I start is, "Lord, empower me to love these people. Connect me with them and them with me. Make me one with them in the Spirit."

Surrendering While Speaking

With all the spiritual preparation that you can make prior to and just before speaking, there is no substitute for being surrendered to the Spirit in the *midst* of speaking. While you are speaking to a crowd, or even when you are witnessing to a single person, there should simultaneously be a prayer going on within the depths of your being in which you are asking God to empower your words. Yes! You can speak and pray at the same time, *but it takes practice.* Many speakers addressing a crowd or witnessing on an individual level can attest to the sense that the words coming out of their mouths are coming from *beyond* themselves. It doesn't happen all the time, but there are those times when you will realize that what is being articulated is beyond human origin. My pastor says that at such times he has "gotten down." To my church audience, that means that the prepared text has been transcended, that our preacher has departed from his manuscript, and that the Spirit of God has taken control of the sermon. Those of us in the pews immediately sense what has happened, and it is then that we begin to react emotionally, shouting out words of affirmation even as our pastor continues to declare the Word of God.

In my own experience as a speaker, I sense when this has happened to me. When it has, there is no hesitation on my part when it comes to issuing an invitation at the end of the talk for people to give their lives to Christ for the first time or to live more radically for Jesus if they already claim to follow him. When the Spirit takes control and I feel the Spirit's presence empowering my words, I *know* that there will be a response. God's Spirit has borne witness with my spirit, and I sense an assurance that many will say yes to the invitation.

The Ending: A Call to Decision Making

Decision making should always lie at the end of every presentation. Over the years, I have had many occasions to make presentations to sales-people in the insurance industry. What I have learned from those who are experts in this field is that the difference between those who are successful in sales or fundraising and those who are not is determined by which of them can "close the deal" or "give 'the Ask.'" Presidents of insurance companies have said that they have had salespeople who know the business inside out and backwards and are able to make presentations that comprehensively cover everything that should be covered in a presentation, but lack the ability to look the client in the eye and ask forthrightly, "Will you say yes? Will you buy the policy?" Those who are unwilling or unable to close the deal never sell insurance. The same is true for preachers, who want their listeners to be not only "hearers of the word, but doers also."

> *Decision making should always lie at the end of every presentation.*

It is always important to have in mind what you want the listener or listeners to *do* in response to your message. Gospel messages require such a focus, which is why I am amazed at how many times such messages do not include a clear and specific call to make a decision.

What's a Clearly Defined Call to Decision?

Several years ago, I was invited to speak at a Governor's Prayer Breakfast for a state out west. As is the custom in most cases, I was invited to the governor's mansion for dinner the night before the breakfast as an act of hospitality. While at the dinner, I asked the governor who the speaker had been at the previous prayer breakfast. He told me about him, whom he acknowledged as one of the best speakers he had ever heard. Evidently, the message was extremely memorable, because the governor could recite the major points the preacher had made. What was evident was that the preacher had clearly outlined the salvation message of the Gospel, but issued no invitation to respond. When the governor finished telling me about the speaker, I asked him, "Have you ever surrendered your life to Christ? Have you ever asked Jesus to become a transforming presence in your life?"

After a long pause, the governor answered, "No, I haven't."

"Why haven't you?" I asked.

"Because nobody ever asked me to," was his answer.

"Well, I am asking you right here and right now," I said. "Will you surrender your life to Christ right now? Will you invite Jesus into your life to be a transforming presence?"

The governor thought over these questions for a few moments, and then answered with a simple "Yes!" Then he said, "Now that we've taken care of that, would you pass the potatoes?"

I was totally depressed by his response, and I thought that he had trivialized the invitation—but I was wrong.

The next morning at the breakfast, as the governor was introducing me, he announced, "Last night was undoubtedly one of the most significant times of my entire life. Last night I responded to an invitation to surrender my life to Christ, and I did it. I am going to be a different kind of person and a different kind of governor from this day forward."

The speaker the previous year had done a brilliant job of articulating the basic truths of the Gospel, but he had never called for a decision to be made. In the end, witnessing on an individual level or speaking to a group should always involve a call to some type of decision making. Arguably no one has done this better in recent years than Billy Graham. When Graham finishes a sermon, he always calls people who are ready to make decisions to leave their seats and come down the aisles to the front of the auditorium or stadium in order to take a stand publicly, declaring that they are giving themselves to Christ. What must be noted, however, is that he always makes it clear just what it is that he is asking people to decide. He can be counted on to say something like, "If you're ready to repent of your sins and ask Jesus to come into your life to make you into a new person, then come forward and stand here with me."

Depending on your audience, you may decide that your talk is aimed at calling people to *rededicate* themselves to Christ because they have slipped away from the zeal and commitment that had once marked their lives. Or you might be asked to speak at a conference that is especially designed to get Christians to consider living out their lives in full-time vocations as missionaries. In either case, you'll want to remind your audience of what it means to "count the cost" of following Jesus.

If you take on the role of a prophet and speak out against injustice or the materialistic consumerism into which we all have been seduced, it is crucial that you offer your listeners reasonable, specific ways to change their lifestyles and respond to the needs of those who Jesus called "the least of these." I often invite young people in my audiences to consider taking a year off to participate in an urban ministry called "Mission Year."[2] Other times I arrange for representatives from Compassion International to be present and offer audience members opportunities to "sponsor" Third World children. I make it clear that if each of them made commitments that would cost little more than $1.50 a day—much less than it costs for a cup of coffee at Starbucks—needy children in Third World countries could be educated, fed, clothed, and evangelized. Following the message, Compassion International workers have packets on hand that contain photos of specific children needing sponsors, and they are prepared to sign up those who are ready to make commitments.[3] Please note that it is important to give audience members options for both charity *and* justice work.

Although a call to decision does not have to involve overt public displays from audience members, I often ask people to stand up from where they are sitting, and I say, "I'm making this as hard as possible, because if you can't stand up for Christ here and now, in front of people who will cheer your decision, you'll not be able to stand up for Christ in a world that is often hostile to the things of God." Then I quote Jesus' words from scripture, "And I tell you, everyone who acknowledges me before others, the Son of Man also will acknowledge before the angels of God; but whoever denies me before others will be denied before the angels of God" (Luke 12:8–9). In most cases, I do not ask the congregation to bow their heads and close their eyes. Citing Romans 12:1–2, I declare that decisions should be made, as the J. B. Phillips translation states, "with eyes wide open to the mercies of God."

One strong bit of advice is for you not to drag out the invitation. Too often there are speakers who, in order to "look good" as evangelists, keep pleading with people to come forward. Perhaps you have been present when that has happened—and, if you are like me, you will confess that it wears on your nerves. If the Holy Spirit is at work in the lives of those in the congregation, then people will come. If it is not the Holy Spirit who leads people down the aisles but the nagging of the preacher, a disservice to the Kingdom has been rendered.

Who Is Responsible for the Outcome?

It takes a certain amount of courage to ask for a decision, because listeners can say no. Always remember that as a speaker you have a responsibility to provide a well-planned and well-delivered call to decision, but you are not the one responsible for the outcome. That's between the Holy Spirit and the listener. Whether people respond to the message or

> *As a speaker you have a responsibility to provide a well planned and delivered call to decision, but you are not the one responsible for the outcome.*

not has much to do with whether or not the Holy Spirit has brought the listener under conviction. You are not God, and only God can lead people to make valid commitments.

I haven't always remembered these truths in my life. The occasion wherein I felt the most pressure to "deliver" decisions for commitments to Christ was when I was faced with having to give an invitation at the famous Urbana missionary conference sponsored by Intervarsity Christian Fellowship. Every three years, upwards of twenty-five thousand college and university students gather on the campus of the University of Illinois over the Christmas break to hear speakers and attend seminars that are aimed at getting them to consider missionary service. I did not understand when I was asked to be one of the speakers at the 1987 gathering that there would be only one invitation given during the conference, and that I had been designated as the one to give that invitation. When I realized how much depended on what was supposed to happen at the end of the message, I was more than a little upset. The director of the conference let me know that there were nine hundred counselors who were prepared to talk and pray with those who made commitments, and that nine hundred packets containing helpful brochures had been prepared to give to the respondents. To add even more pressure, Billy Graham, one of the other speakers for the conference, put a hand on my shoulder and said, "Tony, I know this is going to be a great time for the Kingdom of God as you invite young people to give themselves to the missionary enterprise!"

I was intimidated. I thought, "Even if a couple of hundred collegians make decisions to become missionaries tonight, those who are running this conference will still be disappointed."

As I was wrapping up my message that night, I approached the end with fear and trembling. I would have run away if that had been a possibility, because I felt so much pressure to "bring in the numbers."

When thousands of young people said yes to the call to missionary service, I remembered the One who is responsible for the results. God answered the prayers of Christians around the world who were praying for those young missionary prospects at that Urbana conference that very night. What the Holy Spirit did because of their prayers would reap a great harvest for God's Kingdom. God was working in the lives of the young people who heard the invitation, and their responses were evidence that the prayers of the faithful "availeth much" (James 5:16, KJV).

We must never forget that it is the Holy Spirit who motivates people to make decisions for following Christ, and that the Holy Spirit doesn't even require that the speaker be in a most spiritual mind-set to motivate the listeners into making life-changing decisions. That's a good thing to remember, as not all of us who give invitations always do it in the best frame of mind. There are occasions when God moves people in spite of the condition of the speaker.

What's a Good Environment for Decision Making?

There are many ways to create a proper setting for people to respond. Some have invitational music sung or played in the background. If a worship team is singing or playing, make sure that they do so softly, so as to avoid creating any distractions that could hinder people from paying attention to how the Holy Spirit might be speaking to them. When the invitation is ended, the music should cease completely. Quiet is essential to give those who are prayerfully dealing with "heavy" decision making the chance to do so without interference. Personally, I prefer to have no background music during the invitation, so as to minimize distractions, including the possibility that the music could be interpreted as a manipulative device.

What About Follow Up for Those Who Commitments?

There are a variety of ways to follow up when people make commitments to live for Christ. If there is no one available to provide wise direction for those who positively respond to an invitation, I usually ask those who want to make decisions to raise their hands or to stand up. I pray for them, but then I charge them to contact their pastor, or some respected mature Christians whom they know, and set up specific times to pray and talk with those Christian leaders about the decisions that they have made. During that charge, I require them to make that contact with a telephone call or with a letter within the next twenty-four hours. There are two other things I say after that. One is that if they don't do this, they should look themselves in the mirror the next day and tell themselves that what happened during the invitation was superficial. I explain that in order to live out the commitments they have made, they very much will need the ongoing support and regular counsel of a pastor or a mature Christian teacher. Living out the call of Christ is not a "Lone

Ranger" activity. Furthermore, I tell them to explain to those persons whom they ask to spiritually nurture them that, according to James 3:1, if these newly committed persons drift away from Christ because of the failure to receive the spiritual help they need, those spiritual mentors or pastors will be held responsible by God on the day of judgment.

If you think I am putting an extremely heavy a trip on those making commitments and on those they contact to walk with them in their spiritual journey, I can only respond by saying, "I know I am!" What concerns me is that we often take responses to invitations far too casually and do not press for the kind of follow-through that nurtures those who make commitments to faithfully follow Jesus.

The conditions for decision making should not be too easy. Jesus did not tell us to go into all the world and make believers out of people. He called us to make disciples. We all know that there is a big difference between believers and disciples. Believers are those who only give intellectual assent to certain theological propositions. According to scripture, even the demons believe (James 2:19). Disciples are people who are willing to imitate their teacher. Disciples are those who are willing to do what their leader wants them to do, to go where their leader wants them to go, and to be the kind of persons that their leader wants them to be. No easy believe-ism is being called for by Christ. Instead, what is required is to surrender to Jesus Christ as *Lord*!

If we lose this generation, it will not be because we have made Christianity too difficult for them but because we have made it too easy.

Do not think that putting the cost of discipleship too high will lead to losing people to God's Kingdom. Quite the opposite is true. If we lose this generation, it will not be because we have made Christianity too difficult for them but because we have made it too easy.

The Power of the People

Sooner or later, every speaker becomes aware that whether or not what is said goes over with listeners has a great deal to do with the openness and responsiveness of the listeners themselves. Those with experience know that any given audience can make or break a talk. White preachers often remark that on those occasions when they have had opportunities to preach for African American congregations, those congregations draw out of them their very best sermons. Belonging to an African American congregation myself, I can personally attest to the reputation that African Americans have earned as enthusiastic encouragers of preachers.

The resounding "Amens" and cries of "That's right, preacher!" pick up the energies of just about any preacher. Most preachers will say that they end up preaching at a higher level than they ever thought possible.[4]

I have been told more than once that my delivery style is that of a black preacher, a comment that is a high compliment. I believe that this perception is a direct result of how the people in my home church have encouraged me with their responses when I've preached there.

Several years ago, my home church, which has a couple thousand members, was on a search for a new pastor to replace the founder of the church, who had served faithfully until his death. When I heard that the search committee had settled on a young man just out of seminary, I was a bit upset. I told the deacon who was serving as chairman of the search committee, "Ours is a large and prestigious church, and we ought to recruit some tried and experienced candidate who has proven himself to be a great preacher!"

The response of that deacon was memorable. He said, "We're going to take this young preacher and *make* him great!" And they did!

Sometimes speaking to a particular audience can be disheartening because the people are used to being quiet and not effusive. One time I was invited to preach to a staid and stiff group in a church in Lancaster County, Pennsylvania. I did my best to elicit some excitement from that congregation and gain some kind of emotional rapport with the people, but all my efforts were to no avail. However, as I greeted people as they left the church, I received from one stern-faced man what might have been, for that congregation, a big-time compliment. While firmly but slowly shaking my hand, he said, "Well! We wouldn't be opposed to having you back again."

There are other times when an audience is deadly because of what has gone on before they've had a chance to hear the message. More than once I have been in situations where I had to follow a worship band who for close to an hour played music that seemed both monotonously repetitious and lacking in any kind of inspiring melodies. Situations like this can so deaden an audience that resurrection is nearly impossible. Then there are times when I have felt a *spiritual* deadness evident in the crowd, where the audience seems to be made up of religiously blasé people who come to church out of habit rather than out of any expectation or hope of experiencing a blessing from God. Jesus himself encountered such spiritually dead people on occasion, and scripture says that even he could not do much at times with such people "because of their unbelief" (Matthew 13:58). There are some audiences that can kill the messages of even the best teachers and preachers.

One way you can know if your message was effective is if people come up to you afterwards and say something like, "You said some things today that I have been feeling, but until you said them, I had never been able to put them into words." Your spirit, through the Holy Spirit, was, as it says in Romans 8:16, bearing witness with their spirit. Good messages are those that confirm what the Holy Spirit has already put into a listener's heart. That is what connecting like Jesus is all about. But be careful that you don't let such affirmations go to your head.

> Good messages are those that confirm what the Holy Spirit has already put into a listener's heart.

When I was a twenty-year-old youth leader, the pastor of the church where I was serving, because he had a bad case of laryngitis, asked me to preach what was to be my first sermon. I'll not forget his warning when he said, "When you've finished your sermon and are greeting people at the door, you will be told over and over again how wonderful you were. Remember—the first one in line who will be telling you that will be Satan. He knows that pride goes before destruction."

Frankly, one of the most difficult times for me is greeting people following a service. I know I'm supposed to be a gracious, smiling person, but I find it very hard. Preaching wipes me out, so I have little to no energy for interactions afterwards. It's especially difficult to be gracious if someone wants to argue with me or wants an opinion on a complex question that was brought to his or her mind during the message. I always carry business cards with me so that I can give the person a card and say, "Could you be so kind as to write me a letter addressing the issue you want to talk about or specifically explaining what you want to ask me? I promise you, I will send you a personal response." I have to report that of the hundreds of times I have given out my cards for such purposes, seldom does a person follow through and write to me.

It is very important to put off those who might confront you after an exhausting speaking event, because if you take the time to carry on a discussion right then, not only will you hinder others who are standing in line to greet you, but you are likely to say something out of exasperation that you'll soon regret. Those on-the-spot answers that you might give could be harmfully superficial.

The Personal Aftermath

If the talk has gone well, I am likely to get depressed within a couple of hours after I speak. First, there is the matter of mental and physical exhaustion that results from passionate preaching. In 1 Kings 19, we read about how the prophet Elijah, after his "homiletical" triumph over the prophets of Baal, ran away to a lonely place and wanted to die. Then God told Elijah to eat a good meal and get a good night's sleep—and he'd feel better in the morning. That was good advice because one contributing factor to depression is fatigue, and Elijah was extremely tired.

Second, there has seldom been a time when, following a talk, I did not reflect on how the message could have been better. I think of illustrations that I might have used that would have better driven home certain points I made. Almost always I can think of how I could have improved on some of the words and phrases I used. At the time, this depresses me. I find that writing down suggestions for the future helps alleviate some of my depression and also proves to be a valuable resource in preparation for future talks. In addition, hearing from others can greatly help us determine what we might want to do differently in subsequent speaking situations. Mary told me that our friend Oreon, a seasoned speaker herself, gives Mary specific, helpful feedback on both content and delivery whenever she hears Mary speak in public.

Finally, depression sets in because almost every time I speak, I preach not only to the audience but to myself. Strange as it may seem, I am almost always brought under strong conviction by what I have had to say—perhaps more so than any of the listeners. That is because in preaching, I try as much as possible to put myself in the place of the members of the audience. I try to take on the consciousness of those persons who are listening to what I am saying. I try to feel their feelings and take on their mind-set. I try to imagine what is troubling those in the congregation. Depending on the Spirit to give me empathy with my listeners, I endeavor to connect with their questions and to understand the struggles they are going through. I try to preach to the fears and anxieties that might be unsettling them. In taking on such consciousness, I end up making myself the object of the sermon and preaching to myself. When looking for counsel about this from one of America's greatest preachers, I was told that he too suffered from similar feelings of depression after sermons for exactly this reason.

A Summary of Suggestions

Because my coauthor teaches speech courses that integrate speaking techniques with spiritual practices, I asked her how she succinctly tells students the most important aspects of delivery. Mary has what she calls "Presentation Ps" that serve as a good summary of what I have been trying to get across in these chapters on teaching and preaching.

PRESENTATION Ps

o **Pray.** Pray about your upcoming talk, that the Holy Spirit would guide your planning so that you say what God wants you to, no more and no less.

o **People.** Ask yourself audience analysis questions like the ones I mentioned in Chapter Eleven, and pray for your audience.

o **Purpose.** Think about your specific purpose in talking to a particular audience.

o **Point.** If your purpose is to promote the Kingdom of God, then before you begin preparing your talk, remind yourself that what you say and how you say it are to point to Jesus, not yourself.

o **Pick.** Pick an appropriate topic and supporting materials that match your purpose and lend credibility to it.

o **Passion.** Have passion for your purpose, your topic, and your audience; if you feel you don't deeply care about your talk or your listeners, spend time in prayer before and during the planning of your talk, asking the Holy Spirit to help you care for your listeners and your topic.

o **Prepare.** Structure and organize your talk in a clear manner that will accomplish your purpose; run your outline by someone you trust to tell you whether or not it makes sense.

o **Pepper.** Enliven your talk by finding appropriate materials, such as stories and other illustrations, testimonies, and interesting research. Seriously consider engaging in lectio divina on scripture passages as part of this process. Again, run your ideas by someone who will give you helpful and honest feedback.

o **Plan.** So that you are ready to engage your audience as well as finish your talk in a memorable way, carefully plan how you start and finish. Have your actual opening and closing stories, quotes, engaging lines, and challenges or calls to action ready, recognizing that you can always change them if you discover better ones. Sometimes the Holy Spirit will impress upon you a

better introduction or conclusion than you had planned. Be open
to this.

o **Practice.** Practice your actual talk out loud using vocal and
physical delivery that you believe can best connect with your
audience. Be intentional with how you use eye contact, facial
expressions, gestures, other movement, and vocal volume, rate,
and inflections. Ask a few people to listen to you practice. In
addition, watching tapes of other effective speakers can help you
with technique as well as inspire you.

o **Present.** As you get up to give your talk, ask the Holy Spirit to
calm any nerves, fill you with passion, and give you love for your
audience. Then take a deep breath and speak!

o **Ponder.** Within a few days of speaking, spend some quiet time
with God, reflecting on your talk and any responses to it of
which you may be aware. Ask the Holy Spirit to help you react
to any responses, positive or negative, in ways that glorify God
and help you learn what you need to know about yourself, your
audience, and your speaking.

As you can see, all the suggestions on teaching and preaching in these
chapters require much time. Hastily thrown together and carelessly delivered messages are at best a sign of disorganization and at worst a sign
of disbelief. If we really believe that we are speaking to help advance the
Kingdom of God, then we can never be careless. The Apostle Paul tells
us in Philippians 2:12–13 to "work out your own salvation with fear
and trembling; for it is God who is at work in you, enabling you both
to will and to work for his good pleasure." May we work out our salvation through how we teach, preach, and care for one another's souls—all
the while trusting that God is preparing us, as we are preparing ourselves,
to connect like Jesus.

Postscript for Spiritually Charged Communication

No Exit is the name of a classic play written by the French existentialist philosopher Jean Paul Sartre. In that play, Sartre tried to demonstrate what he believed to be the ultimate tragedy of the human condition: the inability of persons to connect with one another in ways that enable them to escape their feelings of estrangement.

In this book, we have invited you to prove Sartre wrong. We have endeavored to make the case that, empowered by the Holy Spirit, whose relationship with us is nurtured through a variety of spiritual practices, we are able to break down the barriers that separate us from one another. Connecting, we have said, is more than an art form that involves learning how to say things so that people might listen. We have claimed that connecting requires the Holy Spirit to be at work in all we say—and don't say.

It is our hope that what you have read will help you connect like Jesus. We hope that you will try the practices we have suggested or that you will search until you find combinations of spiritual and communication practices that connect you to others in ways that honor and glorify God. Most of all, we hope that one day soon, each of us will find no need to talk about communication and spiritual practices as separate entities because *all* of our communication will have become a spiritual practice. When that day comes, we will be the kind of people God desires us to be: those who show the rest of the world what it means to be unified through our love for one another.

As Dietrich Bonhoeffer wrote in *Meditations on the Cross*, "The world is overcome not through destruction, but through reconciliation. . . . only God's perfect love can encounter reality and overcome it." It is "the love of God in Jesus Christ, a love genuinely lived, that does this."[1] Love cannot be genuinely lived without specific changes in the ways we communicate every day with God, ourselves, and others. May we commit to making the kind of changes in how we relate to one another that will empower us to connect like Jesus and thereby hasten the day when God's Kingdom—the place where God's will is done—is realized on earth as it is in heaven.

"One Another" Verses

1. Show hospitality to one another—1 Peter 4:9
2. Bear with one another and, if anyone has a complaint against another, forgive each other—Colossians 3:13
3. Regard one another as better than yourselves—Philippians 2:3
4. Be subject to one another—Ephesians 5:21
5. Instruct one another—Romans 15:14
6. Bear with one another in love—Ephesians 4:2
7. Be kind to one another—Ephesians 4:32
8. Live in harmony with one another—Romans 12:16
9. Outdo one another in showing honor—Romans 12:10
10. Have fellowship with one another—1 John 1:7
11. Clothe yourselves with humility in dealing with one another—1 Peter 5:5
12. Provoke one another to love—Hebrews 10:24
13. Bear one another's burdens—Galatians 6:2
14. Confess your sins to one another—James 5:16
15. Pray for one another—James 5:16
16. Have the same care for one another—1 Corinthians 12:25
17. Encourage one another and build up one another—1 Thessalonians 5:11
18. Through love serve one another—Galatians 5:13
19. Be at peace with one another—Mark 9:50
20. Encourage one another—1 Thessalonians 4:18
21. Wash one another's feet—John 13:14
22. We are members of one another—Romans 12:5

23. Do not compete against one another—Galatians 5:26

24. Do not envy one another—Galatians 5:26

25. Do not pass judgment on one another—Romans 14:13

26. Do not wrong one another—Acts 7:26

27. Do not grumble against one another—James 5:9

28. Do not speak evil against one another—James 4:11

29. Do not lie to one another—Colossians 3:9

30. Love one another—Romans 12:10; Romans 13:8;
     1 Thessalonians 4:9; 1 John 4:7; 1 John 4:12; John 13:34;
     John 13:35; John 15:12; John 15:17

Using This Book in Small Groups or Classes

Because this book contains several specific spiritual and communication practices for connecting like Jesus, we hope it will be useful not only for your own individual growth but for encouraging one another in small group and classroom settings as well. If you choose to use it in a group context, here are some possible suggestions.

You could focus on the entire book or choose certain sections. The following ideas show how the topics of soul healing and teaching and preaching can each be discussed in twelve-week formats. Or you could tailor the book to suit your group's needs. No matter which format you choose, we propose including Part One and Chapter Nine on storytelling, to lay the groundwork for connecting like Jesus and to highlight the importance of storytelling in all of life.

Soul Healing: Twelve-Week Format

If you focus on *soul healing*, here are the chapters we suggest, as well as a sample format:

Week 1: Introduction and Chapter One, on spiritually charged communication

Week 2: Chapter Two, on soul healing

Week 3: Chapter Three, on self-awareness; stop after the section "Difficulties in Becoming More Aware"

Week 4: Chapter Three, on self-awareness, starting at "Six Crucial Questions for Increased Self-Awareness"

Week 5: Chapter Four, on fears that keep us from others

Week 6: Chapter Five, on listening; stop after the section "Physical Preparation for Sacred Listening"

Week 7: Chapter Five, on listening, starting at "What Keeps Us from Sacred Listening"

Week 8: Chapter Six, on the importance of asking questions

Week 9: Chapter Seven, on conflict as an opportunity to connect

Week 10: Chapter Eight, on redeeming conflict

Week 11: Chapter Nine, on storytelling

Week 12: Review and wrap-up

Teaching and Preaching: Twelve-Week Format

If you focus on *teaching and preaching*, we suggest the following format:

Week 1: Introduction and Chapter One, on spiritually charged communication

Week 2: Chapter Two, on soul healing

Week 3: Chapter Three, on self-awareness; stop after the section "Difficulties in Becoming More Aware"

Week 4: Chapter Three, on self-awareness, starting at "Six Crucial Questions for Increased Self-Awareness"

Week 5: Chapter Four, on fears, including fear of speaking in public

Week 6: Chapter Six, on the importance of asking questions

Week 7: Chapter Nine, on storytelling

Week 8: Chapter Ten, on laying the groundwork for teaching and preaching; stop after the section "Offering Hope and a Future Vision"

Week 9: Chapter Ten, starting at the section, "Three Essential Elements for Teaching and Preaching"

Week 10: Chapter Eleven, on specific suggestions for preparing a talk

Week 11: Chapter Twelve, on delivery and the significance of the ending

Week 12: Review and wrap-up

Homework Ideas

We encourage you and your fellow group members to engage in various communication and spiritual practices in the chapters from week to week and to report your joys and struggles in doing so.

With either of the formats we have described here, when your group gets to the storytelling chapter, we encourage you in the following week to write personal stories of how Jesus has changed your lives, and then perhaps even take an extra week to share your stories.

The following paragraphs describe an idea for homework called "relational transformation," which we highly encourage your group to consider doing if you have chosen to focus on the chapters on soul healing.

After the first group meeting, each of you are to prayerfully identify two relationships in your life in which you would like to connect in more God-honoring ways. *Note:* we recommend that you consider your relationship with God for one of your choices. We also advise that this "assignment" *not* be used to acquire (or reacquire) a romantic interest because it may be hard to discern if one's motives are pure.

Then, following *each* group session (starting with that first week):

- For each person you have identified, write down one or two *very specific* ways that you will try to connect better in the relationship, basing your effort on combining some of the spiritual and communication practices discussed that particular week. These ideas can be the same for both people or can be four different ideas. By *very specific,* we mean setting measurable goals. For example:
  - I will call, text, or e-mail twice this week and ask how the person is doing. When he or she responds, I will sacredly listen and ask appropriate questions by trying to see situations from his or her point of view.
  - I will listen to God in silence twenty minutes a day this week.
- Have a plan to remember to carry out your plan. As Mindy Caliguire put it, the "gravitational pull of daily life" will typically draw our attention away from connecting like Jesus, so along with being willing to engage in these practices, we need *a plan* to remember to engage in them. We are referring to a specific plan, such as the following:
  - I will set my alarm on my cell phone, and when it goes off, I will call, text, or e-mail the person.
  - I will put a sticky note on my mirror to remind myself every morning to sit in silence with God before I leave my room.

It is our prayer that no matter what format you choose, you will consider integrating these practices into your own lives and the lives of your community of believers. We believe that this is the way we can learn to better connect like Jesus so that it will consistently be said of us, "See how they love one another!"

Notes

All scriptural references are from the New Revised Standard Version, unless otherwise noted.

CHAPTER ONE: SPIRITUALLY CHARGED COMMUNICATION

1. Brian McLaren (author, speaker, pastor; http://www.brianmclaren.net), in discussion with Mary Albert Darling, Feb. 26, 2009. Throughout the book, we include segments of personal interviews from Christian speakers and writers Shane Claiborne, Brian McLaren, and Mindy Caliguire to show how certain preachers, teachers, and soul healers in our present time have endeavored to carry out these ministries one-on-one and in larger groups.

2. We have chosen to use "Kingdom of God" language, although as Brian McLaren addressed in our interview, there may be limitations in doing so. If you do perceive the phrase as limiting in today's world, we hope that you find the following words from our interview helpful and that you will feel free to replace "Kingdom of God" for a different phrase that better captures the intended meaning for you:

   "I think when we're trying to understand what Jesus meant by this core message of the Kingdom of God, we have to start by exploring what the term meant in its original context. But then I think we have to realize that if Jesus were here today, it's virtually certain he wouldn't use the phrase 'Kingdom of God' because there is just no context for the term to be used today in the way that it was used in Jesus' day. And then we have to ask how Jesus would communicate the same meaning today. I think when Dr. King said 'I have a dream,' he was in some ways translating the idea of the Kingdom of God. We might talk about the sacred economy of God or the sacred ecosystem of God. We might talk about the dance of God, the community of God, the party of God, the song of God, the school of God, the movement of God, the peaceful revolution of God. I think there's any number of metaphors that we use. You see them in a lot of book titles. *The Divine Conspiracy* is Dallas Willard's way of saying it. Shane Claiborne's is *The Irresistible Revolution.* Tony's is *The Kingdom of God Is a Party.* Matthew, Mark, and Luke talk about Kingdom. I think when John talks about life or abundant life or life to the full or life of the ages, I think that's John's translation of Kingdom."

3. Shane Claiborne (http://www.thesimpleway.org), in discussions with Mary Albert Darling, June 8, 2008, and Aug. 18, 2009.

4. Kinnaman, D., and Lyons, G. *Unchristian: What a New Generation Really Thinks About Christianity—and Why It Matters.* Grand Rapids, Mich.: Baker Books, 2007, p. 15.

5. For an additional look at how Christians are seen by other segments of society, we highly recommend the film *Lord, Save Us from Your Followers,* by Dan Merchant. You can find more information on this film at http://lordsaveusthemovie.com/.

6. Barton, R. H. "*The First Week of Lent: Practicing Repentance,*" Mar. 3, 2009. The Transforming Center. http://www.thetransformingcenter.org/pdf/repentance09.pdf. (Accessed Sept. 14, 2009)

7. Wilson, B. *Christianity in the Crosshairs: Real Life Solutions Discovered in the Line of Fire.* Shippensburg, Pa.: Destiny Image, 2004, p.74.

8. Mindy Caliguire (http://www.soulcare.com), e-mails exchanged with Mary Albert Darling, between Aug. 5, 2009, and Sept. 12, 2009.

9. Wesley, J. *The Works of John Wesley* (A. Outler, ed.). *Sermons I: 1–33.* Nashville: Abingdon, 1984, pp. 236–237.

10. Wesley, J. *The Works of John Wesley* (A. Outler, ed.). *Sermons III: 71–114.* Nashville: Abingdon, 1986, p. 423.

11. *Hymns, Psalms and Spiritual Songs.* Louisville, Ky.: Westminster/John Knox, 1990, p. 322.

12. See the list of "one another" verses after the Postscript. A special thanks to our friend Ron Kopicko, the chaplain at Spring Arbor University, for introducing Mary to this list he compiled several years ago.

CHAPTER TWO: SOUL HEALING

1. We are using the term *soul* to indicate the essence or "center" of who we are—that which lives on after death. For a short discussion of the concept of soul, see Dallas Willard, "Gray Matter and the Soul," *Christianity Today,* Nov. 18, 2002, p. 74. http://www.christianitytoday.com/ct/2002/november18/30.74.html. (Accessed Sept. 20, 2009)

2. Our intent in differentiating between soul healing and physical healing is not to dichotomize body and soul; in fact, much of value has been written about the connections between spiritual and physical healing and wholeness. What we want to focus on specifically, however, are the ways Jesus interacted with people to heal their souls, recognizing that oftentimes healing resulted in physical healing too.

3. Mulholland, M. R. *Invitation to a Journey: A Road Map for Spiritual Formation*. Downers Grove, Ill.: InterVarsity, 1993, p. 12.

4. Wesley, *Works, Sermons III*, p. 416.

5. Blakemore, G. S. "By the Spirit Through the Water: John Wesley's 'Evangelical' Theology of Infant Baptism." *Wesleyan Theological Journal*, Fall 1996, *31*, 175.

6. Fénelon, F. *The Seeking Heart Auburn*. Maine: SeedSowers, 1992, p. 13.

CHAPTER THREE: IT *IS* ABOUT YOU

1. Jacob Atem (president, Southern Sudan Healthcare Organization, http://www.sshco.org), in discussion with Mary Albert Darling, June 1, 2008.

2. Wright, W. M. *The Rising: Living the Mysteries of Lent, Easter, and Pentecost*. Nashville: Upper Room Books, 1994, p. 51.

3. Myers, D. G., and Jeeves, M. A. *Psychology Through the Eyes of Faith*. Washington, D.C.: Council for Christian Colleges and Universities, 2003, p. 160.

4. Niebuhr, R. *The Essential Reinhold Niebuhr: Selected Essays and Addresses* (R. M. Brown, ed.). New Haven, Conn.: Yale University Press, 1986, p. xxiv.

5. Wesley, *Works, Sermons III*, p. 423.

6. Fénelon, *Seeking Heart*, p. 102.

7. Wesley, J. *The Works of John Wesley* (A. Outler, ed.). *Sermons IV: 115–151*. Nashville: Abingdon, 1986, p. 385.

8. Nouwen, H.J.M. *Life of the Beloved: Spiritual Living in a Secular World*. New York: Crossroad, 1992, p. 109.

9. Fénelon, *Seeking Heart*, pp. 131–132.

10. Lewis, C. S. *The Screwtape Letters*. San Francisco: HarperSanFrancisco, 2001, p. 12.

11. Fénelon, *Seeking Heart*, p. 5.

CHAPTER FOUR: FROM FEAR TO FREEDOM

1. Schulz, C. M. *Peanuts for Everybody*. Greenwich, Conn.: Fawcett Crest, 1958.

2. Wesley, *Works, Sermons III*, p. 425.

3. *Harry Potter and the Sorcerer's Stone*, DVD. Directed by Chris Columbus, 2001; Burbank, Calif.: Warner Home Video, 2002.

CHAPTER FIVE: SACRED LISTENING

1. Caldwell, T. *The Listener*. Garden City, N.Y.: Doubleday, 1960, p. 9.

2. Brandi Kendall (student in the Master of Arts in Spiritual Formation program, Spring Arbor University), post to online course discussion board, Feb. 2009.

3. For listening to be empathic, however, the listener only shares his or her own thoughts and feelings if he or she can "speak the truth in love," as Paul tells us to do in Ephesians 4:15. For more on what we think it means to speak the truth in love, see Chapter Eight.

4. Bonhoeffer, D. *Life Together*. New York: HarperCollins, 1954, p. 97.

5. Marin, A. *Love Is an Orientation: Elevating the Conversation with the Gay Community*. Downers Grove, Ill.: IVP Books, 2009, p. 21.

6. Winner, L. "Sleep Therapy." *Books and Culture*, Jan.-Feb. 2006, p. 7.

7. Fénelon, *Seeking Heart*, p. 12.

8. Susan Hric (student in the Master of Arts in Spiritual Formation program, Spring Arbor University), post to online course discussion board, Feb. 2009.

9. Tannen, D. *You Just Don't Understand: Women and Men in Conversation*. New York: Quill, 2001, pp. 141–143.

10. Bonhoeffer, *Life Together*, p. 99.

11. Ortberg, J. *God Is Closer Than You Think: If God Is Always with Us, Why Is He So Hard to Find?* Grand Rapids, Mich.: Zondervan, 2005, p. 72.

12. Chambers, O. *My Utmost for His Highest: Selections for the Year*. New York: Dodd, Mead, 1943, p. 230.

13. Mott, M. "Did Animals Sense Tsunami Was Coming?" *National Geographic News*, Jan. 4, 2005. http://news.nationalgeographic.com/news/2005/01/0104_050104_tsunami_animals.html. (Accessed Sept. 20, 2009)

CHAPTER SIX: CONNECTING THROUGH QUESTIONS

1. Leeds, D. *The 7 Powers of Questions: Secrets to Successful Communication in Life and at Work.* New York: Berkley, 2000, p. 1.

2. Malony, H. N. "John Wesley and Psychology." *Journal of Psychology and Christianity*, 1999, *18*(1), 7.

CHAPTER SEVEN: CONFLICT

1. Barrett, D. B., Kurian, G. T., and Johnson, T. M. *World Christian Encyclopedia: A Comparative Survey of Churches and Religions in the Modern World.* Vol. *1.* Oxford: Oxford University Press, 2001, p. 10.

2. Kinnaman and Lyons, *Unchristian*, p. 36.

3. Wesley, *Works, Sermons I*, p. 107.

4. Merton, T. *Faith and Violence: Christian Teaching and Christian Practice.* Notre Dame, Ind.: University of Notre Dame Press, 1976, p. 208.

5. For further information on the Evangelical Council for Financial Accountability, see http://www.ECFA.org.

6. McLaren, B. "*A Call for Evangelical Rhetorical Accountability.*" Blog post to God's Politics: A Blog by Jim Wallis & Friends, June 26, 2008. http://blog.sojo.net/2008/06/26/a-call-for-evangelical-rhetorical-accountability-by-brian-mclaren. (Accessed Sept. 4, 2009)

7. Briner, B. *Roaring Lambs: A Gentle Plan to Radically Change Our World.* Grand Rapids, Mich.: Zondervan, 1993, p. 38.

8. Wilmot, W. W., and Hocker, J. L. *Interpersonal Conflict.* New York: McGraw-Hill, 2001.

9. Chambers, *My Utmost for His Highest*, p. 28.

10. Day, D. *Dorothy Day, Selected Writings: By Little and by Little* (R. Ellsberg, ed.). Maryknoll, N.Y.: Orbis Books, 1992, p. 213.

11. Norris, K. *Amazing Grace: A Vocabulary of Faith.* New York: Riverhead Books, 1999, p. 126.

12. Chittister, J. *Beyond Beijing: The Next Step for Women: A Personal Journal.* Kansas City, Mo.: Sheed & Ward, 1996, p. 26.

13. Dallas Willard, e-mail message to Mary Albert Darling, June 29, 2009.

CHAPTER EIGHT: REDEEMING CONFLICT

1. Peterson, J. A. *The Myth of the Greener Grass.* Wheaton, Ill.: Tyndale House, 1983, p. 200.

2. McLaren, B. "Prayer Regarding Critics and Enemies." Brian McLaren. http://www.brianmclaren.net/archives/prayer-regarding-critics-and-ene-1. html. (Accessed Sept. 8, 2009)

3. Fénelon, *Seeking Heart*, p. 18.

4. Wesley, "On Love," *Works, Sermons IV*, p. 383.

5. Merton, *Faith and Violence*, pp. 205–206.

6. Ibid., p. 205.

7. Fénelon, *Seeking Heart*, p. 102.

CHAPTER NINE: WHEN STORIES TELL THE STORY

1. Campolo, A. *Let Me Tell You a Story*. Nashville: Word, 2000, pp. 80–81.

2. Myers, B. K. *Young Children and Spirituality*. New York: Routledge, 1997, p. 18.

3. Nichols, D. "The Writer and the Film." *Theatre Arts*, Oct. 1943, pp. 591–602.

4. Maguire, J. *The Power of Personal Storytelling: Spinning Tales to Connect with Others*. New York: Tarcher/Putnam, 1998, p. 7.

5. Smalley, G., and Trent, J. T. *The Language of Love*. New York: Pocket Books, 1991, p. 21.

6. One such urban legend debunking site is http://www.snopes.com.

7. Schultze, Q. J. *An Essential Guide to Public Speaking: Serving Your Audience with Faith, Skill, and Virtue*. Grand Rapids, Mich.: Baker Academic, 2006, p. 71.

8. Campolo, *Let Me Tell You a Story*, p. 19.

9. Maguire, *Power of Personal Storytelling*, p. 221.

10. King, M. L., Jr. "I Have a Dream." American Rhetoric: Top 100 Speeches. http://americanrhetoric.com/speeches/mlkihaveadream.htm. (Accessed Sept. 20, 2009)

CHAPTER TEN: PREPARING THE SOIL

1. In some cases, initial decisions are made at what one theologian called "a crisis moment." However, the early twentieth-century psychologist, William James, who made the first extensive scientific study of religious conversions, pointed out that some come to decisive decisions over an extended period of time, and might even have been unconscious of the exact time when those crucial spiritual decisions were made.

Whether decisions are made suddenly or gradually, preaching should aim at leading listeners to making specific commitments to live their lives more in line with how Jesus wants them to live. This is not only about getting people to affirm certain propositional truths. Acknowledging essential doctrines on the intellectual level is not enough for people to be "saved" and guarantee them free passage into heaven when they die. Although the Bible says in John 3:16 that those who believe in Jesus will have eternal life, we generally have a limited understanding of what it means to believe in Jesus. Just about any biblical scholar will tell you that in the language of the ancient world, to believe in Jesus carried with it a meaning that was more complex. From such scholars we learn that to believe was to be committed totally to all that Jesus was about. It was not solely about accepting doctrinal truths. To believe in Jesus was to be committed to all that Jesus was as a person and to all that he was doing in the world. Believing in Jesus was to be understood as "trusting obedience" to what Jesus called his followers to do and to be.

2. Fosdick, H. E. *The Living of These Days: An Autobiography*. New York: Harper, 1956, p. 94.

3. Brueggemann, W. *The Prophetic Imagination*. (2nd ed.) Minneapolis: Augsburg Press, 2001.

4. Brosend, W. "Blank Stares: Who's Listening to Sermons?" *Christian Century*, Apr. 21, 2009. http://findarticles.com/p/articles/mi_m1058/is_8_126/ai_n32144704/.

5. Aristotle. *The Basic Works of Aristotle* (R. P. McKeon, ed.). New York: Random House, 1941, p. 1329.

6. For more information about this program and Haiti Partners, please visit http://www.haitipartners.org.

7. Schleiermacher, F. *On Religion: Speeches to Its Cultured Despisers*. London: Paternoster, 1893. http://books.google.com/books?id=lH1AAAAAIAAJ&printsec=frontcover&dq=schleiermacher#v=onepage&q=&f=false.

Chapter Eleven: Planning Your Message

1. Barth, K. *Homiletics*. Louisville, Ky.: Westminster/John Knox, 1991, p. 119.

2. Mead, G. H., and Morris, C. W. *Mind, Self and Society from the Standpoint of a Social Behaviorist*. Chicago: University of Chicago Press, 1934.

3. Tillich, P. *Systematic Theology*. Vol. 1. Chicago: University of Chicago Press, 1951.

4. Bonhoeffer, D. *The Cost of Discipleship*. New York: Touchstone, 1995, p. 89.

Chapter Twelve: Presenting Your Message

1. These are stories that are commonly circulated in England. Tony last heard both of them when speaking at Spurgeon College in Croyton, England, in October 1992.

2. For more information on Mission Year, visit http://www.missionyear.org/.

3. There are those who criticize child sponsorship such as that promoted by Compassion International and World Vision, and claim that such sponsorships do not address the structural evils inherent in the political and economic institutions that create poverty. These critics have their point, of course, but they are probably forgetting what we know about the connection between preaching and praxis. They have forgotten that action can create a change in consciousness. In becoming involved in concerns for the poor on the micro level through a child sponsorship program, people just might be led to reflect on the causes of poverty, and follow up with plans to work for the macro political and economic changes that can move the world toward eliminating poverty.

   Jesus taught that God's Kingdom would begin to break loose in history through such small initiatives. In scripture we read, "With what can we compare the kingdom of God, or what parable will we use for it? It is like a mustard seed, which, when sown upon the ground, is the smallest of all the seeds on earth; yet when it is sown it grows up and becomes the greatest of all shrubs, and puts forth large branches, so that the birds of the air can make nests in its shade" (Mark 4:30–32). Jesus is telling us that if we are faithful in doing the little things we can do in the here and now, eventually we will be able to control the big things that must be done if world poverty is to be abolished (Luke 19:17).

4. For a valuable resource on this topic, see Mitchell, H. H. *Black Preaching*. Philadelphia: Lippincott, 1970.

Postscript

1. Bonhoeffer, D., and Weber, M. *Meditations on the Cross*. Louisville, Ky.: Westminster/John Knox, 1998, p. 47.

The Authors

Tony Campolo is a sought-after speaker throughout the United States and abroad, speaking over three hundred times a year, including regular engagements in England, Australia, and New Zealand. He has been considered by *Time* magazine as one of America's best preachers, and *Christianity Today* magazine named him among the most influential preachers in the last half century. He is an ordained minister who has served American Baptist churches in New Jersey and Pennsylvania, and is presently recognized as an associate pastor of the Mount Carmel Baptist Church in West Philadelphia.

Tony is also professor emeritus of sociology at Eastern University in St. Davids, Pennsylvania. He previously served for ten years on the faculty of the University of Pennsylvania. Tony is a graduate of Eastern College and earned a Ph.D. from Temple University.

As founder and president of the Evangelical Association for the Promotion of Education (EAPE), Tony has worked to create, nurture, and support programs for "at-risk" children in cities across North America, and has helped establish schools and universities in several developing countries.

Tony has written more than thirty-five books and is a media commentator on religious, social, and political matters. He has been a guest on such television programs as the *Colbert Report, Nightline, Crossfire, Larry King Live, CNN News,* and *MSNBC News.* He presently hosts *Across the Pond,* a weekly program on the Premier Christian Radio Network in England. He is also a highly respected and sought-after guest on radio stations across the United States, Canada, the United Kingdom, Australia, and New Zealand.

Tony and his wife, Peggy, live in the Philadelphia area and have two grown children and four grandchildren.

Mary Albert Darling is an associate professor of communication at Spring Arbor University in Spring Arbor, Michigan; she also designed and teaches two courses in the university's master's program in spiritual formation and leadership. She is a graduate of Spring Arbor, with a double major in philosophy/religion and psychology.

In November 2002, Mary completed a two-year program in spiritual direction through the Manresa Jesuit House in Bloomfield Hills, Michigan. Mary has also studied spiritual formation under Richard J. Foster and Dallas Willard.

In addition to teaching, for which she has received Spring Arbor University's Teaching Excellence Award as well as its Faculty Merit Award, Mary is a frequent speaker at seminars, workshops, and retreats. She speaks on topics ranging from how to transform our relationships and friendships to spiritual formation and the spiritual disciplines, including what she believes are "lost" ancient spiritual practices. She also does spiritual direction, primarily with university students.

This is Mary's second book with Tony Campolo. Their first book, *The God of Intimacy and Action: Reconnecting Ancient Spiritual Practices, Evangelism, and Justice,* was published by Jossey-Bass in 2007 and released in paperback with a readers' guide in 2008.

Mary is married to Terry Darling, professor of psychology at Spring Arbor University and men's tennis coach. They have two teenage boys, David and Michael; a yellow lab, Amelie; and two cats, Cocoa and Cappuccino.

Index